A HISTORY
OF THE
SINGAPORE VOLUNTEER CORPS
1854 - 1937

being also

An Historical Outline of Volunteering
in Malaya

NOTE

The Government of the Straits Settlements is not responsible for the facts or opinions contained in this volume.

A HISTORY
OF
THE SINGAPORE VOLUNTEER CORPS
1854 - 1937

being also

AN HISTORICAL OUTLINE OF VOLUNTEERING IN MALAYA

The Naval & Military Press Ltd

Published by
The Naval & Military Press Ltd
5 Riverside, Brambleside, Bellbrook
Industrial Estate, Uckfield, East Sussex,
TN22 1QQ England
Tel: +44 (0) 1825 749494
Fax: +44 (0) 1825 765701
www.naval-military-press.com
www.military-genealogy.com

*In reprinting in facsimile from the original, any imperfections are inevitably reproduced
and the quality may fall short of modern type and cartographic standards.*

THE COLOURS

A HISTORY
OF THE
SINGAPORE VOLUNTEER CORPS
1854 - 1937

being also

An Historical Outline of Volunteering in Malaya

by

CAPTAIN T. M. WINSLEY, S.V.C.

With a

Foreword by

H.E. SIR THOMAS SHENTON WHITELEGGE THOMAS, G.C.M.G., O.B.E.
Governor and Commander-in-Chief, Straits Settlements

and an

Introduction by

H.E. MAJOR-GENERAL W. G. S. DOBBIE, C.B., C.M.G., D.S.O.
General Officer Commanding Troops, Malaya

Dedicated to

Singapore Volunteer Gunners, Past, Present and Future

and

Published to Commemorate

The 50th Anniversary of the Founding of

The Singapore Volunteer Artillery
now
The Singapore Royal Artillery (Volunteer)

22nd February, 1888 — 22nd February, 1938

FOREWORD

by

HIS EXCELLENCY SIR THOMAS SHENTON WHITLEGGE THOMAS,
G.C.M.G., O.B.E.
Governor and Commander-in-Chief, Straits Settlements

GOVERNMENT HOUSE,
SINGAPORE, 6*th April*, 1938.

This is history worth recording, and Captain Winsley's book will be valued not only by those who have direct associations with the Singapore Volunteer Corps but also by those who are interested in the Volunteer movement throughout the Empire. Never before has the fine record of the Corps been so completely displayed.

I congratulate Captain Winsley and the Corps and I wish the history all success.

T.S.W. THOMAS,
Governor.

INTRODUCTION

by

HIS EXCELLENCY MAJOR-GENERAL W.G. S. DOBBIE, C.B., C.M.G., D.S.O.
General Officer Commanding Troops, Malaya

Captain T. M. Winsley, the author of this history, is to be congratulated on his concise and clear work.

The records of the Singapore Volunteer Corps shew how success has been gained through self-sacrifice and industry. The Corps has worked with whole-hearted devotion and without advertisement. It is indeed a record of splendid achievement, and one of which we may all be proud.

To those who have served or are serving in the Corps this history will require no recommendation, but I am glad to think that the story will also be valued by a wide public in Singapore and in Malaya as a whole. The close connection between Singapore and its Volunteer Corps, now extending over eighty years, is an association which must be highly prized, especially in view of the important role assigned to the Corps in the Scheme of Defence.

W.G.S. DOBBIE,
Major-General,
General Officer Commanding, Malaya.

SINGAPORE, *March,* 1938.

PREFACE

"He dipped into various books, fluttering over the leaves of manuscripts, taking a morsel out of one, a morsel out of another, here a little, and there a little." Washington Irving.

On the 29th March, 1915, the late Major W.G. St. Clair, S.V.A., published a leader in the *Singapore Free Press* which he finished with the following paragraph:—

"In the above there is presented merely the skeleton of the history of "the Volunteer Forces in Singapore, which may be of use as a means of "reference to those who are interested in that subject. But perhaps what "we have written today will be forgotten soon and in a short time this brief "record will be as though it had not been written, for men come and men go; "for here we have no abiding city!"

The preservation of tradition generally in Malaya has ever been hampered by the constant changes in the community and I realized how true were Major St. Clair's words when I unearthed his leader one evening ten years ago, when searching old *"Free Press"* records in their offices in Robinson Road. His leader had been forgotten, and one of my reasons for compiling this history was that it would take longer to lose than the leader referred to above. My other aim was to give the Volunteer Gunners of Singapore some easy reference book with a more or less complete history of the Volunteer unit to which they belong and thus to help to foster that "Esprit de Corps" which is so necessary in all walks of life and more especially in the Services, be they Regular or Auxiliary forces. I have even hope that it may be of some little use in recruiting Volunteers, especially members to that unit of the present Straits Settlements Volunteer Force with which I have had the honour to be connected ever since I came to Malaya in 1921. Lastly, I have thought that if a record of early Volunteer History is not made now, it may not be made at all, or will indeed in a further ten years time be much more difficult to compile.

Researches in my spare time have been interesting and numerous, though sometimes tedious when information for which I was hunting did not appear to be forthcoming. They have included a complete search through all the old S.V.A. and S.V.C. Orders in existence; searches through old volumes of the *"Singapore Free Press"* and *"Straits Times"*, through old records at Fort Canning and in the Colonial Secretary's Reference Archives: the summarising and collecting together of all references to Volunteering in Buckley's Anecdotal History, The Straits Chinese Magazine, "One Hundred Years of Singapore", "One Hundred Years of the Chinese in Singapore", Mr. W. Linehan's "History of Pahang", and the Official Reports on the Local Forces.

I am indebted to Captain E. Foster Hall, M.C. (The Buffs), for information recorded by him, while he was Staff Officer S.S.V.F., in a digest of the Corps' activities between 1922 and 1935, much of which I have included without alteration, to the memories of many past volunteers, including Major W.G. St. Clair (on whom I called in Colombo, shortly before his death), to the Royal Artillery Institution for the loan of plates of old guns for reproduction, and to the Editors of the *"Singapore Free Press"* and the *"Straits Times"* for their courtesy in allowing me free access to ancient volumes of their respective journals. I must also acknowledge the help and patience of my wife who has always encouraged me in all Volunteer activities.

A business transfer to Penang resulting in my absence from Singapore of five years held up the publication of this history. Since it has been written by a gunner, the 50th anniversary of the founding of the Volunteer Battery seems a most suitable occasion to present it as a permanent record. In doing so, I make no apologies for the inclusion of the doggerrel verse of the 'nineties or for any social or anecdotal weakness in the text, or lack therein of the strong historical data that is the background for the proud histories of the regular forces: I have endeavoured from the material at my disposal to clarify and extol the spirit of the civilian troops in a Volunteer Corps that has never had the chance of creating history by being "Amazing first in War".

In putting this history before the public and ex-public of Malaya I ask them to believe that the difficulties of an amateur historian are legion and, by forwarding any criticisms, corrections or additional data either direct to me or to the headquarters of the Straits Settlements Volunteer Force, to assist in the production, at some future date, of a revised and better edition.

T.M.W.

SINGAPORE, *December,* 1937.

CONTENTS

Page

CHAPTER I

THE FIRST AND SECOND CORPS 1854–1887 1
    EARLY VOLUNTEERING IN SINGAPORE—A RIFLE CORPS

CHAPTER II

THE THIRD CORPS 1888–1900 21
    THE SINGAPORE VOLUNTEER ARTILLERY CORPS

CHAPTER III

THE FOURTH CORPS 1900–1921 42
    ARTILLERY—EUROPEAN RIFLE COMPANY—ENGINEERS—EURASIAN COMPANY—CHINESE COMPANY—MAXIM COMPANY—MALAY COMPANY—THE WAR AND THE SINGAPORE MUTINY

CHAPTER IV

THE FIFTH CORPS 1922–1937 85
    THE S.V.C. AS PART OF THE STRAITS SETTLEMENTS VOLUNTEER FORCE

APPENDICES 131

INDEX 203

LIST OF APPENDICES

		Page
I.	(a) Rules and Regulations of the Singapore Volunteer Rifle Corps 1857	131
	(b) Proposed Volunteer Artillery Corps for Singapore (*Free Press* extract 1887)	134
	(c) Correspondence and other papers connected with the proposal for raising a Volunteer Artillery Battery for Singapore	135
II.	(a) A list of Governors of the Straits Settlements 1826 to 1937 and a list of G.O.C's. of the Straits 1883 to 1937	145
	(b) A list of Commandants, Adjutants and Officers Commanding Units of Singapore Volunteer Corps 1854 to 1937	147
III.	(a) A list of Officers of the Singapore Volunteer Rifle Corps 1856–1887	154
	(b) A list of names of the 96 gentlemen who enrolled in the S.V.A. on its formation 22nd February, 1888	157
	(c) A list of officers of the S.V.A. and S.R.A.(v) 1888–1937	160
	(d) A list of N.C.O's. of the S.V.A. and S.R.A.(v) 1888 to 1937	163
IV.	(a) Notes on Volunteer Decorations and Medals	171
	(b) A list of Volunteers who have received Decorations, Medals and Awards for their work in the Colonial Auxiliary Forces	173
V.	Copies of two letters from the Governor, Sir Cecil C. Smith to Lieut. W.G. St. Clair at Raub during the Pahang Rebellion 1892	187
VI.	A copy of the S.R.A.(v) and S.R.E.(v) Royal Warrant 1923	188

		Page
VII.	(a) SINGAPORE MUTINY CASUALTIES FEBRUARY 1915—SUMMARY AND LIST OF NAMES	189
	(b) SINGAPORE MUTINY SUMMARY OF SURRENDERS, CAPTURES AND SENTENCES	192
VIII.	NOTES ON SINGAPORE FORTS AND BARRACKS	193
IX.	HISTORICAL NOTE ON SOVEREIGNS AND REGIMENTAL COLOURS	196
X.	S.V.A. CAMP SONGS	199

LIST OF ILLUSTRATIONS

	Page
SINGAPORE VOLUNTEER CORPS COLOURS—PRESENTED 1934 ..	FRONTISPIECE
SINGAPORE VOLUNTEER RIFLE CORPS COLOURS—PRESENTED 1857	6
COLONEL W.J. BUTTERWORTH, C.B.	8
COLONEL SIR W. ORFEUR CAVENAGH, K.C.S.I. ..	
LIEUT.-COLONEL RONALD MACPHERSON	9
THE HON'BLE CAPTAIN W.H.M. READ, C.M.G., K.N.L. ..	
A SINGAPORE VOLUNTEER RIFLE CORPS GROUP—1865 *(circ.)* ..	12
A SINGAPORE VOLUNTEER RIFLE CORPS GROUP—1869–70 *(circ.)* ..	13
S.V.A. OFFICERS WITH .405 MAXIM GUNS—1893 *(circ.)* ..	30
AN S.V.A. .405 MAXIM GUN DETACHMENT—1893 *(circ.)* ..	31
THE SINGAPORE VOLUNTEER RIFLE CORPS MARCH ..	36
S.V.A. OFFICERS—1895 ..	37
S.V.A. SERGEANTS—1896 ..	
H.R.H. THE DUKE OF CORNWALL INSPECTING THE S.V.A.—1901 ..	50
THE S.V.A. SECTION S.S. CONTINGENT—CORONATION OF KING EDWARD VII—1902	
S.V.A. 10-PR. 2.75-INCH B.L. MOUNTAIN GUNS—1905 *(circ.)* ..	51
S.V.A. MOUNTAIN GUN PARK AT TANJONG KATONG ..	
S.V.A. CYCLIST SECTION—1896 ..	52
S.V.A. MAXIM GUN SUB-SECTION AT BALESTIER RANGE ..	
S.V.A.(M) KING'S BIRTHDAY PARADE ON THE OLD RACE COURSE—1904	53
DO. PASSING THE SALUTING BASE ..	
THE S.V.A. AT BUKIT PANJANG—ARRIVAL BY TRAIN AND COMING INTO ACTION—1903 ..	58
S.V.C. TEAM—RIFLE MATCH CEYLON/RANGOON/SINGAPORE—1908 ..	59
S.V.C. RIFLE TEAM AT BISLEY, ENGLAND—1910 ..	
S.V.A. DRILL HALL—FORT FULLERTON SITE ..	62
DO. FROM THE PADANG ..	
THE CHINESE VOLUNTEER CLUB BEACH ROAD 1907 TO PRESENT DAY ..	63
THE OLD DRILL HALL AT BEACH ROAD, 1908–1933 ..	
HEADQUARTERS "F" MALAY COMPANY S.V.C.—1910–1937 ..	66
THE CHINESE COY. S.V.I.—1906—AT H.Q. BRAS BASAH ROAD ..	
THE S.V.A.—MOUNTING A 6-INCH GUN, DRILL HALL BEACH ROAD—1912 ..	67
THE SINGAPORE VOLUNTEER FIELD AMBULANCE COMPANY—1917 ..	
S.R.A.(V) TROPHIES ..	74
S.V.A. GROUP—WINNERS OF THE FINDLAYSON CARBINE TROPHY—1906 ..	

	Page
Collar Badges, Shoulder Titles & Buttons P.V., P.W.V.R., M.V.R., M.V.C., P. & P.W.V.C.	75
M.S.V.R. Maxim Gun & Carriage trailed by a two-seater car—1916 Do. Mounted on a Motor tricycle—1916	82
S.R.E.(v) and 41st Coy. R.E.—Group at Pulo Brani—1918 Malay Company P. & P.W.V.C. in Mess Dress 1936	83
S.V.C. Collar Badges & Buttons	98
S.V.C. Shoulder Titles	99
Penang & Province Wellesley Volunteer Corps Colours and Malacca Volunteer Corps Colours—Presented 1934	116
The S.V.A.—1895 The S.R.A.(v)—1935	118
Armistice Day Minute Guns 4.5-inch Howitzer 1928—3.7-inch Howitzer 1936 S.R.A.(v) coming into Camp at Siglap with 4.5-inch Howitzer lorry drawn 3.7-inch Mountain Howitzer on Trailer Carriage	119
King's Birthday Parade on the Padang, Singapore 1935 The Officers Singapore Volunteer Corps—Group 1934	124
The Straits Settlements Volunteer Air Force—Group 1936 The S.S.R.N.V.R., Patrol Launch "Panglima" 1937	125

THE SINGAPORE VOLUNTEER CORPS

CHAPTER I

THE FIRST AND SECOND CORPS 1854–1887

EARLY VOLUNTEERING IN SINGAPORE—A RIFLE CORPS

The History of the Singapore Volunteer Corps is tantamount to a history of Volunteering in Malaya because for the first forty-six years, 1854 to 1900, there were practically no other Volunteers in the Country and although the activities of the Singapore Corps are recorded in greater detail, there is running through these pages a general outline of Volunteering throughout the Country which, including Malay States under British protection, is more generally known as British Malaya.

Since it might be said that there have been five Volunteer Corps in Singapore, it seems necessary, in compiling a History of Volunteering in the Colony that may be followed easily, first to give a precis of the formation of the various Corps during the last eighty-three years.

The First Corps formed in 1854 was called the Singapore Volunteer Rifle Corps and was of a private nature, though it had the support of the Governor, Colonel W.J. Butterworth, C.B.

The Second Corps dates from 1857. It was in reality the First Corps being officially recognised by the Indian Government after the Indian Mutiny broke out; it became embodied under Act dated 23rd October, 1857.

The Third Corps was an Artillery Corps, formed on the 22nd February, 1888 after the disbandment of the Second Corps, and was known as the Singapore Volunteer Artillery Corps, (S.V.A.).

The Fourth Corps came into existence in 1901 and was known as the Singapore Volunteer Corps, being the Singapore Volunteer Artillery and three new units, The Singapore Volunteer Rifles, The Singapore Volunteer Engineers and The Singapore Volunteer Infantry. This Corps was formally disbanded in 1921 for reorganisation.

The Fifth Corps, formed in December, 1921 and existent today, was the outcome of the reorganisation, when all Volunteer Corps of the Straits Settlements became the Straits Settlements Volunteer Force, under one Commandant, a regular officer, who is also the Officer Commanding the Singapore Volunteer Corps.

1846. *The Raising of a Volunteer Corps.*—The raising of a Volunteer Corps for Singapore was first mooted in 1846 after the settlement had been disturbed by Chinese riots, but this was not achieved until nearly ten years afterwards[1]. In spite of this delay it is interesting to record that the institution of a Volunteer force in Singapore took place several years before the great Volunteer Movement in the United Kingdom, which did not commence until 1859, and, since it was acknowledged to be the first movement of its kind in India, it may be considered to be the first official Volunteer Organisation in the British Empire[2].

1854. A Volunteer Corps was formed in Singapore in 1854 after the recurrence of further Chinese riots[3], which upset the Island for ten or twelve days. It arose between the Hokiens, from the province of Hokien in China, and the Teo Chews from the province of Quantung, because the Hokiens refused to join in a subscription to assist the rebel Teo Chews who had been driven from Amoy by the Imperial Chinese Troops.

As the formation of a Volunteer Corps in Singapore was primarily for purposes of internal security, which was constantly being disturbed by riots, the following passages, from the remarks to the Grand Jury, made by Sir Wm. Jeffcott about the riots in 1854, will serve to illustrate the nature of such trouble and what the authorities and Volunteers had to contend with on and off over a long period of years:—

> "These people had hitherto lived peaceably together, transacting business with each other and living intermingled in the same streets. Without any apparent cause, however, a spirit of discord appears suddenly to have arisen amongst them, which on the 5th of May last broke out in acts of violence, riots occurring in different parts of the town, and at length resulting in houses being attacked and plundered. This state of things continued for seven or eight days, although after the first three days the rioting in town gradually diminished. The police were incessantly employed, the military were called out, and the marines landed from the ships-of-war: and with a most praiseworthy alacrity, the European inhabitants came forward and offered their services as Special Constables and had afforded most valuable

---

(1) Buckley's "Singapore" p. 446—"One Hundred Years of Singapore" I p. 384.

(2) The Shanghai Volunteer Corps was formed in the International Settlement in 1853 and first tasted fire at the Battle of Muddy Flat (now the Shanghai Race Course) on the 4th April, 1854. On this date which is incorporated in their badge they suffered casualties to the extent of four killed and fourteen wounded. As the Corps is international and consists of companies drawn from various nationalities, the statement in the text is still correct.

(3) "Our Tropical Possessions In Malayan India" by John Cameron—1864 and Buckley's "Singapore" pp. 585/595.

assistance in preserving order, for which they were entitled to the gratitude of the community.

After the first two days, the disturbances spread into the country, where, they assumed a very different character. The riotous proceedings there were much more serious and aggravated, and quickly led to the plundering and burning of property, and eventually to the destruction of life and the committal of excesses of every kind of the most barbarous nature. The Grand Jury could easily understand how this difference should have taken place. While in town the people are comparatively civilised, the mass of the population in the jungle consists of men who have never for any length of time come in contact with Europeans or with the more orderly part of the town residents and who lived in a state of secluded semi-barbarism in the jungle, with little or no idea of what law or order is. When, therefore, the disturbances spread amongst them, they naturally plunged at once into far greater excesses than had characterised the town population, and the consequence was, that for a series of days the rural districts were the scene of the most lamentable outrages—huts and villages being burnt down in every direction, and murders committed, many of which had come to their knowledge, while it was to be feared many more had been perpetrated but remained unknown. Another cause, perhaps, of the different character which the disturbances in the country had assumed compared with those in the town, might be found in the fact that while in the town the two parties were nearly equal, in the country one of them had a great preponderance, and had the other party in a great measure in their power."

The Sessions lasted seventeen days and about two hundred and fifty prisoners were tried. Six men were sentenced to death, but only two were executed; sixty-four were sentenced to various terms of hard labour, and eight were transported for fourteen years.

These riots, and the outbreak of the Crimean War, led to a public meeting[1], which was held on Saturday, the 8th July of that year, with the concurrence and support of the then Governor, Colonel W.J. Butterworth, C.B. Mr. John Purvis was in the chair and the meeting decided to form a Volunteer Corps under the name of the "Singapore Volunteer Rifle Corps". The following resolution was finally passed:—"Proposed by H.C. Caldwell and seconded by M.P. Davidson—That it is the opinion of the meeting that a Volunteer Rifle Corps will be of manifest advantage to the Settlement; that the following gentlemen do form a Committee *viz.;* Messrs. Purvis, Guthrie, Napier, and W.H. Read, to offer the services of the Corps to Government, and that His Honour the Governor be requested to propose a set of Rules and Regulations for the guidance of the Corps." Before the meeting broke up thirty-two signatures were affixed to the Volunteer Roll. More were added later making up a total

---

[1] Buckley's "Singapore" pp. 606 & 607.

membership of sixty-one when the Corps was raised. The name of Mr. W.H. Read was the first on the roll. The Governor became its first Colonel and Captain Ronald Macpherson, Madras Artillery, (afterwards Colonel and first Colonial Secretary, S.S.) its first Commandant. The fact that its first Commandant was an artillery man probably accounts for the early interest in gunnery in the Corps in 1868.

1855. On Thursday the 8th March, there was a review of the newly enrolled Volunteer Corps of which the *"Free Press"* wrote as follows:—

> "The Singapore Rifle Corps paraded on Government Hill (Fort Canning) on the afternoon of Thursday last, and went through a pretty stiff drill, after which they were reviewed by the Hon'ble the Governor (Colonel Butterworth) who then addressed them in complimentary terms on the efficiency they had attained, and assuring them how proud he should have been to have headed them in actual service. His Honour requested that his name might remain upon their roll,[1] and concluded by reading some dispatches from the Court of Directors and Supreme Government of India, noticing in terms of approbation the promptitude with which the Singapore Volunteers had come forward with the offer of their services and expressing the hope that their example might be followed in other parts of India. The Corps, although they turned out on this occasion in somewhat diminished numbers, appeared, as far as the unprofessional eye could judge, to go through their manœuvres with steadiness and precision, and we have no doubt that they will highly distinguish themselves whenever they may be called upon to take the field."[2]

1857. In the early days of the Singapore Volunteers, the staff was composed of a Captain Commandant (Capt. R. Macpherson of the Madras Artillery), an Adjutant (Capt. Robert Church of the 47th Regiment Madras Native Infantry,[3]) two Lieutenants (W.H. Read and C.H. Harrison), three Sergeants and three Corporals. There were however some slight changes in 1857 after the Volunteers were officially recognised by the Indian Government and over the next two decades there was in addition to the Captain Commandant,—who from December, 1857 was always a Volunteer officer,—a Colonel Commandant usually the senior regular Military officer stationed in Singapore. Capt. W.H. Read was promoted on the 1st January, 1858 to become first Volunteer Captain Commandant and Brigadier McLeod of the Madras Native Infantry was the first Colonel Commandant. A "Second Captain" was added to the establishment, Mr. J. Purvis being the first to hold the position. The work of Adjutant

---
(1) This parade was immediately prior to his retirement.
(2) Buckley's "Singapore" p. 619.
(3) Capt. Church was also Secretary and A.D.C. to the Governor.

and Quartermaster was assigned to Volunteer officers and the strength was consequently increased by an additional Lieutenant making three in all. Dr. R. Little M.D. was appointed Hon. Surgeon to the Corps and the old title of Sergeant accorded to Senior N.C.O's was abolished in favour of "Sub Officers" of which there were four and four Corporals.

In January of this year, the state of affairs in China led to another riot in Singapore and Buckley[1] tells us that "The Military and Volunteer Rifles were in readiness, and large guns were mounted on Government Hill (Fort Canning) and Pearls Hill. An additional Regiment was soon afterwards sent from Madras".

Up to 1857 the Madras Native Artillery used to supply detachments for Singapore, Malacca and Labuan, but a small force of Madras European Artillery (regular army) was sent to Singapore in this year, and constituted the first European regular troops of any arm to be stationed in the settlement of Singapore.

[2] On the evening of Saturday, the 14th February, 1857, the Singapore Volunteer Rifle Corps was presented with a set of colours which had been prepared for it by Mrs. Butterworth, the widow of the late Governor, under whom the Corps had been embodied, and who had continued to be its Colonel up to his death. Brigadier McLeod permitted all the troops in Singapore to be paraded on the Esplanade. The Corps wore a band of crape on the arm as a sign of mourning for their late Colonel (Butterworth). Governor Blundell presented the colours to Mr. W.H. Read, the Senior Lieutenant, and addressed the Corps.

Mr. Read replied; the following is the final passage of his reported speech:—"We seek not glory of the battlefield, nor to embroider the names of victories on these colours. Ours are less martial, more peaceful aims. Our object is to assist in protecting the lives and property of the public, and to shew the evil-disposed how readily Europeans will come forward in the maintenance of order and tranquility. Should we ever be called upon to act, we shall be found prepared to do our duty, contented with the approbation of the Government and the applause of our fellow citizens."

These Colours lasted for over twenty-five years and after the silk had rotted away from damp and insects, the bare pikes were deposited at the Central Police Station, but these too disappeared as lumber.

It was not until September, 1937 that the design of the Colours presented by Mrs. Butterworth was discovered. When hunting for illustrations for this history the chronicler found, among a pile of old unframed

---

[1] Buckley's "Singapore" p. 645.
[2] Buckley's "Singapore" p. 647.

photographs in Raffles library, an S.V.R.C. group, very faded, dating about 1870, with the Colours shown very clearly in the centre of the background(1) and from this the coloured reproduction contained herein has been drawn. It will be observed that it is a Regimental Colour of the old Ensign design (before 1868) which differed from present day Colours in that it was of larger dimensions(2) and had a Union Jack in the top corner near the pike, the main field being the same colour as the regimental facings, while the pike had a spear head instead of the present day crown and lion. The photograph naturally contained nothing to indicate the main colour of the field (*i.e.* main flag) so it has been assumed that it would probably have been green, since the Corps facings were green(3).

At this time the Corps being a Rifle regiment was not really entitled to carry Colours, but this point seems to have been ignored as it was in England years later where Volunteers, originally all "Rifles", were occasionally presented with Colours.

That there was only one Colour and not a stand of two, Queen's and Regimental, can be accounted for by the fact that though most regiments now have two, in the early days there were some that had one only while others had as many as three.

On the 18th July, 1857 the Legislative Council of India, with the assent of the Right Honourable the Governor General, passed an Act (No. XXIII) "to provide for the good order and discipline of certain Volunteer Corps and to invest them with certain powers". This was the first Volunteer Ordinance and through it the Singapore Volunteer Rifle Corps ceased to be a private Corps.

Other than this first Volunteer Ordinance very little information was available to show how the Volunteers of the period were administered, until the discovery in June 1937 of an original copy of the Rules and Regulations of the Singapore Volunteer Rifles dated Singapore 1857(4).

Authorative information regarding the badge of the Corps between 1854 and 1887 is still lacking, though a microscopic examination of an enlargement of the photograph opposite page 12 suggests that the badge used in 1865 was a grenade with the motto "Primus in Indis" in a scroll beneath it. From this, and the fact that all infantry regiments of the Old East India Company were Fusiliers, it would seem possible that the

---

(1) *See* illustration opposite p. 13.
(2) *See* appendix IX on "Colours"
(3) *See* 1885 re uniform p. 16.
(4) *See* Appendix I for a copy of these Rules and Regulations, the original of which belonged to the Singapore Free Press. It has now been presented to the S.V.C. by the Straits Times Ltd. and is in H.Q. Mess.

A History of the Singapore Volunteer Corps.

A Reproduction of
THE COLOURS
presented to
THE SINGAPORE VOLUNTEER RIFLE CORPS
by
Mrs. BUTTERWORTH
1857.

original badge was a grenade without other adornment. It is nevertheless amazing that all efforts to obtain further information regarding the early badges of the Corps have proved fruitless. The ever changing community seems to have passed on and taken all record with it.

The Corps was uniformed in dark-green (Rifleman Green) to indicate its status as a Rifle Corps; an historical feature handed down from the Royal American Regiment (afterwards the 60th Rifles) whose 5th battalion was first uniformed in green in 1798 for distinctive purposes since it was expressly raised as a rifle battalion in the comparatively early days of the rifling of hand guns.

Rule IX of the S.V.R.C. in 1857 states:—

> "At Full Dress Parades the members shall wear a Green Uniform of "the material and pattern originally agreed upon; and at all other times "they shall appear, when called on duty, in White Jackets, White Trousers, "and Cap-covers, Black Neck Ties and Black Shoes".

It is probable that the S.V.R.C. was first armed with the Brunswick Muzzle Loading (M.L.) percussion rifle with two grooves and .704 bore since this weapon was the British Army armament from 1838 onwards.

POSSIBLE DESIGNS OF THE OLD S.V.R.C. BADGES
Not authentic but drawn after microscopic inspection of old photographs
1 & 3 Alternative Shako and/or Cap Badges 2 Shako plate

The Minié Rifled Musket though adopted in a small way in the British Army in 1851 and used by some troops in the Crimea was not generally issued but a few may have found their way to Malaya after the Enfield, also a muzzle loader with percussion cap, was adopted in the Army in 1853. It is hardly probable, however, that any of this new, Enfield, pattern weapon came into the hands of the Singapore Volunteers until some years later.

1858. On the morning of the 19th November at seven o'clock, the Queen's Proclamation of 1st September, by which Her Majesty took upon herself the direct government of her Indian dominions, was read by the Governor from a platform under an attap covering in the centre of the Esplanade. The troops in garrison, the 43rd Madras Native Infantry and Madras Artillery and the Singapore Volunteer Rifle Corps were paraded, together with the Marines and a party of sailors from H.M.S. "Amethyst" with the band of that ship[1]. The Proclamation was read first in English by the Governor and then in Malay, after which a Royal Salute was fired by the Artillery and a 'feu de joie' by the troops. The Governor proposed three cheers for the Queen and the day was observed as a holiday.

1860. [2] On the evening of Monday, 26th November, 1860, the Singapore Volunteers were reviewed by the Hon. the Governor, Colonel Cavenagh, on the Esplanade. The volunteers mustered in full force under their commandant, Captain Read, and on the arrival of His Honour, accompanied by Brigadier Burn and Staff, presented arms. They then marched past in slow and quick time, and went through a number of Light Infantry manoeuvres, advancing, firing, halting, changing front in one direction and in the other, forming square, retiring, and finally, having fired two volleys with remarkable precision, they formed up in their original position and again presented arms.

The Governor then addressed the corps in animated language. He alluded to the formation of the corps, which had the honour to be the first enrolled in India and was therefore entitled to bear upon its colours the inscription "Primus in Indis". He dwelt upon the great utility of volunteers in general, and adverted to his own experience as having commanded the Calcutta volunteers during the Indian rebellion, when they were found so eminently useful in preserving confidence and order in the capital, and in allowing the regular troops to be employed in active

---
[1] Buckley's "Singapore" p. 665.
[2] Buckley's "Singapore" p. 682.

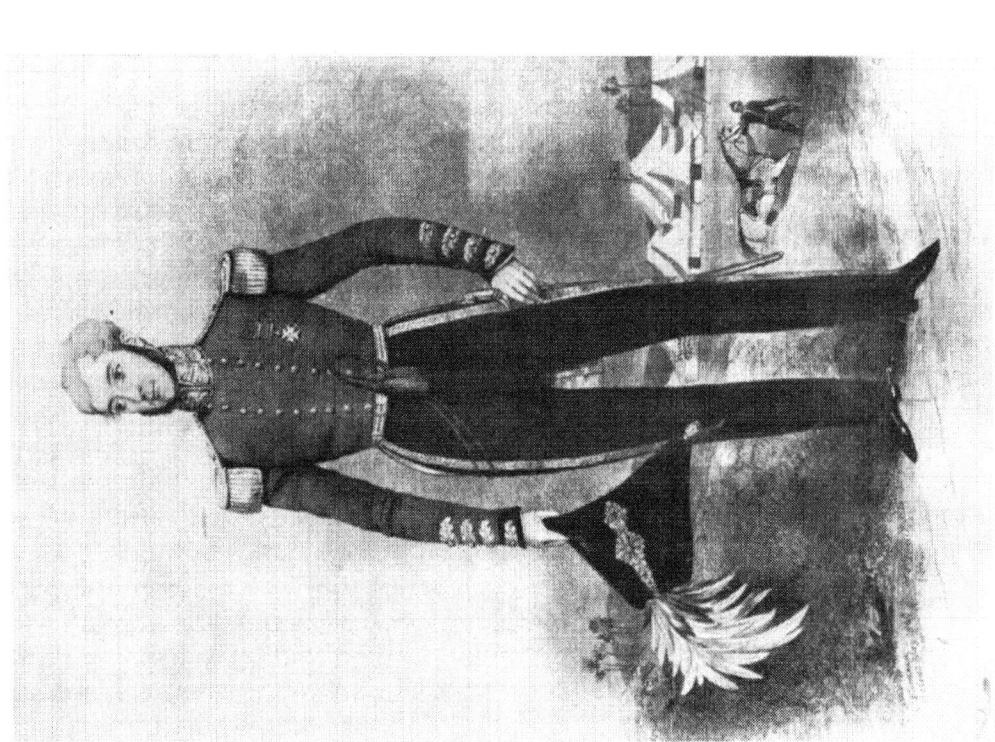

COLONEL W.J. BUTTERWORTH, C.B.,
Governor 1843–1855
First Honorary Colonel of the S.V.R.C. 1854

COLONEL SIR W. ORFEUR CAVENAGH, K.C.S.I.,
Governor 1861–1867
Honorary Colonel of the S.V.R.C. 1861–1867
Responsible for the first S.V.C. motto "Primus in Indis"

THE HON'BLE CAPT. W.H.M. READ, C.M.G., K.N.L.
(born 1819—died 1909)
The first Volunteer in Singapore
Captain Commandant S.V.R.C., 1857–1864 & 1869–1874

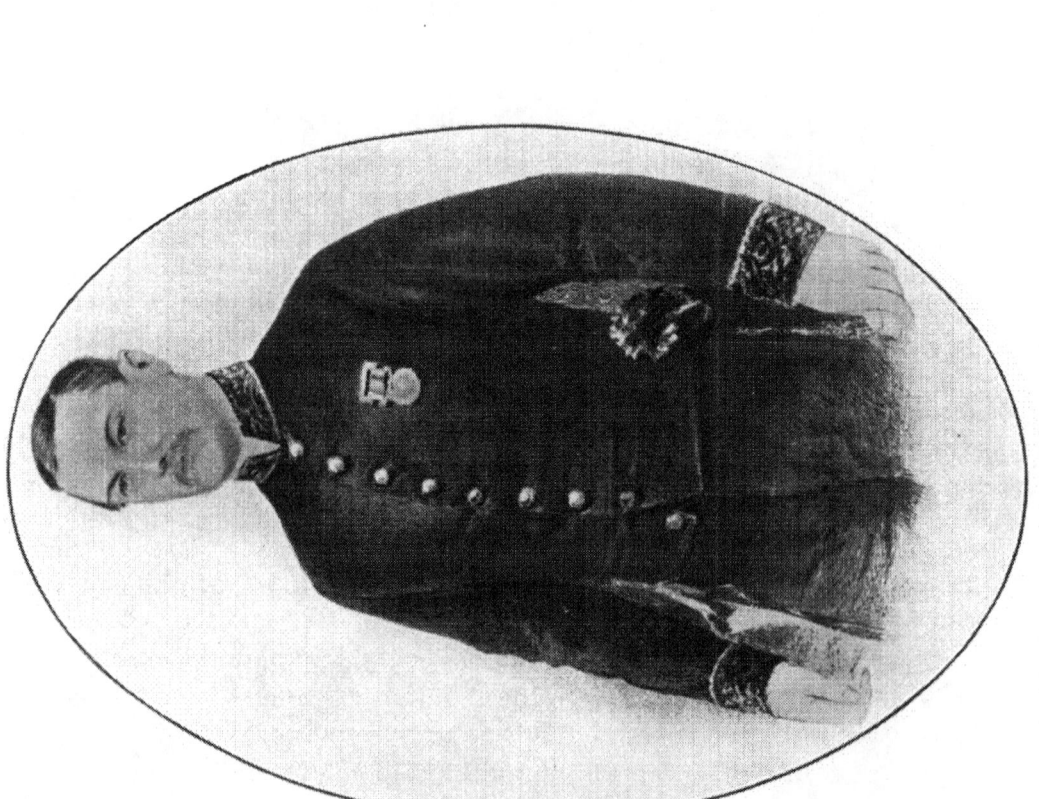

LIEUT.-COLONEL RONALD MACPHERSON
Madras Artillery; Capt. Commandant S.V.R.C., 1854–1856
Honorary Colonel S.V.R.C. 1864
Resident Councillor, Singapore, 1855–1867
Colonial Secretary, S.S., 1867–1869

operations against the mutineers. His Honour adverted to the great and wonderful progress such institutions had made in the mother country of late, and as in these days no dependence could be placed in the duration of peace, the speaker said he thought it behoved all good and true subjects to stand forward in the general defence. Colonel Cavenagh then eulogised those citizens who, though not British subjects, yet showed their appreciation of the protection bestowed by the law and of the benefits they thereby derived, by swelling the numbers of the volunteers, and he concluded by expressing a hope that those young men who had not yet joined the corps would no longer hesitate to enrol themselves as members of the Singapore Volunteer Rifles.

The Governor complimented the volunteers on their soldierly appearance and the steadiness and precision with which the various manoeuvres had been gone through. Much of this was owing to the indefatigable exertions of the Captain and other officers of the Corps, who were no doubt highly gratified at the result of their assiduity having elicited the commendations of so competent an authority in these matters as Colonel Cavenagh. The spirited address of the Governor was followed by three hearty cheers for His Honour. The spectators then gave three cheers for the corps, which marched off to the Masonic Lodge. The excellent Band of Her Majesty's 40th Regiment M.N.I. attended, by the kind permission of the officers of the Regiment, and added much to the gaiety of the scene[1].

The Motto[2]. Singapore was under the Indian Government in the first days of the Volunteer Corps, and this accounts for the allusion by Colonel Orfeur Cavenagh to the formation of the corps which had the honour to be the first enrolled "in India", and was therefore entitled to bear on its colours the motto "Primus in Indis". This continued to be the corps' motto from that day until the formation of the Singapore Volunteer Artillery in 1888 when it was changed to "In Oriente Primus" which motto the Corps of to-day still bears.

1861. Volunteering commenced in the Settlement of Penang (Prince of Wales Island) in May, 1861 with the formation of the Penang Rifle Corps, the Officers being, Corps Commandant Major H. Mann, Madras Staff Corps (Resident Councillor, Penang), Captain L. Nairne (of Nairne & Coy.) and Lieutenant G.M. Sandilands (of Lorrain, Sandilands & Co.[3]),

---

[1] Buckley's "Singapore" p. 682.
[2] "One Hundred Years of Singapore" I pp. 384/5.
[3] Partners—W.S. Lorrain (Glasgow) G.M. Sandilands (Penang) and J. Buttery (Singapore).

all appointed on the 15th May, 1861. This list was added to by the Commission of Mr. J.P. Stewart as a Lieutenant on the 13th February, 1862 and although the Corps existed, at any rate on paper, for nearly nine years, according to the directory the officers were the same throughout the years 1863 to 1867 and in 1868 and 1869 the commissioned strength seems to have been reduced to one officer only, Captain L. Nairne. The Corps appears to have been disbanded in 1870, though it was possibly moribund for three or four years before that and throughout its nine years it probably had about six years active existence.

In 1861 the barracks on Fort Canning (Bukit Larangan) were completed and the European Artillerymen were removed there from their previous quarters on Pearls Hill (Capt. Pearls Plantation)[1]. A Gunner Officers Mess remained at Fort Canning until as late as 1907 when the barracks there were turned into Headquarter Offices. These were pulled down in 1927 when the water reservoir for the Gunong Pulai scheme was built on the site and the Military Headquarters offices were moved outside the old fort wall to magnificent new quarters which had been built for the purpose further down the hill.

1862. Volunteering in Hongkong commenced in March, 1862 with the formation of the Hongkong Artillery Volunteer Corps, which was first armed with 3-pounders and 4.4-inch howitzers[2].

1864. For Queen's Birthday celebrations on the 24th May, 1864, about 80 Volunteers, dressed in white trousers and light coloured hollands, turned out for review on the Esplanade at a little after five in the morning. The Sepoys on this occasion numbered 800 men, all in red turbans, red coats, black trousers and sandals, and the Artillery (British) numbered over 120 with white pith helmets, blue trousers and jackets[3]. There was a "feu de joie" and twenty-one rounds from the guns at Fort Canning before the review was over at about 8 A.M. The occasion was further celebrated by the lighting of Singapore streets with gas for the first time.

In the Eighteen Sixties one of the guns (68 pounders) at Fort Canning ushered in the dawn with a round of blank at five o'clock.

1867. The Volunteer Corps consisted at the May 1867, birthday parade, of Captain Commandant C.H.H. Wilsone (Hamilton Grey & Co.),

---

(1) Buckley's "Singapore" p. 686 and "One Hundred Years of Singapore" Vol. II p. 507.
(2) Hongkong Volunteer Defence Corps Year Book 1934–1935 p. 19.
(3) "One Hundred years of Singapore" II p. 512.

Lieut. Von der Heyde (a partner of Behn, Meyer & Co.), Ensign A. Duff (William Macdonald & Co.), Hon. Surgeon Dr. Little and forty-seven N.C.O's and men. It is recorded that they did well at drill during this year and were complimented by Major General Sir Orfeur Cavenagh [1].

1867 was the year of the transfer of the Straits Settlements from the East India Company to the Colonial Office. The Military expenditure at the time was again the subject of much discussion by the mercantile community as it swallowed up, in 1863, nearly one half of the Colony's revenue (the gross amount of which was about £100,000). The fortifications at the time were Fort Canning and Fort Fullerton and two small earth works at Mt. Palmer and Mt. Faber containing in all 36 guns.

1868. *Volunteer Field Artillery* [2].—In the early part of 1868 the Corps was augmented by the loan of two 12 pr. Howitzers and the formation of a half Battery of Field Artillery. The officers and N.C.O's had to provide themselves with horses and the members to find a pair of ponies for each gun and ammunition wagon. These field guns formed an active section of the Singapore Volunteers for some years, but for want of interest, owing to lack of firing practice, it gradually declined, and in October, 1875 the guns and horse equipment were handed over to the Perak Government for the use of Mr. Birch [3]—first British Resident, Perak.

On the 4th August, 1868 Captain W.H. Read, who had resigned from the S.V.R.C. in 1864 owing to other heavy public duties, was reappointed Captain Commandant while still a member of the Legislative Council. The reappointment seems to have been due to an effort to revive interest in the Corps as members including officers had fallen off considerably for over two years.

The rank of Ensign first appears in 1868 when on the 26th June, Sergt. Charles Dunlop was promoted to it. The Corps had Ensigns up to 1872 when the title was changed to Sub-Lieutenant [4] and Ensign Robert Dunman became Sub-Lieutenant and Sergt. C.H. Harrison Jr. received promotion to that rank.

12-pr. Howitzer—S.V.R.C. 1868

---

(1) "One Hundred Years of Singapore" I p. 402.
(2) "One Hundred Years of Singapore" I pp. 385 and 403.
(3) Ref. letter 7341-76 dd. 6.12.76 from C.R.A.S.S. to Commandant, S.S.
(4) The title was changed in the Regular Army in 1871, Ensigns and Cornets becoming Sub-Lieutenants. In 1876 they were renamed Second-Lieutenants. In 1881 the rank of Second-Lieutenant was abolished but reintroduced in 1887.

Captain Read having again assumed command of the S.V.R.C. found that his predecessor, Captain Wilsone, had organised a band consisting of a bugler, drummers and fifers. In September, 1868 the Drummers had reached that state of efficiency to make the supply of Corps drums necessary; on indenting for Drum Heads, a query was raised which resulted in Capt. Read replying to Government that he had never heard of a Rifle Corps with a Drum and Fife Band but that not liking to disturb the arrangements already in hand he had indented for Drum Heads. Apparently they did not get them as a note on the letter covering the indent suggests that it was returned for cancellation[1] and a Drum and Fife Band with borrowed instruments under the Drum-Major of the Madras Native Infantry continued to encourage the Volunteers, until the regiment left Singapore and the band failed for want of an instructor and instruments.

1869. The Duke of Edinburgh visited Singapore in 1869 and the Volunteers provided a mounted escort and a guard of honour of sixty-two men. The mounted escort was much admired and praised and the members of it were Messrs. R. Dunman, McPherson, J.C. Ker, R.W. Maxwell,[2] G.A. Maclaverty, Bligh, Rae, C.E. Velge, O'Laughlin and C. Phillips[3].

The first Volunteer Ordinance in the Straits Settlements was made law and cited as the "Volunteer Ordinance 1869".

This year saw the change from the old Enfield rifle, known as the "Brown Bess" presumably after a more ancient flintlock weapon with the same nickname, to the short Snider carbine[4], chosen by Col. Macpherson; it proved a fairly good weapon from 100 to 300 yards. This stimulus to rifle-shooting created a new interest and raised the strength of the corps to over 100 men and many competitions were arranged on the old Race Course Range (400 yards), prizes for shooting being given by the

---

(1) Ref. C.S.O. Permanent Records—letter No. 1468 mil. dd. 24.9.68.
(2) Youngest brother of Mr. (later Sir) William E. Maxwell.
(3) "One Hundred Years of Singapore" Vol. I. p. 403.
(4) "One Hundred Years of Singapore" Vol. I. pp. 395 and 403.

*Enfield Muzzle Loading (Percussion) Rifle ("Tower 1863")
used by the S.V.R.C. up to 1869*

A SINGAPORE VOLUNTEER RIFLE CORPS GROUP—1865 (circ.)
At Fort Fullerton

A SINGAPORE VOLUNTEER RIFLE CORPS GROUP—1869-70
The Colours presented by Mrs. Butterworth, 1857 in the background
Back Row Standing—Extreme left—Tessensohn—Extreme right—Sgt. A. Clarke
Front Row Standing—Cpl. E. Reutens—Extreme right—Sgt. C.B. Buckley

Captain Commandant (Mr. W.H. Read), Lieut. R. Duff, Sergt. R. Dunman, and Sergt. C.B. Buckley([1]).

1870. The Volunteer Depot about this time was next door to the Sailors Home in North Bridge Road and the headquarters of the European Police Force, known as Police Bahru, where the Volunteers were drilled. Target practice took place at the Race Course where George Samuel Reutens, in 1919 the doyen of the Eurasian community, was one of the best marksmen of the day. In those days snipe abounded in the district round the Race Course (now Farrer Park) and rifle practice was profitably intermixed with pleasure([2]).

1871. Mr. Henry Barnaby Leicester records in his "Personal Recollections"([3]) that the uniform of the Singapore Volunteer Rifle Corps in 1871 was a "scarlet tunic with green facings, white trousers and a shako." It would seem, however, that he has reversed the order and the uniform actually was the original green tunic with the subsequent addition of scarlet facings and was the dress uniform only, as from a photograph taken about 1865([4]) it would appear that there was also a working kit composed of a brown holland tunic, trousers and shako with sun flap. It is interesting to note that the corps colours of today, green and scarlet, are the colours of the dress uniform of this period.

During the riots in 1871 the Volunteers were again called out to perform duties which Capt. W.H. Read described in 1857 as "more peaceful aims"! While on patrol at Kampong Glam (the residential quarter of the day situated between Beach Road and Rochore Canal) some of the men got so excited at seeing the Chinese breaking into and looting shops, that they broke the ranks and started belabouring the rioters until the Commanding Officer (Capt. Read) managed to get them to fall in again([5]).

1872. In 1872 it was proposed to established a militia to be armed with the Snider rifle as the reorganised police force was not considered strong enough. A "Militia Bill" was introduced in 1873 but "objected to on the grounds of Prussianism"; at least this was the ostensible reason([6]).

---

[1] Responsible for the standard work "An Anecdotal History of Old Times in Singapore" by Charles Burton Buckley (Fraser & Neave 1902) and referred to in this History as "Buckley's Singapore".
[2] "One Hundred Years of Singapore" Vol. I. p. 392 and Vol. II. p. 530.
[3] "One Hundred Years of Singapore" Vol. II p. 530.
[4] *See* reproduction opposite page 13.
[5] A good account of this period and these riots is to be found in Mr. W.H. Read's rare book "Play and Politics" by an "Old Resident".
[6] "One Hundred Years of Singapore" I p. 395 and 591.

1873. The Rifle Association was formed in 1873([1]). In the two previous years matches had been fixed against the Gordon Highlanders and the 80th Regiment (Staffordshire Volunteers), but the short Snider was too great a handicap against the military long weapon([2]). At first few civilians joined the Rifle Association as they were unable to get rifles suitable for competition the difficulty, however, seems to have been overcome as the Association has continued with only short periods of inactivity right up to the present day.

1877. Correspondence took place during the year between the Colonial Secretary, S.S. and the Resident, Perak regarding the return of the two 12-pr. Howitzers mentioned in 1868 as having once been part of the Singapore Volunteer equipment and transferred to Perak in 1874. These letters also give the distribution of Artillery in Perak at the time, which as a point of interest was Qualla Kangsa—two–7 pr. M.L.R.; two–9 pr. Krupps; two–3 pr. Boat Guns; two–6 pr. Rocket Tubes; one Hales Rocket Tube; Larut—two–12 pr. Krupps; Durian Sebatang—two–9 pr. Vavasour M.Y.R.; Kinta—one–4.25 Howitzer, and Bandar Bahru two–12 pr. Howitzers and two–4.25 Mortars.

On the 30th November, 1877 the Rangoon Volunteer Rifles were raised under command of Mr. H. Krauss, but subsequently it was decided that a Military Officer should be in command and Major Evanson (then a Magistrate in Rangoon) was appointed with Captain Cuthbert, 89th (P.V.) Regiment, as Adjutant. Two Cadet Companies were formed in 1878 from the boys of St. Pauls School and the Diocesan Boys School. These were the first School Companies in the history of Volunteering in Burma and they also seem to have been before Malaya in this respect.

1878. In 1878 the Race Course Rifle Range, being only 400 yards long, was abandoned and the old Artillery Range at Balestier was taken over and continued as the Volunteer Rifle Range until 1922, when the Government decided that as a range it was a danger to the community, Singapore having grown round it.

Lieut. C.B. Buckley held a commission in the Volunteers from 1871 to 1878 when he retired to allow Major Grey to reform the Corps which had fallen off sadly in numbers.

---

(1) "One Hundred Years of Singapore" I p. 404.
(2) The Snider-Enfield versus the Martini-Henry.

1879. The Rangoon Volunteer Artillery was formed on the 20th October, 1879 as one Company of Artillery. Whether Coast Defence or mobile is not on record but in 1892 it was definitely a Coast Defence Unit with a war role of assisting the Regular Companies of Royal Artillery in Rangoon in manning the forts on the river. Before Major St. Clair arrived in Singapore he was in Burma and a member of the Moulmein Volunteer Rifles and without doubt the war role of the Rangoon Volunteer Artillery made such an impression on his mind that later, in 1888, it was responsible for his sponsoring the Singapore Volunteer Artillery when he found that the conditions in Singapore undoubtedly warranted a similar role in the Volunteer movement.

1880. *The Volunteers as The Local Fire Brigade.*—In 1880 and 1881 the Singapore Fire Brigade was a voluntary organization mainly supported by the members of the Singapore Volunteer Corps. Captain H.E. McCullum (in 1888 Commandant of the Singapore Volunteer Artillery Corps) and Mr. E.M. Merewether (in 1895 a Subaltern in the S.V.A.) were volunteer officers of the efficient fire brigade of those days and up to 1896 the Guns at Fort Canning were used to signal an outbreak of fire in the City.

The Volunteer Ordinance of 1869 was amended during this year to include provisions made in the "Army Discipline and Regulations Act 1879".

Officers Badges of Rank.—The Stars and Crown used in the badges of rank of the Officers of the Corps have always been the same as those generally used in the Regular Imperial Army; the Star being first mentioned in the Dress Regulations of 1822 but probably introduced somewhat earlier. Since the origin and formation of this Star worn by so many Volunteer Officers is known to so few it may be of interest to detail them here as on the 20th October, 1880, was introduced the system of Badges of Rank which has held sway ever since, together with a change of position from collar to shoulder-strap.

The original Star used to indicate an Officer's rank in the army was an accurate representation of the Star of the Knights Grand Cross of the Military Division of the Most Honourable Order of the Bath (founded 1399 and revived 1725), which briefly described was round in outline having flame shaped rays of silver upon the centre of which was set a Maltese Cross in gold. In the middle of this surrounded by a wreath of green laurels with three berries, was a circlet of crimson edged and inscribed with the words "TRIA JUNCTA IN UNO" in gold. This enclosed a silver Centre Piece charged with three gold Albert Crowns placed one over two. Across the inferior arm of the Maltese Cross was a blue scroll edged and inscribed "ICH DIEN" in silver.

The Star now worn by Officers of the Regular and Auxiliary Forces is a modified version of the original and dates from 1880 differing in the following heraldic particulars. The Maltese Cross of its illustrious forbear has become a Cross pattee (*e.g.* that of the Victoria Cross), the Crowns of the three Kingdoms (England, Scotland and Ireland) have become reversed and are now set two over one, the scroll bearing "ICH DIEN" has disappeared and the flame rays of the original star have become straight and with only twenty points.

Up to 1904 Second-Lieutenants had shoulder-straps without any badge of rank, Lieutenants had one and Captains two stars on the shoulder-strap; after this date Second-Lieutenants received one, Lieutenants two and Captains three stars. The badges of Field Officers (those of rank of Major and higher) remained unchanged, being distinguished by a crown for a Major, a crown and one star for a Lieutenant-Colonel and a crown and two stars for a full Colonel.

1885. To revert for a moment to Volunteering in Burma. In November of this year the first outstation Company, a mounted Infantry unit, was formed at Akyab which was later sent to Pegu with the regular punitive expedition to assist in dealing with dacoit bands in the third Burmese War.

That the uniform of the S.V.R.C. underwent a change about this time seems certain as mention of it suddenly appears in the old directories of the day together with the motto immediately under the Corps title. From 1869 to 1875 "Facings—Green" was regularly recorded though no mention of the actual uniform, but in 1885 the entry is "Uniform Red—Facings Green" and in 1886 and 1887 "Uniform Invisible Green—Facings Green"; it is therefore just possible that Mr. Leicester's recollections[1] of a red uniform with green facings in 1871 were correct after all and that the change of colour was being so discussed at the time that prominence was given to it in print thereby placing the colour of the old uniform and its facings on record a year before they were changed back to the original green adopted on the formation of the Corps or at any rate in 1857. On the other hand the entry in 1885 recording a Red uniform may have been an error as it is really improbable that the colour of the uniform, originally

---

(1) *Vide* p. 13.

green should have been changed to red and then back to green again. One other alternative suggests itself as a solution to the problem of the old S.V.R.C. uniform and that is that a change from green to red took place in 1868 when patterns of uniform were submitted to His Excellency the Governor for approval, just after the separation of the Straits Settlements from the Indian Government, and that having made the change the error of departing from green for a Rifle Corps was pointed out and subsequently corrected to conform with custom which according to an authority([1]) on Military uniform is as follows:—

"The Rifles have dark green uniforms, similar in cut to that of the "foot soldiers of the line; Collar and facings of the King's Rifles are scarlet, "of the Rifle Brigade black, of the Irish Rifles grass green, and of the "Scottish Rifles dark green; the buttons of all of them bronze. Their head-"dress is a low fur cap with upright horsehair plume. The Scottish Rifles "have uniforms of Scotch cut, tartan trousers and shakoes."

The patterns of the uniform submitted to the Governor were, however enclosed in a letter to the Colonial Secretary dated 19th May, 1868([2]) which also mentioned that they were for the S.V.C. Rifle Company and Artillery, the change might equally have been due to the fact that a separate uniform was required for the newly formed Artillery unit and that the opportunity was taken to make certain adjustments to the Rifle Company uniform at the same time. The letter does not state details though and the patterns were presumably returned.

According to information received by Major St. Clair from Sergt. Major Charles Phillips, drill instructor to the S.V.R.C. from 1866 to 1887 and later Superintendent of the Sailors' Home, the Minutes of Volunteer Committee Meetings, which might have assisted in defining the old uniform more accurately, were, together with the Muster Rolls, deposited in the Central Police Station, presumably at the same time as the bare pikes of the first Colours and disappeared with them as lumber.

The Singapore Volunteers' head dress during the first twenty-five years of the Corps existence was the shako. The shako was adopted in 1800 as the general head dress of the British infantry soldier, in place of the three cornered cocked hat. It originated in Hungary where the word for a peak is "csak", so that when the Hungarians added a peak to their previously brimless round hat (or cap) it was called a schako (chaco or shako). The shape of the British shako varied according to fashion over the period of years it was in general use by the British infantryman. The

---

(1) "The British Army" by a Lieutenant-Colonel in the British Army (Introduction by Major-General F. Maurice, C.B.) (Sampson Lowe 1899) p. 38.
(2) C.S.O. Permanent Records No. 718 of 19.5.1868 heading "Military."

following is a list of different types of which the S.V.R.C. probably wore the last three; the main difference lay in the height which was gradually reduced.

1800–1812	Stove-pipe Shako
1812–1816	Waterloo Shako
1816–1829	Regency Shako
1829–1844	Bell-topped Shako
1844–1855	Albert Shako
1855–1861	French pattern Shako
1861–1869	Quilted Shako
1869–1878	The Last Shako.

Fixed to the front rim of the crown of the shako the S.V.R.C. adopted the drooping horse-hair plume, about 5″ in height and dark green, of the Light Infantry and Fusiliers[1] (*See* photograph p. 13). Below the plume was the cap-plate or badge which in one photograph seems to have been a grenade[2] and in another a bugle-horn[3] and in neither does it appear to be as large as usual for a shako cap-plate or helmet plate.

There are no existing specimens of the badges, shako-plate, shoulder belt plates (Officers), pouch plates (Officers) and waist belt plates worn by the Singapore Volunteer Rifle Corps between 1854 and 1887. In the one photograph[4] the Officer's shoulder belt plate is distinctly a garter surmounted by a St. Edwards Crown, but whether the former is inscribed with their motto "Primus in Indis" or "Honi Soi qui Mal y pense" is a matter for conjecture; the badge in the centre might be a combination of both grenade and bugle horn.

The disappearance of all specimens of these articles, now historical relics, issued to so many men over a period of thirty-three years (1854–1887) the last date being only about fifty years ago is a complete mystery which the chronicler is still endeavouring to solve. The only solution for the present is that owing to the market among the Chinese for old brass most of them went to the melting pots and any retained as souvenirs have left the country with the retirement of Europeans.

The S.V.R.C. Shako

(1) Adopted by Light Infantry and Fusiliers in 1856.
(2) *See* photograph opposite p. 12.
(3) *See* photograph opposite p. 36.
(4) *See* photograph opposite p. 12.

With such a sad lack of evidence to corroborate the exact uniform and equipment of the period it almost seems as though the Corps was a free lance in the matter of its dress and custom. Though a Rifle regiment it carried Colours and seems to have had the bugle-horn badge of a Light Infantry regiment, though the Lancashire Rifles (1853–81) had a Pouch-Belt plate containing a bugle-horn badge; then the grenade badge may have been a Fusilier grenade due to their connection with the 'John Company', most of whose infantry regiments were Fusiliers, or an Artillery Grenade owing to the early formation of a battery in 1868; their shako plume seems to show that they wished to have direct connections with both Light Infantry and Fusiliers while their uniform which, though it may at one time have been red, was originally green denotes their real status as a Rifle Regiment.

1886. Up to now the S.V.R.C. had been drawn from all nationalities of the civilian European and Eurasian population of the Settlement but Mr. A.H. Carlos writes in his Article on "Eurasian Volunteers" in "One Hundred Years of Singapore" that "Through indifferent recruiting and scant recognition of Imperial needs the Eurasian began gradually to disappear from the ranks of the Volunteers, and in the latter part of the 'Eighties there remained hardly one member of the community in the Corps. The continued influx of Europeans began to make itself felt in Singapore about that time, and the separation into social planes in the island made itself evident. The Eurasian is by temperament retiring and by training unable to make himself heard, and this tended for many years to keep him from participating in the defence of the Colony". Mr. Carlos was somewhat hard on his community of the times when he wrote this. To indifferent recruiting, yes, and perhaps also to scant recognition *by the Imperial Government* might well be attributed the falling off in Volunteering in all Communities during those days, both being due to many years of peace as such was always the case. War in the Crimea, the Indian Mutiny, the Boxer Rebellion, the South African War and the Great War of 1914 all revived Volunteering as they broke out and the fact was, and is, that Defence of the Realm is only seriously considered by the majority of the Civilian population when war clouds are actually gathering or war has broken out.

1887. *Disbandment of Singapore Volunteer Rifle Corps.*—In 1887, the year of the Jubilee of the reign of Her Majesty Queen Victoria, the S.V.R.C. had again dwindled to a mere remnant[1] and a small half company was

---

[1] "One Hundred Years of Singapore" Vol. I p. 385.

all that Major W.R. Grey(¹) then commanded as its Captain Commandant. They, however, turned out for the Jubilee Parade a weak Company which had been got together for the purpose, in which Lieut. C.B. Buckley reappeared for duty.

It is about this period that we first hear of Mr. W.G. St. Clair's interest in the S.V.A. which as the History of Singapore (*One Hundred Years of Singapore*) puts it was his "Sturdy Youngster". Mr. St. Clair was the Editor of the "Singapore Free Press" and he used his journal to urge the value of a Volunteer Artillery Corps as a local reserve to the Garrison(²). As a result the Governor, Sir Cecil Clementi Smith, G.C.M.G., after granting an interview on the 1st December 1887 to a small Sub-Committee headed by Mr. St. Clair, accepted the services of a roll of Volunteers for a Volunteer Artillery Corps and asked a provisional Committee to proceed with the work of organization. For this purpose the Singapore Volunteer Rifle Corps was disbanded by proclamation on the 16th December, 1887.

---

(1) Major W.R. Grey had been in the 30th Regiment and served in Ceylon, and the campaigns in China (1857–60) and New Zealand (1860–66) before coming to the Straits as Superintendent of the Singapore gaol 1875, and Inspector of Prisons 1880. He retired in 1893 when he was succeeded by Mr. (later Sir) E.M. Merewether, an early subaltern in the S.V.A.

(2) Appendix I(*b*).

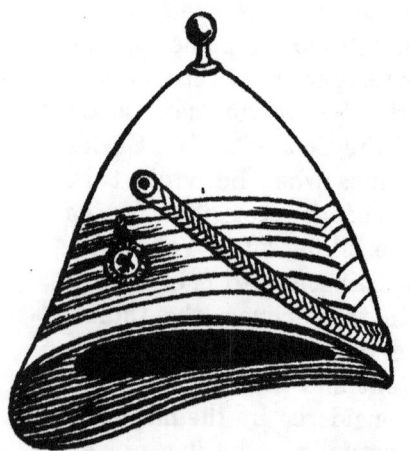 

S.V.A. Helmet 1888–1900 and Present Day Sun Helmet
(Note badge on opposite sides)

CHAPTER II

THE THIRD CORPS 1888–1900

THE SINGAPORE VOLUNTEER ARTILLERY CORPS

Data for the period during which the Corps was an Artillery one has proved plentiful. In the first place Mr. St. Clair was a journalist by profession and, in the style of those Victorian days of profuse verbiage, let his pen flow freely for the benefit of the Corps and public in the columns of the *"Free Press"*. Secondly, by a stroke of luck the Chronicler was able to save the Corps Orders from 1888 to 1906 from destruction when in 1927 they were cast out for the incinerator together with a lot of straw and packing from Camp crockery; they were then rebound for permanent record. In the third place we have many of the Camp Songs still on record. The Camps of the period and the "Sing Songs" after dinner were always a great feature. Major MacCallum was a splendid force in himself, brimful of energy and high spirits and always ready to unbend when play followed work: his voice was more than a parade one and his ready wit, and Mr. St. Clair's vamping and improvisations, resulted in a general feeling of good spirit in the Corps.

1888. *Singapore Volunteer Artillery Embodied.*—The Singapore Volunteer Artillery, which the members of to-day rightly consider to be the nucleus of the present Corps from which sprang or around which formed all the other existing units, was embodied by proclamation on the 22nd February, 1888. The number of enrolled members at this date of formation numbered ninety-six[1]. The last of these original members of the S.V.A. to remain on the active strength was Lieut. Colonel G.A. Derrick, C.B.E., V.D., who retired from the position of Commandant in 1919.

The Governor, Sir Cecil Clementi Smith, G.C.M.G., became the Honorary Colonel of the Singapore Volunteer Artillery on the 1st February, 1890 and remained so until his death on the 7th February, 1916.

1888. With the constitution of a new Corps came a change of motto. The Volunteer Gunners adopted the motto "In Oriente Primus" in place of "Primus in Indis" which had been the Singapore Volunteer Corps motto

---

[1] *See* Appendix III(b).

since 1860. That the Singapore Volunteer Artillery were responsible for the present day motto there is no doubt as "Primus in Indis" appeared in the old Straits and Singapore directories under the Corps title right up to 1887, and while the Volunteer Artillery have the honour of being the first bearers of the present day motto "In Oriente Primus" it seems a pity that the original motto was not carried down through the ages. The reason for the change remains unexplained though it is possible to surmise that the separation of the Straits Settlements from the jurisdiction of the Indian Government, when the transfer to the Colonial Office took place in 1867, must have had some bearing on the point and the newly formed Artillery Corps also thought that it was a good time to indicate that the Corps was entitled to a motto which made it clear that it was the first British Volunteer unit in the whole East.

Mr. W.G. St. Clair joined the S.V.A. on its formation as a Sergeant, refusing a commission, and remained an active member until the 5th February, 1903 when he commanded the S.V.A. and as Senior Major was Second in Command of the S.V.C. Besides being the prime mover in the formation of the S.V.A., he also carried out the organization and equipment of the Singapore Volunteer Rifles in 1901 at the request of the Government so that to both Gunner and Infanteer of the present day S.V.C. he may be justly termed the "Father of the Corps."

Major H.E. McCallum, C.M.G., late Royal Engineers (Colonial Engineer S.S.) commanded this newly formed Artillery Corps and continued to do so up to 1897 when he was promoted to be Governor and Commander in Chief in Lagos.

Drills.—There being no Drill Hall proper, the headquarters of the unit were in the Town Hall where Signalling, Squad, and Carbine Drill took place at regular and frequent intervals. The S.V.A. general Committee however met monthly in the Committee Room of the Singapore Cricket Pavilion.

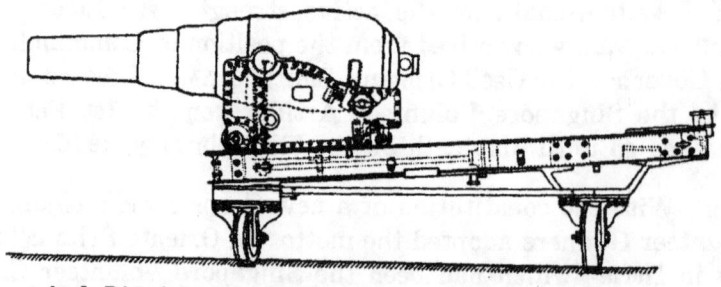

7-inch Rifled Muzzle Loading Gun—("Bottle Gun")

Gun Drill was carried out on the 7 inch R.M.L. at Fort Siloso, and later for extra efficiency on the 8 inch B.L. at Fort Tanjong Katong and on the 7 inch R.M.L. at Mount Palmer. Launches left Johnson's Pier for Siloso (B. Mati) and Katong at 5.15 on Drill evenings, but it having been very quickly realized that these two places were really too far away for week day drills, it was decided to bring a 7 inch R.M.L. gun from Mount Palmer (which was not a healthy spot owing to the unpleasant smell that arose from Teluk Ayer Bay at low tide) to a more central spot where drills could be comfortably attended after business hours; it was decided that this spot should be behind the Master Attendant's office (present Post Office) on the site of the old Fort Fullerton. An appeal was made for 50 Volunteers to parade to move the 7 inch R.M.L. to this latter position, and there it stayed for some years.

Major W. Brooke-Hoggan R.A. compiled an S.V.A. Drill Manual in 1888 (dedicated to H.E. Sir Cecil Clementi Smith G.C.M.G.). This manual[1] was in two parts neatly bound in red leather, Part I being 7 inch R.M.L. Gun Drill and Part II 8 inch B.L. Gun Drill.

Twelve Drills on the 7-inch M.L. qualified a member of the S.V.A. to commence a voluntary course of 8 drills on the 8 inch B.L. at Tanjong Katong Fort, while the required number of drills under Regular Army instruction at Siloso was fixed at 10 per annum. The drilling in the several different types of ordnance was at the suggestion of the G.O.C. Commanding China and the S.S. (General W.G. Cameron).

Membership.—Membership was by election. Candidates for admission were proposed and seconded and balloted for by the general committee. Membership by election was in force right up to the reorganization of the S.V.C. in 1921 after which members were enrolled as in the Territorial Forces in England.

Promotion.—The method of promotion of all ranks was by qualifying examination; this method also was retained up to the reorganization of 1921 and in the case of N.C.O's of the S.R.A.(v) was reinstituted in 1927.

1888. *Dress.*—The uniform of the S.V.A. on formation was similar in general detail for both officers and other ranks. *Khaki Helmet* surmounted by the Artillery metal ball, chin chain and blue puggaree with the S.V.A. badge fixed into it on the right hand side. *Khaki Glengarry cap* with badge on the front left hand side—(the Glengarry cap was

---

[1] A copy of this 1888 Manual in two parts has recently been presented to the S.V.C. Headquarters Mess where it is on view.

abolished in 1894 on the introduction of a new Field Service Cap of blue cloth with folding peak in front and flaps at the sides to let down and fasten under the chin with two small buttons, the regimental badges being worn as in the case of the Glengarry on the front left hand side). *Khaki Tunic* ("tutup") of the patrol type with roll collar and, later, for officers a white stiff collar inside (the officers open jacket with khaki shirt, collar and tie did not come in until 1915). *Khaki trousers* and short blue gaiters (Marine Artillery style)—*Black Boots*. *Solar Topees* were also worn for gun drill at the forts. All ranks carried *swords*. Officers wore *Sam Browne belts* with khaki uniform. In addition to the *badges of rank* worn on the shoulder strap by officers they also wore, for some years, decorations of blue braid on their sleeves commencing with one or more rings about two inches above the edge of the cuff and continuing with a mass of braid almost up to the elbow, the number of rings and amount of braid increasing according to rank. These elaborate decorations from the cuff to the elbow, as badges of rank, were handed down from the days when the Corps was a Rifle Regiment and were abolished after a few years. Other Ranks also wore blue braid round the cuff decorated with a "Crow's Foot" at the point but this was abolished at the same time as the officers' decorations of this kind. *Buttons* were all of the regulation Artillery type except that the officers wore the bullet shaped button on the tunic front and two on each cuff after the elaborate braid decoration had disappeared from the sleeve. *White Uniform* was worn by all ranks for full dress.

The Rangoon Volunteer Artillery was in existence long before the S.V.A. and at the time of the forming of the latter, the former's smoking concerts earned an amount of praise and newspaper comment in Singapore.

The First S.V.A. Camp—at Blakan Mati, Easter 1888.—Over the Easter Holidays the first camp (for future N.C.O's) was held at Blakan Mati, arrangements having been made for the S.V.A. to occupy a bungalow at Blakan Mati East on the hillside about a hundred yards from the drawbridge leading to the fort. The following formed the first "Blakan Mati Squad" and were transported to Blakan Mati with their boys and "barang" (luggage) by the launches "Laju" and "Alberquerque" at 2.00 P.M. on Thursday, the 29th March, 1888:—

Major McCallum, Capt. Bruce-Webster, Lieutenants R. Dunman and Wade-Gardner, Gunners Alexander, Ayre, Bean, Hutton, Moffat, Morrison, Skene, St. Clair, and White, with Trumpeter Ryan and Signaller Pierce.

After corners had been chosen, mattresses laid down and mosquito curtains rigged up, a cup of tea formed a pleasant prelude to the S.V.A's first introduction to the 7-inch R.M.L. Gun on the left of the entrance to the fort.

There were four parades daily, two of these being gun drills of about an hour and a quarter's duration, one carbine drill of an hour and the other parade for a lecture. Two main lectures were given, one by the Commandant upon the disposition of the defensive works at Singapore and their armament, the other by Major Brooke-Hoggan, R.A., who was acting as Adjutant to the S.V.A., upon the construction and use of the Watkins depression range finder, and the construction of the 7-inch R.M.L. Gun, while the nature of its ammunition and fuzes were discussed at other lectures. Sergeant Grimmer, R.A., acted very efficiently as Sergt. Instructor during the stay of this detachment at Blakan Mati East. The detachment stood together for the first time behind a 7-inch gun on a Thursday evening and on Monday evening were able to fire the gun with blank ammunition, the weapon being trained and laid upon a moving steamer (s.s. *"Horsburgh"*) at about 2,000 yards, electric light playing full upon her from Fort Teregah.

As a wind-up to a real working holiday, the Blakan Mati Squad of the S.V.A. gave an "At Home" to their fellow gunners, and other friends, on the Monday evening (Easter Bank Holiday). There was a certain amount of novelty about the invitation that encouraged the guests, not a few of whom were ladies, to try and penetrate the mysteries that surrounded the "terra incognita" of Blakan Mati. The guests, about a hundred and fifty, were brought over by various launches including the paddle steamer *"Bangkok"*[1] (by Capt. Blair's kind permission). They witnessed the first "Action" by the S.V.A. and the "destruction" of the s.s. *"Horsburgh"* with blank ammunition, Major Hoggan taking command and giving orders to the detachment (whose acting No. 1 was none other than Major McCallum himself) to "Take post under cover", "Prepare for action" and then "As with Palliser shell, load". After the demonstration a "Jamboree" took place by the light of an immense camp fire. The band of the Royal Artillery from Fort Canning played lively tunes to begin with and the Commandant S.V.A. and his detachment paraded at tattoo to the rollicking "Babylon is falling", the Blakan Mati whistlers made their debut, and four sturdy Caledonians danced a spirited reel on the very

---

(1) 1928 the "Bangkok", a two funnelled paddle boat, has for the last decade been gradually falling to pieces in the vicinity of the Boat House at the R.S.Y.C.

edge of the fiery furnace, to the strains of an accordion! Gunners H. Brett, Currie and E.A. Thompson carolled comic songs with splendid choruses assisted by Lieut. Tyler (a regular soldier) who nearly brought down the marquee (there being no "house" handy) with his song "I'm getting a big boy now".

Gunner H. Brett, mentioned in the previous paragraph is a good example of the old saying "Old Soldiers never die". In 1888 he attended the first Camp of the S.V.A. at Blakan Mati and forty-one years later we find him as Battery Quartermaster Sergeant again attending a Blakan Mati Camp, amusing Volunteer Gunners with his comic recitations after their days work. What a magnificent example to follow! But, alas, this old gunner has now "faded away" in true soldier style, for he retired to England in 1930 with colours still flying.

On the 26th October, 1888 the "Volunteer Ordinance 1869" and the "Volunteer Amendment Ordinance, 1880" were repealed, and a new Ordinance was provided for the establishment of the new Corps and was cited as the "Volunteer Ordinance, 1888".

The Adjutants, from the formation of the S.V.A.C., were regular Officers serving in the Colony, who undertook this work in addition to their regular duties, and it was not until 1901 that a regular Adjutant was permanently appointed to the S.V.C.

1889. Colonel Anderson of the Northamptonshire Regiment (O.C.S.S.) was deputed by the Governor to make the first annual inspection of the S.V.A. this year. The inspection took place at Fort Fullerton on the 7-inch R.M.L. Gun at short notice owing to the War Office instructions to remove the gun and re-convey it to Fort Blakan Mati East. Col. Anderson in alluding to the great difficulty in training if the Corps had to drill at Blakan Mati promised to write a strong letter protesting against the removal of the gun; as a result the gun was left at Fort Fullerton. Present at the inspection were 4 Officers and 58 rank and file, 6 being on leave.

S.V.A. Maxim Gun Section.—Sir Hiram Maxim, it is recorded, perfected a machine gun about 1885 after having fired an old "Brown Bess" rifle during a visit to America and been surprised by the recoil or "kick" which he turned to good account. According to *Chambers Journal* (19.3.1887) General Stanley took one of the first Maxim machine guns for defensive purpose on his expedition for the relief of Emin Pasha. Many countries purchased considerable numbers following the publicity given to the weapon when it was awarded the gold medal at the Inventors' Exhibition in 1886, China being one of the largest purchasers and Malaya not so far behind the first purchasers.

In 1889 four of these Maxim guns (calibre ·450) were publicly subscribed for, and it is interesting to find the *"Lat Pau Press"* of March 9th making a strong appeal to the Chinese merchants to contribute liberally to the Subscription List for the purchase of Maxim Guns for the S.V.A.

> "The volunteers," says the editor, "are not lawless vagrants who are fond of fighting and quarrelling, but are all merchants or gentlemen of reputation, who are most energetic in protecting the Settlements, and being prompted by a sense of duty do not shrink from any dangers or troubles ......
> Now, supposing the volunteers do not care to make preparations for the future, but prefer a life of idleness, who can punish them for so doing? But no, they are most ardent to make their Corps efficient, and those who hear of them ought to be just as ardent in responding to their appeal, which consists in merely subscribing money."

The total amount subscribed was $10,524, of which $7,000 came from the Chinese (including $2,500 from Mr. Cheang Hong Lim). The translation of this *"Lat Pau"* appeal, which was published in the *"Free Press"*, was reproduced in several English papers, including *"Reynold's Weekly"* where it appeared under the title "Bravo, Singapore!" commending highly the generous action of the Chinese community.

Mr. Cheang Hong Lim's subscription covered the entire cost of one gun, another subscription from H.H. the late Sultan Abubakar of Johore covered the cost of one more and the remaining two were purchased from the subscriptions of the Chinese, Arab, Malay and Chetty communities.

The new Corps earned a grant of $1,800 for the official year ending 31.3.89 and began the new year with a credit balance of $1,269.30. A telephone was installed at the temporary S.V.A. Headquarters office at the Cricket Pavilion.

The Dress Regulations included Gaiters, Waist belt, Sword, Field Cap and two suits of uniform, one white and one khaki, the last being supplied by Messrs. Robinson & Co. All ranks possessing Mess Uniform were requested to wear it at the Queen's Birthday Ball and a note in July, 1889 on the Mess Dress states that the G.O.C. was pleased to allow members of the S.V.A. to continue the use of red cummerbunds until gilt buttons were procured from England for use with white waistcoats and also to wear red waistcoats in cloth uniform until silver-plated buttons were procured.

At 5.45 A.M. on the 24th May, 1889 the S.V.A. paraded at Fort Fullerton in preparation for their first public appearance—the 6.30 A.M.

Queen's Birthday Parade at the Race Course, now Farrer Park. On this occasion they wore their new khaki uniforms, gilt buttons and regulation helmets.

1889. ([1])Six Hotchkiss guns arrived in Singapore this year for the protection of mines defending the New Harbour. These early machine guns were manned by regular troops and some were placed in the subterranean casemates, to be seen to-day, near "Lot's Wife" (Tanjong Belayar Point) at the narrow western entrance of the harbour opposite Fort Siloso.

In September on the holiday for the Prince of Wales birthday the Volunteers ran a picnic (stag party) to the Carimons (Karimon) Islands, landing on Greater Carimon, and visited the waterfall.

In December they were inspected by Colonel Craster, R.A. from Hongkong.

Medical and Pay Work was under Honorary Surgeon Mugliston and Captain and Honorary Paymaster J. Fraser.

1890. The second annual inspection by General Sir Charles Warren took place at Fort Siloso on the 22nd March when 70 Volunteers were present.

Over Chinese New Year the S.V.A. held a firing practice on the two 7-inch guns at Fort Pasir Panjang and the following month they held 7-inch gun drills at Fort Siloso (Blakan Mati) being brigaded with the Regular Artillery for gun manning during the visit of the Duke and Duchess of Connaught. Later, between the 26th February and the 3rd March, a Camp was held at Katong for 8-inch gun drill where a "Camp Fire Entertainment" took place on the last day at 9.00 P.M., invitation being by ticket, Corporal Fabris and Gunner Brett rendering a genuinely unique impersonation of a Chinese domestic drama which raised loud laughter from the audience.

The Establishment of the S.V.A. in 1890 was 104 and the Corps was complete to this figure. The War Office raised the question of forming a Eurasian Volunteer Artillery Battery for Singapore for affiliation to the existing European Corps; the Government discussed the proposition with the Eurasian residents but nothing came of it.

1890. For the Queen's Birthday parade on the 21st May, 1890 at a review by General Sir Charles Warren, the 7-pounder Battery from Fort

---

(1) "One Hundred Years of Singapore" Vol. I. p. 383.

Canning was marched on to the Esplanade where it fired the salute, the order of march being:—

>7-pounder Battery Royal Artillery
>Royal Artillery
>Singapore Volunteer Artillery
>58th Regiment of Foot.

The Drill Hall.—Up to this date the Town Hall had been used for drilling and as a meeting place for instruction of the Volunteers. The Singapore Volunteer Artillery seemed, however, so firmly established and so likely to remain as a flourishing Volunteer unit (as indeed it has), that the first Volunteer Drill Hall was erected in this year.

Early in 1890 the plans were prepared for the proposed building, "80'×52' of simple and neat design, to be constructed of light materials, iron, wood and zinc and thereby easy to transfer if necessary". A site was chosen on that previously occupied by Fort Fullerton, beyond the Master Attendant's Office and adjoining the old Post Office. Sanction from home was received in June to proceed with the work and tenders were submitted in July. It was built by the first S.V.A. Commandant, Major McCallum who was at the time Executive Engineer, P.W.D., S.S. This building proved to be a fine example of a good "temporary building", lasting for 43 years! It was removed after sixteen years to the present position of S.V.C. Headquarters in Beach Road, being finally demolished in 1933, when its place was taken by the fine new building of to-day. At the same time that the first Drill Hall was built, a gun emplacement for a 7-inch muzzle loader was constructed for S.V.A. drill purposes, and this finally disappeared when the reclamation from Johnson's Pier to the mouth of the river was made in 1907.

The Hongkong Government having heard of the generosity of various public spirited people in Singapore in subscribing $10,000—for 4 Maxim guns for the S.V.A.—voted $37,275 for the purchase of 12 Maxim guns for the Hongkong Volunteers.

1891. An S.V.A. Chaplaincy was established in 1891.

It is interesting to note here that the Pioneer Company of the Calcutta Volunteers saw active service in April, 1891 being sent to Manipur to serve with the Manipur Expedition.

The O.C. Hongkong Volunteers wrote wishing to arrange a competition on the 64-pounder gun but it was found to be impossible as the S.V.A. could not spare the time from their training on the 7-inch R.M.L. and

8-inch B.L. guns to get over to a fort possessing 64-pounders on which to train.

In March Major McCallum went home to Chatham for six months to complete his examination in the Royal Engineers, and during his absence Captain R. Dunman commanded the S.V.A.

The uniform is again mentioned in connection with a camp as "White Clothing; Gaiters; Sun Hats (Forage Caps to be taken), Regimental Shirts, Waist belts, Swords and Rolled Coats." As regards the Mess Dress, White Waistcoats came into use in March, 1890 on arrival of the silver-plated buttons from home (50 cents for a set of five) and the scarlet cummerbund was discontinued from this date. When in Mess Dress all Volunteers wore a small gilt "V" on their shoulder straps to distinguish them from regular soldiers; this was discontinued in 1921.

Most camps were under canvas. There was one at Tanjong Katong (on the site of the present Katong Park) from Wednesday, 5th November, to Tuesday the 11th November. Camp orders mentioned the fact that a messing allowance of 75 cents per diem was granted for each man sleeping in Camp and that members not sleeping in Camp would pay for their own messing! To compare with the present day the following Camp programme is quoted.

Reveille	5.30 A.M.
Launch Singapore to Katong	6.00 "
Parade 8-in. gun Drill and Foot Drill	6.15 "
Launch Katong to Singapore	8.00 "
Launch Katong to Singapore	9.00 "
Launch Singapore to Katong	5.00 P.M.
Parade 8-in. Gun Drill and Foot Drill	5.30 "
Launch Singapore to Katong	6.15 "
Lecture	6.30 "
Launch to Singapore	7.45 "
First post and launch to Singapore	10.00 "
Second post	10.30 "

Swim after morning parade and before breakfast.
Swim after evening parade and before dinner.
Sunday morning included a short Church parade.
The Officers of the R.A. would dine with the S.V.A. on Saturday evening.

In this year the four Maxim Guns subscribed for in 1889 arrived in Singapore on the 4th April by *s.s. "Glenshire"*. This acquisition made the

S.V.A. OFFICERS WITH .405 MAXIM GUNS—1893 (circ.)

L to R Standing—Capt. G. Bruce-Webster; 2nd/Lt. E.M. Merewether; 2nd/Lt. J. Fabris; Lt. W.G. St. Clair; Capt. R. Dunman
Sitting—Capt. & Paymaster F.W. Barker; Major H.E. McCallum; Lt. & Adjutant W. Jennings, R.G.A.
Sitting Front—Capt. & Surgeon T.C. Mugliston; Lt. C.J. Davis

AN S.V.A. .405 MAXIM GUN DETACHMENT—1893 (circ.)

The 7-inch R.M.L. Gun in the background—Gnr. J.M. Rodesse & Lt. W.G. St. Clair on extreme right
Behind the Drill Hall, Fort Fullerton Site

Singapore Volunteer Artillery the first Maxim Gun Company in the British forces, regular or auxiliary.

As the G.O.C. at the time (Sir Charles Warren) was not in favour of it the Regular Troops were not present at the Queen's Birthday parade on the 29th May, 1891, and the S.V.A. had the Esplanade to themselves to demonstrate the loyalty of the Colony. At this parade they were formally presented with the four Maxim Guns. The disappointment of the populace that the S.V.A. Maxim Guns were not fired immediately after presentation and the Major's horse (Major McCallum was mounted) were subjects remarked upon during the parade and after it the excellence of the S.V.A. gin slings and cocktails!

The press were caustic about the exclusion of the regulars; the following is an extract from the *"Singapore Free Press"* (Weekly Edition, Tuesday, 9th June, 1891) :—

> "Singapore celebrated the Queen's Birthday sporadically owing to the "danger of letting British soldiers go out in the sun. It is fortunate we have "so considerate a G.O.C. for, if the customary review had taken place, the "whole battalion might have had to go to hospital, and left us defenceless!
>
> "Singaporeans were interested only in the S.V.A. parade and the Ball "at Government House, as the troops are Imperial and have no connection "with the Colony! .... our fears as to the safety of the town "are allayed when we know that the S.V.A. can take the field when the "regular troops are carefully kept under shelter for fear of sunstroke!"

The S.V.A. Maxim Section was an active section and part of the S.V.A. up to April, 1904 when H.E. the Officer Administering the Government was pleased to authorise the formation of a Maxim Section of the S.V.C. Forty names having been received for the newly organised section, the guns themselves were handed over by the S.V.A. and the section came under command of Capt. F.J. Benjafield. The new unit, however, was still attached to the S.V.A. for administration purposes, and still drilled Artillery fashion. They used the original 4 Maxims of .450 calibre, converted later to .303, up to 1914 when two were lent to the Imperial Government and sent to South Africa and one lent to the Penang Volunteers; none of these actual guns were ever returned to Singapore although they were replaced. The last gun out of the old original four machine guns is preserved as a relic at the Headquarters of the Corps [1].

Regarding the manning of the Maxim Guns the arrangements (made and published in July, 1890) were adhered to, that crews were only picked from members of the Corps who were already efficient in heavy gunnery, and the drivers for the Maxim Battery (until the battery had properly

---

[1] For disposal of these old Guns refer Report on the Local Forces of Malaya 1914-1918 page 21.

been set agoing and some permanent arrangement made about horsing) consisted of those members who possessed the proper sized galloways or ponies in their private stables.

At a route march at 5.15 one evening in May, 1891 the Volunteers wore their white dress uniforms, with side arms, because a halt was made at "Cairnhill," the residence of Mr. and Mrs. Budd, who entertained them to dinner on the tennis lawn, after which the march was continued to Raffles Museum where it dismissed at 9.45 P.M.!

The third inspection of the Corps at Fort Pasir Panjang in May, 1891, was made in the absence of the G.O.C., Sir Charles Warren, by Colonel Barton Brown, C.R.A.

On Monday evening the 13th April, 1891 the S.V.A. had a route march. Numbering forty-five in all, headed by the Drum and Fife Band of the 41st Battery Southern Division (then at Fort Canning), they marched *via* Esplanade Road, Stamford Road and Wilkie Road to Government House domain where they had a little practice in ceremonial movements against requirements at Queen's Birthday Parade. From Government House grounds they continued *via* Cavenagh and Bukit Timah Roads round to Tanglin Club where there was a brief halt for refreshment. The Battery falling in again, the march was resumed by way of Scotts Road, Paterson and Grange Roads to "Balado", the residence of Hon: Surgeon Murray Robertson, where dinner was served to the S.V.A. on the tennis lawn. After dinner and three cheers for "our hostess" the march was continued and finally the parade was dismissed opposite Raffles Museum. Owing to the halts which took place so conveniently, this march was known as "The Battle of Tanglin" and the following verse was written regarding it:—

THE BATTLE OF TANGLIN

To Arms! To Arms! and forward to the fray!
   Each Volunteer obeys stern duty's call,
See them march forth in martial proud array,
   A band of heroes, forty-five in all!

And now their Captain issues bold command:
   "High Tanglin must be stormed and sacked to-night."
Undaunted e'en by this the gallant band
   In serried ranks marched forward to the fight.

Each knows how great the perils are, and yet
   No coward fear can chill their warlike hearts:
Onward! A 'rickshaw coolie they've upset,
   And now they swiftly pass three bullock carts.

> Thus press they onward to the towering height
>   Where Tanglin Club their way doth seem to bar.
> With loosened ranks they rush in to the fight
>   On every side arise loud sounds of war.
>
> The quick reports of fusilade resound
>   Who thinks of sore feet now, or heads more sore?
> 'Ere long "dead men" lie piled upon the ground
>   Thus fight the warriors of Singapore!
>
> Zeal so unquenchable what can withstand?
>   Within brief space their victory's complete,
> The ranks reform, on marches this brave band
>   Though some perchance can scarcely keep their feet.
>
> Go waft the message forth across the sea:
>   When these can do such gallant execution—
> Our Soldier Citizens—what need have we
>   Of increased Military Contribution?

1892. It is interesting to note that in 1892 the Regular Gunners in Singapore numbered only 211 and were distributed roughly as under:—

Blakan Mati—
Fort Connaught (Blakan Mati East)	44	
Fort Siloso	18	
Fort Serapong	36	
		98

Pulau Brani—
Fort Teregah	8	
		8

Singapore—
Fort Pasir Panjang	34	
Fort Tanjong Katong	30	
Fort Palmer	26	
Fort Canning	15	
		105
		211

Captain Bruce Webster assumed command of the Corps during Major McCallum's absence in Pahang and camps for the year were commenced with one at New Harbour[1] over the period 29th January to 2nd February. The Volunteer Gunners were keen and commenced work early in the day, which is vouched for by the fact that, in addition to the tram

---

(1) Known as "Keppel Harbour" from April 1900 onwards.

service, an extremely efficient daily launch service ran from Johnson's Pier, starting as early as 5.30 A.M. and returning from New Harbour at 8 A.M. and 10 A.M. so that daily business could be attended to during routine hours. Many volunteers would leave Johnson's pier by evening launches, attend the evening parades and stay the night in camp. On occasions when the commissariat shared the baggage trucks attached to the steam tram running to New Harbour, we are told that the onlooker might be reminded of the well-known "Latin" verse:—

    Isabile eris ego   I say Billy 'ere's a go,
      Fortibus es in aro,   Forty busses in a row,
    O Nobile themis trux   Oh! No Billy, them is trucks,
      Soevat sinem pes au dux.   See what's in 'em, peas or ducks.

Peas and ducks most likely, for they did themselves well, in spite of there being no Cold Storage. The Camp was under canvas and pitched on the top of the hill at the entrance to Bukit Chermin, a large bungalow belonging to the New Harbour Company being used as a Mess. During the long week-end, launches left Bukit Chermin for Fort Siloso where drills took place on the 7-inch guns. Among the chief features of this camp are reported to have been the Church Parade in the New Harbour Reading Room which was well attended, and the succeeding bathing parade that took place in the dock and included water polo and other amusements. This programme was fitted in between early morning Gun Drill and the midday Gun Drill lecture, which was followed in the afternoon by Maxim Drill. Sentries were posted throughout the night, taking one hour shifts.

On occasions when 7-inch R.M.L. gun practice took place at Fort Pasir Panjang, the S.V.A. previously made up the cartridges themselves at Fort Canning.

Games between Volunteer and Non-Volunteer teams are frequently recorded during this decade and they were no doubt responsible for the enlistment of many a recruit for the Volunteers. Among these games a Rugger Match is recorded in February, 1892 as having taken place between the Volunteers and the Services, resulting in a win for the former by one goal and one try, or eight points, to nil. The Volunteer team consisted of:—

    Back.—Scoular; Threequarters.—Raymond, Firmstone and Lightfoot; Halves.—Gibbs and Miller; Forwards.—Martin (Captain), Barnes Holloway, Douglas, O.V. Thomas, Bruce Webster and W.W. Cook.

The Services, however, reversed the order within a fortnight when, at a return match, they won by eighteen points to two.

About this time the Lee-Metford rifle was taken into use by the Corps.

Our neighbours in Burma formed, in this year, two additional units, the Rangoon Naval Volunteers (with an Artillery war role) and the Rangoon Engineer Volunteers, the latter expanding to a Submarine Mining Company.

The Pahang Rebellion [1].—First news of disturbance in Pahang was received in Singapore on the 23rd December, 1891. On January 20th, 1892 Major McCallum left by the S.Y. *"Sea Belle"* with Raja Impey, for Selangor and Pahang to assist in quelling this rising of the Orang Kaya (Headmen and Tributary Chiefs) and the *"Singapore Free Press"* remarked on the fact that the Major had gone to the front in S.V.A. uniform which would "thus be christened and have its virtues as a serviceable equipment thoroughly tested". Major McCallum was not the only S.V.A. Officer to test the S.V.A. uniform in the Pahang Rebellion, however, as Lieut. W.G. St. Clair followed at a later date.

The rebellion is known as the "Revolt of the Orang Kaya of Semantan" because Abdul-Rahman or Bahman, a Chief in the district of the Sungei Semantan (between Bentong and Temerloh), was the instigator of most of the trouble. Of humble origin, partly Jakun. Bahman in his youth had been a servant in the household of Sultan Ahmad of Pahang but, being a born fighter, had later rendered his Sultan considerable services in war against troublesome chiefs, thereby obtaining from the Sultan some lenience when he refused to obey orders prohibiting him from collecting illegal taxes even before the British came to Pahang. In 1888, however, on the appointment of the first British Resident of Pahang (John Pickersgill Rodger) there started a general tightening up of the laws governing taxes in order that the revenue of the country should be sufficient to cover administration and allowances granted to Chiefs and Headmen in place of taxes which they had previously levied and collected themselves. New laws were also drafted for the eventual abolition of slavery and for land registration. All these changes, including the occupation of lands by mining companies, were of course not too popular to commence with and the Semantan Chief, fearless and turbulent, stood out against them and boasted that he alone had not submitted to the British Government. Bahman's attitude eventually resulted in his rising on December 15th, 1891 at Lubok Trua where he ambushed a party composed of the Collector

---

(1) This account of the Pahang Rebellion has been compiled mainly from "A History of Pahang" by W. Linehan, M.A., M.C.S.

(Mr. C.E.M. Desborough), the Inspector of Mines, 15 Sikhs and 6 Malay police, in the Semantan River inflicting severe casualties and mutilating the bodies of three of the Sikhs. Matters got worse and it being evident that the Pahang police, who numbered less than three hundred, would be unable to cope with the situation, the British Resident determined to concentrate them in the more important stations surrounding the Semantan, namely Bentong, Tras, Raub, Kuala Lipis and Kuala Tembeling, and to rely on the Sultan and his forces to suppress the outbreak. Hugh Clifford (then Assistant Resident) with sixty Sikhs and, the Sultan being an old man, the Regent Tengku Mahmud, with about two hundred followers, entered the Semantan on the 29th December.

In January the Resident accompanied by the Sultan, in person, one of his sons and about a thousand men entered the Semantan district. A force of Selangor and Perak police under the command of Major McCallum, S.V.A. had been despatched to Pahang to assist in the operations on the Bentong side. The rising continued to increase in size and numerous District and Police Officers received orders to command detachments of the Sultan's forces which were strengthened by Sikhs and Malay police. On May 5th Lieut.-Col. Frowd Walker, Commandant of the Perak Sikhs, arrived with some of his men at Raub where one, Mat Kilau, threatened attack. Mat Kilau, whose support of the Semantan Chief (Bahman) continued throughout the campaign, was the son of To' Gajah, Orang Kaya of Lipis, who led a war party in Sultan Ahmad's inner Council and pressed him hard to declare against the British. The old Sultan's attitude was not easy to gauge accurately at this period as he felt keenly the loss of power and privileges which the new regime, and the appointment of Tengku Mahmud as Regent, imposed on him.

[1]At the beginning of August Colonel Walker had in Pahang thirteen European Officers including Capt. Byrne, R.M.L.I., from H.M.S. "*Hyacinth*", Capt. W.A. Cuscaden, Superintendent of Police, Malacca and Lieut. W.G. St. Clair, S.V.A. (in charge of Raub)[2]. The last named Officer's own account (written in 1929, at the request of the Chronicler) of how he got to Pahang and his impressions, is perhaps best quoted verbatim.

"About the end of April 1892, I was at Kuantan having gone up in
"H.M.S. "*Plover*", and found there Lieut. W.B. Jennings R.A., our Adjutant
"in the S.V.A. And while there, staying with Johnny Owen, who was District

---
(1) "A History of Pahang" by W. Linehan, M.A., M.C.S. p. 154.
(2) *See* Appendix V for two letters written to Lieut. St. Clair by the Governor, re this appointment, the originals of which were given by him to the writer of this history just before his death and have recently been presented to the Corps. They are to be seen in the H.Q. Mess.

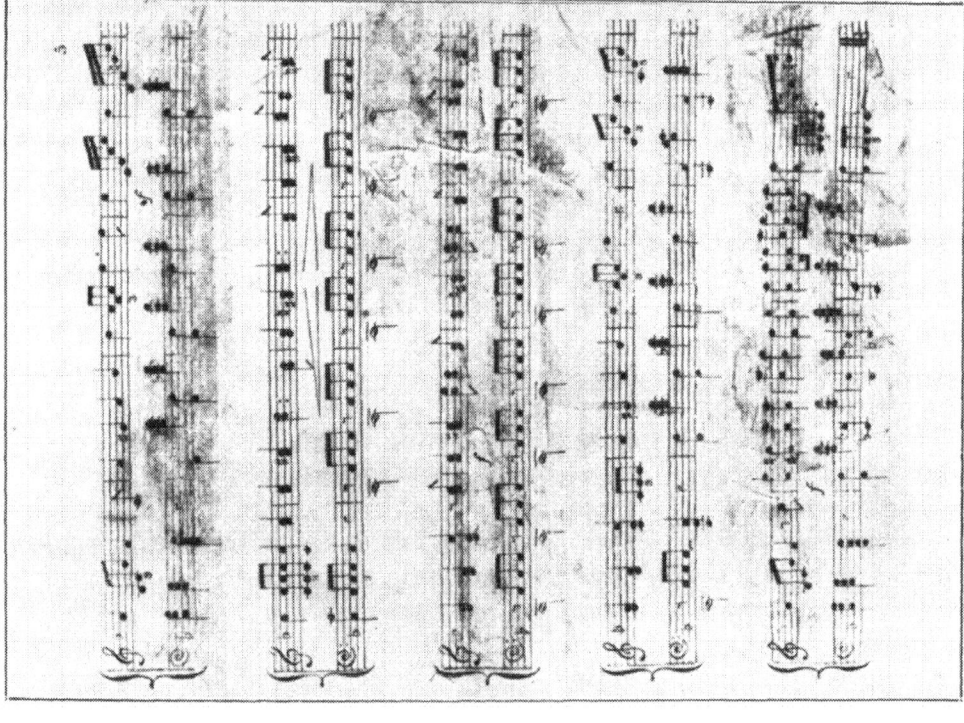

THE SINGAPORE VOLUNTEER RIFLE CORPS MARCH

Composed by Clayworth Hall possibly during the Governorship of Col. Orfeur Cavenagh to whom it is dedicated but presumably reprinted after 1888 since the motto is "In Oriente Primus".—Original presented by Lt.-Col. D.G. McLeod to be seen in H.Q. Mess

S.V.A. OFFICERS—1895
Lt. Sisson, Lt. Cockrane (Adjt.), Lt. G.A. Derrick, Lt. E.M. Merewether
Lt. W.G. St. Clair, Major H.E. McCallum, Capt. R. Dunman, Lt. F.W. Barker

S.V.A. SERGEANTS—1896
Major McCallum, Sgt.-Major Skaw, Adjutant Cockrane
Sgt. Hilton, Sgt. Makepeace, Sgt. Batty, Sgt. Morrison, (behind), Sgt. Benjafield

"Officer, news came that Rodger, the Resident, was going up the Pahang
"River That was my chance. So I walked from Kuantan along the beach
"to Kuala Pahang, and found that I was in time. A strong detachment of
"Perak Sikhs had just arrived by steamer from Singapore, with one 7-pr gun
"and its Pathan detachment. Rodger asked me to go up in charge, which
"I did in S.V.A. khaki, naturally. I spent the month of May at Temerloh,
"during which Rodger one day delivered the historical ultimatum of the
"Governor to the Sultan, that he must "personally direct", and "take part in",
"the operations to deal with the Orang Kaya and his Semantan followers.
"It was an interview of grave importance. The Sultan, To' Gajah and three
"or four other Pahang Chiefs, and three Europeans, Rodger and Teddy Wise
"in sarongs and I standing at the door in uniform. If the Sultan had not
"been overawed by the terms of the ultimatum, we might have all three been
"scuppered on the spot. But he knew enough to know what he was likely
"to be up against.

"I left my detachment and the gun at Temerloh, went up river to Kuala
"Lipis and with Mr. Rodger in the stern wheeler *Sinjunie* and about a
"fortnight later walked across from Kuala Lipis to Raub. I there found
"Colonel Walker and the main body of the Perak Expeditionary Force, with
"the other two 7-pr guns and Pathan detachment under Buswell. Events
"and the Governor's appointment compelled me to stay on there in charge
"for five months while Walker and his flying column, Clifford with him as
"political officer, were trying to follow up the retreating rebels with the
"Orang Kaya, who were trying to make for Kelantan."

There being hardly any roads in those days the rivers were the highways and by-ways for communication in Pahang, Trengganu and Kelantan and indeed have remained so, to a great extent, in the hinterland of these three adjoining states. This war in Pahang was, therefore, one of desultory fighting in jungle and on rivers. Bahman and Mat Kilau had expert knowledge of the country and such fighting and were therefore able to elude the Government forces again and again; in fact they were never caught as they always retreated up the rivers to Trengganu (which together with Kelantan was at that time under suzerainty of Siam) whose Sultan sympathized with them.

In August, 1892 the Governor accompanied by Major McCallum visited Pekan and held a consultation with Sultan Ahmad of Pahang. The Sultan of Johore also attended. A general amnesty was proclaimed applicable to all except the two rebel leaders (Bahman and To' Gajah) and in September the Sultan of Pahang visited Singapore, so that by the end of 1892 there was a marked improvement between the relationship of the people and the Government. With the rebel Chiefs still at large, however, the unrest continued through 1893 at the end of which year, due to certain sympathies given to the rebels by the Jelai Chief and some fanatical support from

Trengganu, the situation became serious again, remaining so throughout 1894, during June of which year Mr. E.A. Wise (Superintendent Ulu Pahang) and four Sikhs were killed and Captain H. Talbot (Perak Sikhs) and four Sikhs were wounded when they met the rebels at Kuala Tembeling on their return from Trengganu.

On March 17th, 1895 Hugh Clifford, with Siamese Commissioners, started on a punitive expedition *via* the river Sepia into Trengganu to capture the rebel leaders who were then established in Besut. At Kuala Pring ninety-five bearers and personal attendants were sent back to Pahang. Owing to difficulties in transport, all Clifford's men, including Europeans, were required to live on a diet of rice, an exception being made in favour of the Sikhs who though they behaved well, seemed totally unsuited for jungle operations. The expedition was a failure though, as the Trengganu rulers, while pretending to be friendly and render assistance, actually concealed the rebels, six of whom (including Bahman) eventually surrendered to the Siamese Authorities and were taken to Siam in November 1895, while To' Gajah and his son, Mat Kilau, were reported to have died in Trengganu.

Thus ended a jungle campaign with its many difficulties, illness, lack of food and medical comforts but in which the Singapore Volunteer uniform was "christened".

This narrative concerning the Pahang Rebellion may appear rather long since only two Volunteer Officers took part. It might have been shortened accordingly to cover their particular activities and the christening of the S.V.C. uniform, but since there has been, really, very little change in the topography of the hinterland of these States of the East Coast of Malaya since 1892 it is felt that it will give Volunteers a good general idea of the difficulties which would still be encountered in any defence operations on the East Coast of Malaya.

1893. In August, 1893 the Volunteers, together with the members of the Straits Civil Service, entertained their Honorary Colonel and Governor, Sir Cecil Clementi Smith, and Lady Clementi Smith, to a luncheon at the Drill Hall being a farewell prior to his retirement. A feature of the special decorations were two big medallions, bearing the monograms "C.C.S." (Cecil Clementi Smith) and "T.C.S." (Theresa Clementi Smith) and ever since these decorations have retained an honoured place in the Drill Hall as a memento of the Governor who took such a keen personal interest in the creation of the S.V.A.C. For that farewell tiffin, Major McCallum, characteristically, designed a delightful menu in the form of a Government minute paper correct even to a little patch of green paper affixed to it, meaning "For immediate attention", and tied up with very thin red tape!

Mondays and Thursdays were "Club Nights" at the Drill Hall, which was lighted at 8 P.M., and a hope was expressed that members would use it as a club. It was open to Active, Honorary and Retired members and to those on the Reserve.

The Rifle Association was amalgamated in 1893 with the Volunteer Artillery Corps, members of which were entitled to join free. The subscription for non-Volunteers was $10 per annum.

1894. A cyclist detachment was added to the S.V.A. Their uniform was khaki helmet, tunic and knickerbockers, dark blue stockings and brown canvas boots. The usual dress for the Gunners at that time was, helmet or field service cap, khaki tunic or regimental shirt, khaki trousers, brown gaiters (of the Marine type) and brown boots. Sun hats of the "beehive" type (light pith) for drill and work in the sun were also used when shirt sleeves were the order.

1895. Camps have always been a feature of the S.V.C. and in 1895 there was a regular "Camp Gazette", copies of which still survive and show that slang and humour are not the products of the present day generation alone(1).

1896. In 1896 the S.V.A. were supplied with six 2.5 R.M.L. (7-pounder) Mountain (Screw) Guns with jungle transport from which in later years they used regularly to fire the salutes on Queen's and King's Birthday celebrations.

On the 2nd March, the S.V.C. held a farewell parade in honour of Major McCallum who was proceeding on leave to England. It proved, however, to be a final farewell because while in London he was appointed Governor and Commander-in-Chief of Lagos and never saw the Straits again.

---

(1) "One Hundred Years of Singapore" p. 397.

2.5-inch, 7-pr. Mountain Screw Gun S.V.A. 1896–1903

1897. For firing practice with the 7-pr. Mountain gun Major McCallum had a land range made at Bukit Panjang, on the Bukit Timah Road, and practice was carried out there for a short period. Unfortunately the targets were on such swampy ground that the shell would never burst on impact([1]).

Puttees of dark blue were first taken into use in 1897 in place of brown gaiters and it follows that boots must also have been changed from brown to black to match the puttees.

A detachment composed of Malay States Guides and Malay Police went home to England this year, under Lt.-Colonel R.S. Frowd Walker, for H.M. Queen Victoria's Diamond Jubilee Celebrations. That Volunteers did not also form a part of the detachment caused some comment at the time.

1898. The Singapore Cricket Club instituted cricket tournaments in the Settlement in 1898 and the shield, presented by a member of the club for competition at these tournaments, was first won by the Singapore Volunteer Artillery skippered by Captain W.G. St. Clair. The shield is still to be seen in the Cricket Club.

1899. On the 29th June, 1899 the second Volunteer Corps was enrolled in Penang (the first being in 1861). It came into existence by proclamation dated 17th May. It was an Infantry Corps constituted under the Volunteer Ordinance of 1888 and composed of Europeans and Eurasians; the original enrolment of 60 members was increased to 158 by the end of the year. Mr. A.R. Adams, who was gazetted Captain on the 31st August, 1899 was also appointed Acting Commandant([2]).

The S.V.C. continued to be the sole Volunteer unit in Singapore until after the outbreak of the South African War in 1899 when the British battalion of the regular garrison of the Settlement was withdrawn for active service and replaced by a native battalion of the Indian Army. This war, just as the Crimean War did in 1857, brought home to a peace-loving,

1899–1921
Penang Volunteers

---

(1) "One Hundred Years of Singapore" Vol. I p. 397.
(2) The appointment was confirmed in 1900 and only relinquished on the 30th April, 1919 when Lt. Colonel Sir Arthur Adams, K.B.E., V.D. retired and left the Colony. This service of practically 20 years as Commandant of the Penang Volunteers earned for Col. Adams the well deserved honour of Knighthood which he received just prior to his retirement.

care-free public the fact that defence of the realm was a duty calling for more support by the ordinary civilian, in the shape of volunteer soldiering; the immediate result was the formation in 1900 of the Singapore Volunteer Rifles.

The Belt Plate worn by Singapore Volunteers 1888–1921

CHAPTER III

THE FOURTH CORPS 1900–1921

ARTILLERY—EUROPEAN RIFLE COMPANY—ENGINEERS—EURASIAN COMPANY—
CHINESE COMPANY—MAXIM COMPANY—MALAY COMPANY—
THE WAR AND THE SINGAPORE MUTINY

During the twenty years covered by this chapter public ideas were generally warmed towards Volunteering; two Kings were crowned, two wars were fought and the population and importance of Singapore increased with the commercial expansion following the demands for rubber and tin. Although with the increase of sport and other pastimes the rising generation of these two decades gradually looked less to Volunteering for exercise and distraction from the every day job, Volunteering never looked back but progressed steadily with an ever increasing public spirit that is proved by the number of new units raised before the advent of the War of 1914.

1900. On the 5th May, 1900 Sergt. W. Cloke of the S.V.A. died in Intombi Hospital Ladysmith, Natal, while serving with Thornycroft's Mounted Infantry in the South African War. A memorial service was held on the 6th January, 1901 in the Presbyterian Church for the unveiling of a tablet erected by the S.V.A. to the memory of Sergt. Cloke.

In addition to the salute at the Queen's Birthday Celebrations, the S.V.A., on the occasion of a loyal public demonstration of British subjects in connection with the surrender of Pretoria, paraded at the Drill Hall, at 8.00 P.M., on the evening of the 7th June, 1900 marched to Government House and fired a salute of 21 guns, from their battery of six Mountain Guns.

In this year (1900) the Rifle unit was formed. It was promoted by Mr. Arnot Reid (Editor, *Straits Times*) so that resident Europeans who were outside the Artillery Corps could assist in the local defence. The organisation of the new Rifle unit was carried out by none other than Major St. Clair who was then (1900/01) acting in command of the S.V.A. Corps.

On the retirement of Major R. Dunman, S.V.A. to England, Mr. Egerton, acting Colonial Secretary, asked Major St. Clair if he would accept the command of the new S.V.C., but, ever without thought of personal advantage, Major St. Clair called on H.E. Sir J.A. Swettenham (Officer Administering the Government) and, under the excuse of preferring to stick to the S.V.A., suggested the appointment of Major A. Murray, who had just been appointed from Ceylon to succeed Major McCallum as Colonial Engineer. Major Murray had been in command of the Ceylon Light Infantry and Major St. Clair submitted that, as a member of the Executive Council, he would be in a good position to represent all Volunteer interests including finance. Major Murray subsequently accepted the command. On Major Murray's arrival back in the Colony (from leave in Tasmania) the Acting Commandant, S.V.A. Corps had the pleasure and honour of handing over to him the Singapore Volunteer Rifles, two strong companies, fully equipped under immediate command of their first officers, Capt. W. Macbean, No. 1 Company and Capt. E.G. Broadrick,(1) No. 2 Company.

1901. When in England in 1901 Mr. Tan Jiak Kim, a leading Chinese citizen of the day, strongly supported the memorial of the Straits Chinese British Association offering the services of Straits-born Chinese, as British subjects, in the defence of the Colony. He interviewed Lord Onslow, Under-Secretary of State for the Colonies, on the subject and on his return to this Colony had the satisfaction of seeing the Chinese Company of the S.V.I. formed in November 1901. Among its original members were Dr. Lim Boon Keng, Mr. (now Sir) Song Ong Siang, Mr. Tan Soo Bin (son of Mr. Tan Jiak Kim) and Mr. Song Ong Joo. Mr. Song Ong Siang became Colour Sergeant of the Company in 1905, on Dr. Lim Boon Keng's resignation, and subsequently the first Chinese officer, being appointed a 2nd Lieutenant in April, 1907; still later, in 1915, he was promoted to Captain when some S.V.C. units were formed into double companies. Mr. Tan Soo Bin later had the honour of being the first Chinese to be promoted to the rank of Major in the S.V.C. while Mr. Song Ong Joo retired as a Sergeant when he left the Colony for Samarang in 1909.

Singapore Volunteer Engineers.—A committee of S.V.A. and S.V.R. Officers, N.C.O's and

S.V.A. 1888–1908

S.V.C. 1900–1928

---

(1) President of the Singapore Municipal Commissioners in 1904.

men sat in December of this year to report on the organization and conditions of service of the proposed Singapore Volunteer Engineers and on the 12th December, 1901 the Singapore Volunteer Engineers were raised and the S.V.A., S.V.R. and S.V.E. became known as the "Singapore Volunteer Corps", which was further added to by the raising of the Singapore Volunteer Infantry, No. 1 Company being Eurasian and No. 2 Company Chinese. Hence the Singapore Volunteer Artillery Corps ceased to exist as a Corps of its own and became the first unit of the S.V.C. which at that time consisted of:—

> Singapore Volunteer Artillery (European)
> Singapore Volunteer Engineers (European)
> Singapore Volunteer Rifles (European)
> Singapore Volunteer Infantry No. 1 Company (Eurasian)
> Singapore Volunteer Infantry No. 2 Company (Chinese).

The S.V.A. Bearer Section was formed by sanction of the Government on the 27th April, 1901 under command of the Hon. Major T.C. Mugliston and later became the S.V.A. Ambulance and Bearer Section. Its designation seems to have been changed many times for it afterwards became the Bearer Coy. S.V.A. and then the Medical Company, S.V.C. (1913) which was reconstructed and reorganised in 1914 into the Singapore Field Ambulance Coy., S.V.C. In 1922, when the Corps was reorganised after the war, this offshoot of the old S.V.A. received its present designation, The Singapore Volunteer Field Ambulance.

The Rifle Range at Balestier.—During 1901, on the request of Major St. Clair, the rifle range at Balestier was widened and extended to take 6 Jeffrys targets (as at Tanglin). This work cost $13,000 and was carried out with the assistance of Mr. Eyre Kenny, P.W.D., indents being submitted to the Ordnance Store on Pearls Hill. This was done to meet the musketry necessities of the new S.V.R.

Reserve of Officers.—The Reserve of Officers for the S.V.C. was formed under the provisions of Rule XVIIA of the Regulations made by H.E. the Governor under Sections 9 and 12 of the Ordinance VII 1888.

Visit of H.R.H. The Duke and Duchess of Cornwall and York.—The S.V.A. under Capt. C.J. Davies fired a Royal Salute from their Mountain

Gun Battery on Collyer Quay(¹) on the 23rd April, 1901, on the occasion of a visit to Singapore of T.R.H. The Duke and Duchess of Cornwall and York (afterwards H.M. King George V and Queen Mary) on their way to Australia on H.M.S. *"Ophir"*. The S.V.A., S.V.R. and a detachment of the Penang Volunteers helped to line the greater part of Connaught Drive.

1902. *The Coronation of King Edward VII.*—The Volunteers, especially the newly formed Companies, were immensely pleased at the receipt of a telegram in March 1902, from the Secretary of State for the Colonies, announcing that a contingent of fifty members selected from the whole of the Volunteer Corps in the Colony should proceed to England to represent the Straits Settlements at the Coronation of His Majesty King Edward VII. One week before the detachment of the S.V.C. left, there was an inspection of the whole Corps on Raffles Reclamation by the Governor, Sir Frank Swettenham, who, addressing the contingent, reminded them that they were going to represent the Colony at the Coronation Celebrations and not on a pleasure trip. The contingent left Singapore by s.s. *"Ceylon"* on the 26th April, 1902; the eight representatives of the S.V.A. being B.S.M. T.O. Mayhew, Corporal F.G. Allen, Gunners Austin Jackson, C.H. Darke, H.G. Darke, L.E. Koek, Webb, and J. Marshall, while the Chinese Company S.V.I. were represented by seven members, Sergt. Lim Boon Keng, Corpl. Song Ong Siang, Lance-Corpl. Chia Keng Chin, and Privates Tan Chew Kim, Seah Cheng Joo, Cheong Choon Beng and Tan Kwee Wah, while Privates Tan Boon Liat and Tan Hood Guan also went at their own expense. The detachment was under command of Major Murray and on arrival in London camped in the grounds of Alexandra Palace. During their stay in England many members of the contingent were able to be present at the annual dinner on June 18th of the Straits Settlements Association, held at the Hotel Metropole and presided over by Sir Cecil Clementi Smith(²). In consequence of the serious illness of the King, the Coronation ceremony was postponed for a couple of months and the contingent did not return to Singapore until the 26th September, 1902, by the s.s. *"Java"*.

A full account of the Colonial Volunteers "Life in Alexandra Palace Camp", as the article is titled, appears in *"The Straits Chinese Magazine"* Vol. VI No. 24 p.p. 123/149, by Mr. Song Ong Siang.

The arrival in London of the Straits Coronation Contingent was apparently hailed by London girls and caused a member of the Volunteer

---
(1) *See* photograph p. 50.
(2) This gathering also included H.H. the Sultan of Perak, Sir Charles Warren, G.C.M.G., K.C.B., Rear Admiral Angus MacLeod, Sir Ewen Cameron K.C.M.G., C.P. Lucas, Hugh Clifford C.M.G., Colonel Dunlop C.M.G., Colonel Frowd Walker C.M.G. and Officers of the Straits Settlements Coronation Contingent.

Artillery to be responsible for the following ditty, the poetical weakness of which was no doubt due in some measure to the vagaries of the tune to which it was voiced:—

>   Kita pergi London Town
>   Tengok Raja pakei crown
>   Inggris - Missi - Missi - suka - S. - V. - A.

but when the Rifles or Infantry Volunteers were within hearing loud protests were heard correcting the last line by shouts of "Tidak, S.V.R." or S.V.I. accordingly.

Some idea of the numbers of colonial troops that attended the Coronation of King Edward VII is given by a passage in the above mentioned article, which tells us that the Banqueting Hall at Alexandra Palace, which was in a bad state of repair, was occupied by the Sikhs, Malay R.E.'s, the Borneo and one or two other native contingents, while

Cover of the Volunteer Coronation Contingent 1902 Magazine published on board S.S. "Ceylon" (From a reproduction in the Straits Chinese Magazine)

on the two sides of another slope facing the Hall were pitched the tents of a part of the colonial troops comprising both Volunteers and Regulars from Bermuda, Jamaica, St. Lucia, Trinidad, Hong Kong, North and South Nigeria, Wei-Hai-Wei, West Africa, Sierra Leone, Gambia, Gold Coast, Lagos and the King's African Rifles (Uganda) with a total strength of about 650. On the opposite part of the Park near Muswell Hill Station, was the "Grove Camp" of tents of the colonial Troops from Cape Colony, Natal, Cyprus, Straits Settlements, Ceylon and Malta, with a total strength of 350 men. Near the Priory Gate were situated the Canadians, Australians, New Zealanders and Maoris, numbering 986 strong.

On June 1st, 1902 the peace treaty between the Empire and the Boers was announced and a big "fraternization" took place among the colonial contingents in Alexandra Park to commorate the occasion when "large smiles and larger drinks were bestowed on all and sundry".

Part of the Coronation Contingent Volunteers received pay at the rate of 2/6 per day on board ship, 5/- a day while in England and an additional 3/6 a day ration allowance when on leave visiting relations and not being fed by the Palace caterer though *"The Lyre"*, the details of which publication are recorded below, published a reputed London telegram on the homeward journey of the Contingent, running "London—Rumour afloat in the city, Chamberlain offers pay Straits Contingent per diem, 1d. per man, 1½d. for each N.C.O. 2d. for each officer. Consols have risen 25 per cent in consequence."

"The Lyre", "published in obscurity" according to the title page which is reproduced in these pages, was a journal of the Straits Coronation Contingent, published in two issues on the homeward voyage on board the P. & O. Steamship *"Ceylon"*. The contingent was fortunate in having on board a Private Mulvany, who, though no relation to Kipling's hero of the same name, appeared to be a "most prolific poet who knocked off poems while you waited". He declared one of the objects of *"The Lyre"* in the following verse:—

> "Subscriptions from all we earnestly ask
>   Though not to pay for the Editor's task,
> The money collected we hope to send
>   To the Party in London the Children's Friend
> And if we are able e'en only to pay
>   For a dozen chicks for a trip away
> From the smoke and the soot of the city streets
>   To taste the woodlands and meadows sweets
> Who'll say the Lyre though birth obscure
>   Has not done a little for the London poor.

The subscription to *The Lyre* was 1/- for members of the Contingent or, as the journal itself put it, "soldiers in uniform" and 2/6 to the outside public, and as the "printing" was done on the ship's cyclostyle, they were able to forward the profits of £4 to the Children's Fresh Air Fund.

A Fancy Dress Ball was advertised poetically in *"The Lyre"* by Mulvany:—

> "To all within hearing of bugle call
>   Take notice we give a fancy ball
> At 8 p.m. of the moon's 9th day
>   So all who won't come can stay away
> 'Tis patronised by the officers all
>   Of the Straits Contingent so when you call
> Bring the dollars with you to help to pay
>   For the claret cup, the whisky and tay".

It was appropriate, says the Straits Chinese Magazine, that one of that line of steamers—the first in the East—should carry the representatives of a Volunteer Corps whose motto is "In Oriente Primus", and in his usual spirit of levity Private Mulvany sang the praises of the P. & O.:—

> Some praise the German Mail Sir
>   Some French, some Japanee,
> For every form of comfort
>   In travelling o'er the sea.
>
> But if as a Contingent
>   To England you would go
> You take the tip from me, Sir,
>   And travel P. & O.
>
> For the comfort of the berth, Sir,
>   Provided for the men
> Is not to be surpassed, Sir,
>   What's that you say? Ahem!
>
> Well even that admitting
>   I'll state beyond a doubt
> That at the bugles calling
>   For "makan", every mouth.
>
> At once begins to water,
>   And men with glist'ning eye
> At once rush to the tables
>   Prepared to do or die.
>
> And to hear the tables groaning
>   With the weight of roasts and stew
> Would make a rank outsider
>   Wish he was contingent too.
>
> Some of those savoury dishes
>   Whose names you can't make out
> But whose taste, Ye Gods and Fishes
>   Of that there is no doubt.
>
> But the curries and the puddings
>   Here the chef doth all excel
> For he works on those grand lines
>   That a Rose will as sweet smell
>
> If by chance you call it Pansy
>   So his puddings just the same
> Day by day are "sama juga"
>   Though they are called another name.
>
> So to your feet Contingent:
>   And take your time from me
> Three cheers and one cheer over
>   For those ships that sail the sea.
>
>   For comfort, food, civility,
>   Excel where'er they go
>   Attention: Present Arms:
>   Hurrah: for the P. & O.

In 1902 a Volunteer Cadet Corps was formed from the boys of Raffles Institution and attached to the S.V.C.; their number was added to in 1906 by the inclusion of companies from St. Joseph's Institution and the Anglo-Chinese School. As the boys were mostly Eurasian and Chinese it was hoped that the Cadet Corps would act as a feeder to the Singapore Volunteer Infantry. This, however, failed to be the case and in the early part of 1918 the Cadets ceased to be attached to the S.V.C. and School Cadet Companies unconnected with the Volunteer Corps were formed in substitution.

A treaty constituting the Federation of the States of Perak, Selangor, Negri Sembilan and Pahang was signed in 1895 and in 1902 Volunteering started in the Federated Malay States with the formation of the first unit of the Malay States Volunteer Rifles. Following the example of the origin of the S.V.C. Maxim Guns, Dr. Loke Yew, C.M.G., presented the M.S.V.R. with two Maxim Guns in this year of their constitution.

The Singapore Volunteer Engineers were granted the title of Singapore Royal Engineers (Volunteers) by Royal Warrant dated 29th May, 1902.

Singapore having just established a Volunteer Engineer unit we find that our friends in Burma were about the same time reorganising their Engineer unit, formed ten years before, and that they disbanded the Submarine Mining Company in this year forming, to take its place, an Electrical Engineer Company. For the benefit of our Gunner Volunteers it is also interesting to mention that the Artillery of the Rangoon Port Defence Volunteers of 1902 consisted of one Artillery Company, two Naval Divisions and two Cadet Companies; the last named became, in 1908, Naval Cadet Divisions, remaining so until 1913 when the Naval Divisions of the Rangoon Volunteers were abolished.

A Malacca Company, S.V.C. was also formed this year (having been sanctioned by the Secretary of State on the 25th October, 1901) under the Command of Captain R.N. Bland. Forty-seven British subjects joined including Europeans, Chinese, Malays and Eurasians. It existed as part of the S.V.C. until its disbandment in 1906.

1903. In this year the S.V.A. changed their armament, the 7-Pr Muzzle Loading Mountain Guns being withdrawn and replaced by the more up-to-date 2.75 inch (10-Pr) Breech Loading Mountain Guns, also known as "Screw Guns" owing to the barrel or piece being in two parts called the "Breech" and the "Chase".

1904. At the end of 1903 the Singapore Volunteer Rifles "died" from lack of support after the South African War scare was over and on the 1st January, 1904 they were disbanded. There was consternation as to what could be done with the few remaining members who would not resign, so it was decided to start a Maxim Gun Company, using for the purpose the four guns presented in 1892 to the S.V.A. but which they were unable to man owing to the popularity of the Mountain Guns with which they were also equipped. The Maxims were rather grudgingly handed over by the S.V.A. on the 7th April, 1904 to the newly formed Maxim Gun Section, on the understanding that, though they might be manned by the latter they were still the absolute property of the former unit, having been presented to them. It also appeared that the S.V.A. maintained the proprietary rights of the Old Drill Hall which they stated was theirs, (a superiority complex, which the S.V.A. is alleged to have held right up to 1914!); a compromise was, however, effected and finally it was settled that the title of the new unit should be the S.V.A. Maxim Gun Section, and that they should discard the khaki puttees of the S.V.R. and take to the Artillery Blue and wear as shoulder titles S.V.A. (M) instead of S.V.R. On the 1st November, 1904 the Maxim Section became a Company and was known as the S.V.A. Maxim Company being to all intents and purposes a separate unit. Lieut. J.A.R. Glennie from the S.V.R. was the first Officer Commanding the S.V.A., M.G. Section with Lieut. F.J. Benjafield as one of his Subalterns and among the first N.C.Os were, No. 1 Gun Detachment Sergt. J.G. Mactaggart, Corporal J.T. Lloyd and Lance-Corporal P.S. Falshaw (Veterinary Officer) No. 2 Gun Detachment Sergt. D.Y. Perkins, Corporal A.S. Mullholland and Lance-Corporal C.C. Mactaggart, No. 3 Gun Detachment Sergt. E.A. Brown, No. 4 Gun Detachment Sergt. W. Berry.

The mounting of the S.V.A. Maxims at this time was the light field artillery carriage with a limber to which the trail of the gun carriage was hooked. The limbers which had shafts (like those for the S.V.A. mountain guns) were pulled by gharry ponies with N.C.O's. sitting on the limbers, driving with long reins and many were the "chariot" races which took place, in clouds of dust, back to the Drill Hall after the day's work. When the guns were unlimbered, drag ropes were provided for hauling them over rough country. As long as the guns were on wheels the Volunteers declared the game an easy one, but when they had to be dismounted and carried then the real work began. The gun weighed 48 lbs. and the tripod nearly as much. The box of ammunition carried

H.R.H. THE DUKE OF CORNWALL (LATER KING GEORGE V)
Inspecting the S.V.A.—Collyer Quay, Singapore, 1901
Major Murray (near camera), Major St. Clair (in khaki)
7-pr. Screw Gun in Background

THE S.V.A. SECTION S.S. CONTINGENT TO THE CORONATION OF H.M. KING EDWARD VII—1902
In Alexandra Palace Grounds, London
Standing Behind—C.H. Darke, A.G. Darke, L.E. Koek. Standing Front—F.G. Allen, Webb, J. Marshall, A. Jackson. Sitting—B.S.M. T.O. Mayhew

S.V.A. 10-pr. 2.75-in. B.L. MOUNTAIN GUNS
Firing practice near Fort Tanjong Katong 1905 (circ.)

S.V.A. 10-pr. 2.75-in. B.L. MOUNTAIN GUNS
Gun Park near Fort Tanjong Katong 1905 (circ.)

on the limber contained four belts (1,000 rounds) and the spare parts box was the same size and nearly the same weight. The drill was the same as the field artillery with commands that would puzzle the present day machine gunner, such as "Action Front", "Action Right", "Front Limber Up" and so on.

The Volunteer Infantry formed in 1900 with 100 members had during the years of the Boer War, and those immediately after, increased to nearly double that number. The national crisis being well over and the regular garrison brought up to its normal strength again, the S.V.I. was reduced in 1904.

1905. A new book of "Regulations and Rules of the Singapore Volunteer Corps" was published in 1905 and the following are some interesting points extracted therefrom.

Regulations.—
 3. Establishment.—

	Lieutenant-Colonel.	Majors.	Captains.	Lieutenants.	Second-Lieutenants.	Quarter-Master.	Surgeons.	Quarter-Master Sergeant.	Armourer.	Sergeant-Major and Colour-Sergeant.	Sergeants.	Corporals.	Trumpeters.	Buglers.	Gunners.	Sappers.	Privates.	Total.	Maximum & Minimum.	Permanent Staff. Adjutant, Instructors.
Staff	1	1	..	..	..	1	3	1	1	..	..	..	..	..	..	..	..	..		1 2
S.V.A.	..	1	1	2	2	..	..	..	..	1	6	6	2	..	86	..	..	107/80		..
S.R.E.(v)	..	..	1	1	1	..	..	..	..	1	3	3	..	1	..	53	..	66/55		..
Maxim Company	..	..	1	1	1	..	..	..	..	1	6	6	1	2	..	..	41	66/55		..
S.V.I. per Coy.	..	..	1	1	1	..	..	1	..	1	4	4	..	2	..	..	89	104/80		..
Malacca Company	..	1	1	1	1	..	..	..	..	1	4	4	..	2	..	..	89	103/80		1
Bearer Section S.V.A.	1	..	..	..	..	..	..	..	..	..	1	1	..	..	..	..	..	8	} 11/8	..
„ „ S.V.I. per Co.	..	..	..	..	..	..	..	..	1	..	..	2	..	..	..	..	..	10	}	

7. *S.V.A. Sections and Sub-divisions.*—The Singapore Volunteer Artillery was divided into Sections each of which was sub-divided into two sub-divisions each under Command of a Sergeant or other Non-Commissioned Officer.

28 and 29 Officers Examination and Outfit Allowances.—Officers were required to pass an examination within two years of their first Commission and upon receiving his certificate of proficiency each officer received $150 outfit allowance (which covered mess dress).

30 Non-Commissioned Officers' Examination.—No member was appointed to or promoted in Non-Commissioned rank unless he had passed the qualifying examinations except in cases of emergency when the appointment or promotion was subject to the individual passing the next examination held.

31. *The Duties of N.C.O's in Command of Sub-divisions, Sections or Squads.*—

    (a) To keep a nominal roll of their Sub-divisions, Sections or Squads.

    (b) To see that each member of their respective Commands carries out the prescribed number of drills each year with the least possible delay.

    (c) To use every endeavour to maintain their Sub-divisions, Sections or Squads in a good state of discipline and efficiency.

39. *Qualification for Efficiency—Artillery.*—

Recruits & Non-Efficients	Efficients
1. 12 Drills 10 pr. jointed Gun.	1. 10 Drills 10 pr. jointed Gun.
2. 8 Drills Maxims.	2. 6 Drills Maxims.
3. 8 Squad or Carbine Drills.	3. 4 Squad or Carbine Drills.
4. 2 Lectures.	4. 1 Annual Inspection.
5. 1 Annual Inspection.	
31 Total	21 Total

Similar tables for other units followed.

43. *Liability as to Capitation Grant.*—Members resigning without good or sufficient reason were liable to the Corps for any loss of Capitation Grant thereby incurred.

49. *Issue of Rifles.*—Only members who were passed by the Adjutant or O.C. Unit as competent to have the care of arms were allowed, on depositing a guarantee in the sum of $50, to take rifles to their houses.!

S.V.A. CYCLIST SECTION 1896

S.V.A. MAXIM COMPANY
Sub-section at Ballestier Range

KING'S BIRTHDAY PARADE 1904—ON THE OLD RACE COURSE
*No. 1 Sub-Section S.V.A. Maxim Company (Sergeant E.A. Brown)
with pony transport, (Gunner H.R.W. Lobb leading pony)*

S.V.A. MAXIM COMPANY—KING'S BIRTHDAY PARADE 1904
"Passing the Saluting Base"

53/58 Capitation Allowance.—Each Officer, N.C.O. and member returned as efficient for the year earned for the Corps the Capitation Allowance of $20 and in addition a further $5 per year was paid to the Corps for each Officer and Sergeant who held a certificate of proficiency in accordance with the Regulations in force.

60 Camp Allowances.—To cover expenses (catering, etc.) of camps the sum of $2.50 per day for a period not exceeding seven days annually was allowed for each Officer, N.C.O. and member who attended and slept in camp and $1 per day for those who attended during the day but did not sleep there at night.

Rules.—

II. *Election of Active Members.*—Candidates for admission to any unit of the Corps as Active Members were proposed and seconded on a form obtained from H.Q. and after being passed by the Medical Officer of the Corps were ballotted for by at least two thirds of the Committee of the unit of the Corps for which the candidate was proposed. One black ball in five excluded.

VI. *Honorary Members* who were approved by the Central Committee of the Corps paid an annual subscription of not less than $25 or became life members on payment of a sum not less than $250 to the funds of the unit for which he was proposed, but they had no voice in matters connected with the interior economy of the Corps.

VII. *General Meetings.*—The Annual General Meeting of the Corps was fixed for July each year. Special Corps General Meetings could be called upon written requisition of 50 members of the Corps and Special Unit General Meetings upon a written request of 20 members of the unit, in both cases definitely stating the object for calling the Special Meeting.

XIV. Every member on enrolment was supplied with a copy of the Regulations and Rules of the Corps.

Service Decorations.—At the end of the book various appendices shewed the regulations for the award of the Colonial Auxiliary Forces Officers Decoration and the Colonial Auxiliary Forces Long Service Medal, followed by rules governing the competition for the various trophies belonging to, or for competition, by the Corps or any of its units.

1906. In 1906 the 2.75 inch 10 Pr. B.L. Mountain Guns, with which the S.V.A. had been equipped since 1903, were withdrawn from their command and the S.V.A. reverted once more to its original role of Garrison Artillery in which capacity it continued to act until after the Great War,

1914/1918. Up to this time, *i.e.* as long as they had been equipped with Mountain Guns (1896–1906), the S.V.A. fired the salute of 21 guns at Queen's and King's Birthday Parades.

From this year the Regular Adjutant, S.V.C. also undertook the duties of Staff Officer Colonial Forces, Straits Settlements and later, in 1913, of Staff Officer Local Forces (S.S. and F.M.S.) [1].

1907. Owing to the growth of the Chinese Company, S.V.I. the old Waterloo Street Club house became quite inadequate and a new Chinese Volunteer Club was built. It was opened on the 4th May, 1907 by H.E. the Governor, Sir John Anderson, a memorable event for the Chinese Volunteers. The premises, situated at the end of Beach Road Reclamation, included a Central Meeting Hall, bar and billiard room and side rooms. Among those present were Major General Perrott (G.O.C.), Captain Young (Colonial Secretary), Colonel Fitton (Royal West Kents) Lieut.-Col. Broadrick (Commanding, S.V.C.) Major Ellis (late O.C. Chinese Coy.) Captains Hilton, Colbeck and Phillips, the Hon. Mr. Tan Jiak Kim and many prominent Chinese. On arrival the Governor was received with the General Salute, the Guard of Honour consisting of the entire Chinese Company under command of Capt. J.A.R. Glennie and Lieut. E.A. Brown. The Cadets band played the National Anthem.

During the ceremonial speeches it was stated that the cost of the building had been met by voluntary subscriptions ranging from $1 to $1,200 and totalling $17,500, collected by the Hon. Mr. Tan Jiak Kim from among the Chinese themselves. Government itself had helped most generously with a donation of $3,000, had given the site and the services of the P.W.D. Staff to oversee the work. The interest shown by the Chinese as exemplified in the building of the New Club house indicated that the movement for a Straits Chinese Volunteer Unit was no ephemeral one, for there were then eighty candidates waiting enrolment and it looked as if permission to form a second company might have to be asked for.

The Governor referred to his having recently conferred a commission on one of their members (Song Ong Siang, the first Chinese Volunteer Officer).

Towards the end of 1907 the Fort Fullerton site was required for other buildings, so the S.V.A. Drill Hall was removed to Raffles Reclamation in Beach Road, adjoining the Chinese Volunteer Club, where it was reopened on 22nd January, 1908. It here remained in continuous use

---

[1] On account of the growth of the S.O.L.F. work, a Volunteer Assistant Adjutant was appointed in 1914.

until 1932 when the present S.V.C. Headquarters were completed on the adjoining ground.

Up to this time the Drill Hall for all the S.V.I. had been in the Old Gaol in Bras Basah Road. The Chinese Company now, however, had Headquarter offices in their new Club House, but the Eurasian Company still continued until their disbandment in 1909, to use the Old Gaol.

1908. Corps Orders for 1908 mention practice by the S.V.A. from the 1-inch Aiming Rifle, with moving Target, round which regular gun drill was performed; also that Gunner D.T. Lewis was the winner, in March, of a laying prize presented by Major G.A. Derrick.

An order dated the 18th September mentions the issue of a new cap badge to the S.V.A. This badge was a gun with two scrolls, one above the gun bearing the Motto "In Oriente Primus" and one below the gun "Singapore Volunteer Artillery". It was worn from 1908 to 1915 when a crown was added above the top scroll. The new Gun badge of 1908 was for the Artillery only and replaced the old S.V.A. Cypher badge in a garter with a grenade over the top portion, but the latter continued to be worn by the S.V.A. Maxim Company up to 1921 with shoulder titles S.V.A.(M) and buttons the same as the S.V.I.

From the formation of the S.R.E.(v), S.V.I. and S.V.A.(M) and the introduction after the Boer War of the khaki field service cap with black patent leather peak and chin strap, the units of the Corps were also distinguished by a coloured band worn round the cap:—

S.V.A., and S.V.A.(M)., Red, with blue piping round the rim of the crown.

S.R.E.(v)., Blue with red piping round the rim of the crown.

The Eurasian Company, S.V.I. continued to wear the khaki forage cap without any coloured facing, while the Chinese Company, S.V.I. wore a khaki field service cap with a segment of green cloth (measuring about 6 inches at the base) as a background for the badge, but with no peak, similar to that introduced for the Malay Company, S.V.I. on their formation in 1910 and worn up to the present day, though the Malay Company have round their cap a complete band of red cloth.

All these various forms of headdress of the Corps are

S.V.A. 1908-1915

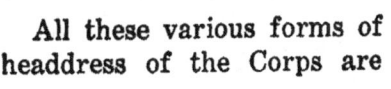

S.V.A. 1915-1923

illustrated in the photograph opposite p. 59 of the S.V.C. Rifle Team that took part in and won the Ceylon—Rangoon—Singapore Rifle Match in 1908.

The all-khaki service dress cap was subsequently issued during the war in place of all these different types of head dress, except for the Malay Company.

1909. In February, 1909 for various reasons, including deficiency in members, the Eurasian (No. 1) Company, S.V.I. was disbanded and not re-formed again until the 4th July, 1918. Mr. Carlos([1]) tells us that "Why and how this happened need not be gone into, although, in passing, the Corps was not wholly to blame. The want of "Esprit de Corps", the absence of sympathy between officers and men, the absence of continuity and regularly trained officers and a feeling of injustice (right or wrong) that the authorities did not appreciate their services were no doubt contributing causes".

Though the Eurasian Company was disbanded in 1909 several keen members of the unit were kept on the strength of Headquarters on account of their ability as marksmen, and two of them (including Sergeant Edgar Galistan) represented Singapore at Bisley in 1910.

1910. ([2]) In the last days of January, 1910, in response to an enquiry from General French as to why there were no Malay Volunteers, the Malays being considered in England to be a fighting race, Mr. Noor Mohamed Hashim and Mr. E.E. Coleman (Hon. General Secretary and President of the Malay Football Association respectively) attended Fort Canning and made proposals for the formation of a Malay Volunteer Unit and due to the G.O.C's (Major General Perrott, C.B.) impending departure from the Colony within a few days, arrangements were made to fill an historical deficiency with military rapidity. On the 7th February

The Slouch Hat— Worn by the S.V.I. instead of a Sun Helmet

(1) "Eurasian Volunteers" p. 393 "One Hundred Years of Singapore".
(2) Memoir of the Malay Company Jubilee 1910–1935.

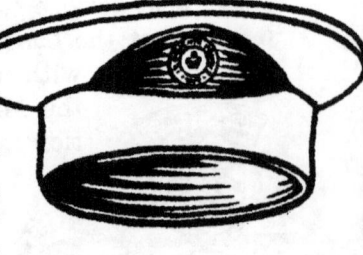

Chinese Coy., S.V.I., Cap

Mr. E.E. Coleman was appointed by the Executive Council to "collect the names of those willing to be enrolled". The following day the Governor offered as Malay Headquarters the old Gaol in Bras Basah Road (previously occupied by the Chinese and Eurasian Companies, S.V.I.) of which "F" (Malay) Company are still proud possessors as their separate headquarters of historic and fort-like military appearance. The Malay representatives at once accepted and a night campaign among the forty-two M.F.A. Clubs immediately opened, Mr. Noor Mohamed Hashim speaking everywhere with great force on the duties and rights of modern Malays. Government decided to accept only a half Company of 60 for the first year so that 61 specially selected athletes were enrolled and about 40 more who had decided that the best way to lead a double life was to be civilian and soldier too, were disappointed until 1911!

The S.V.C. sent a team of eight (not its best but those who were able to obtain the necessary leave) to Bisley in 1910 to compete for the Empire Shield and the Kolapore Cup. The team was composed of Major F.M. Elliot, Capt. C.M. Phillips, Lieut. W. Lowther Kemp, Lieut. Cuthbert, Sergt. D.A. Walker, Sergt. J. Long, Sergt. E. Gallistan and Sergt. Tan Cheow Kim (the first Chinese to shoot at Bisley).

1911. The 11th May, 1911 was the gazetted date for the increase of the strength of the Malay Company, Singapore Volunteer Infantry to 120 men formed into four Sections. Every original member of the Malay Volunteer Company was an athlete and a member of that very patriotic British body the Malayan Football Association, as also have been nearly all the recruits for the twenty-five years since. For a long period no "professional" instructor was allotted to the new unit, as it was decided that the solidification of a Malay *Esprit de Corps* was best left to the Malay experts. The first Commanding Officer was Lieut. G.S. Carver, who proved an excellent leader and instructor, "already built", the reference being to a note from the G.O.C. to the Governor saying "We are unable to build an Officer to order".

Malayan Volunteers were represented at the Coronation of King George V. in July, 1911 by a composite party drawn from members of all Corps in Malaya who happened to be in England on leave during that year.

At the Annual Meeting of the S.V.C. on the 5th May, 1911 it was suggested that the Maxim Gun Company, S.V.A. should re-amalgamate with the S.V.A. and form a section of that unit as in the early days. This suggestion was seriously considered but not acted on, though the President even stated in a reply to a question that the Maxim Guns still belonged to the S.V.A.!

In 1911 the S.V.C. consisted of:—
    S.V.A.
    Maxim Company, S.V.A.
    S.R.E.(v).
    S.V.I. (Chinese and Malay Companies).
    Cadets.
    Bearer Company, S.V.C.
    S.V.C. Band.

1912. In 1912 the establishment of the S.V.A. was reduced from 107 to 85 of all ranks, and the actual strength rose from 66 to 73. Increased facilities for training were also afforded in this year by the mounting of a 6-inch. Q.F. Gun in the compound of the Drill Hall at Beach Road.

A new S.V.A. handbook was published and entitled "Handbook of the Singapore Volunteer Artillery 1912". Under *General* it dealt with:—

The Period of Enrolment, not less than two years. *Qualifying Drills* from which it is interesting to note that the previous year's efficient volunteer got off more lightly than Recruits of the year current and the previous year's non-efficients. *Clothing and Equipment*, a detail of the items provided free by the Government. The detail of various *Orders of Dress* in Drill Order, Review Order, Manoeuvre Order, and Mess Uniform. Active members of the S.V.A. were acquainted with the fact that they were ipso facto members of the *Singapore Rifle Association*. Recommendations to various training books. This was followed by the 6 inch Q.F. Gun Drill, Definitions, how to use the Depression Range Finder, a section on the Sights and a further one on the Ammunition. Altogether a very handy little book of 39 pages.

New Regulations for the S.V.C. were gazetted in December, 1912, similar Regulations for the Penang Volunteers having been published in 1910.

1913. Late in 1913 the Bearer Section S.V.A. was reconstructed, reorganised and formed into that very useful and important unit of the Corps, the Medical Company, S.V.C.

In the Federated Malay States the Volunteer Enactment, 1913 was passed repealing the Volunteer Enactment 1910.

Departure from Bukit Panjang Station

Arrival at Bukit Panjang Station

A steep ascent with ponies, all hands and local help

Moving into action at the Artillery Range

S.V.A. AND 2.75-INCH MOUNTAIN GUNS AT BUKIT PANJANG—1903

RIFLE MATCH, 1908—CEYLON—RANGOON—SINGAPORE

L to R Standing—Sgt. J. Long S.V.I., Gnr. C. Curtis S.V.A., Clr. Sgt. Tan Soo Bin S.V.I., Sgt. M.K. Watt S.V.A., Cpl. Tan Piak Eng S.V.I., Sgt. De Silva S.V.I. Sitting—Clr. Sgt. E. Galistan S.V.I., 2nd/Lieut. W.L. Kemp S.R.E.(v), Captain F.M. Elliot S.V.I., 2nd/Lieut. E.A. Brown S.V.I., Cpl. R.W. Chater S.R.E.(v). Front—Sgt. Tan Chow Kim S.V.I.

S.V.C. RIFLE TEAM AT BISLEY (ENGLAND)—1910

L to R Standing—Lieut. Cuthbert; Sgt. E. Galistan; Pvte. Tan Chow Kim; Sgt. J. Long; Sgt. D.A. Walker. Sitting—Capt. C.M. Phillips; Major F.M. Elliot; Lieut. W. Lowther Kemp.

1914. The Singapore Garrison at this time comprised one British Regiment and one Indian Regiment in addition to the R.G.A. manning the Fort guns but at the end of 1914 the 1st K.O.Y.L.I. left for the front and garrison duties were performed by the native regiment, (the 5th Light Infantry), and the Singapore Volunteer Corps.

The S.V.C. was mobilized on the 6th August, 1914, the strength being about 450. Next day a Cyclist Company was formed with one Cyclist Section and one Motor Cyclist Section.

The Medical Company S.V.C., a development of a Bearer section forming part of the S.V.A., was reconstructed, reorganised and formed into the Singapore Field Ambulance Company. The S.F.A. Company's officers replaced the R.A.M.C. officers of the Garrison, and the men were occasionally mobilised for hospital duty[1].

On the 21st September the German Cruiser *"Emden"* appeared in the Bay of Bengal and started her career in local history by the capture of the *"Indus"*, *"Lovat"*, *"Killin"*, *"Diplomat"* and *"Trabboch"* and all trade routes from Singapore westward were closed. On the 26th September she shelled Madras and on the 1st October captured the *"Tymerie"*, *"King Lud"*, *"Ribera"*, *"Foyle"*, *"Buresk"* and *"Gryfervale"*. In the meantime the British cruiser *"Yarmouth"* sank the *"Markomania"*, one of her tenders, and recaptured the Greek collier *"Pontoporus"* with a prize crew on board, and brought her to Singapore. This was followed by a third list of mercantile victims on the 23rd October the *"Chilkana"*, *"Troilus"*, *"Benmohr"*, *"Clan Grant"*, *"Benzevell"*, *"Exfort"* and *"Egbert"* off the Minicoys. Then on the 28th October the *"Emden"* made her daring attempt on Penang which resulted in the sinking of the Russian cruiser *"Zemchug"* and the French torpedo-boat *"Mousquet"* but this was her last exploit for, on November 9th, while raiding the Cable Station on the Cocos Islands, she was intercepted by H.M. Australian Ship *"Sydney"* and destroyed.

During the time of the *"Emden's"* activity it became evident that the numbers of the local Volunteer Forces were insufficient for the work of manning the forts and miscellaneous garrison duty and a movement was set on foot which culminated in a meeting on the 23rd October at which the reformation of the Singapore Volunteer Rifles (disbanded 1903) was decided upon and one European Company was enrolled under command of Captain C.W. Darbishire. Later a Veterans Company was formed and at the end of 1914 the strength of the S.V.C. stood at 687.

---

[1] "One Hundred Years of Singapore" Vol. I pp. 388 and 389.

It will have been noticed that these pages have included notes on the formation and progress of Volunteer Corps in adjacent territories and Colonies and although this history is primarily of our own Corps, it is of interest to look upon the Volunteer movement in Malaya from a broader aspect. We shall therefore from time to time turn to the activities of our contemporaries, who from the outbreak of war in 1914 up to the present day, have, like the S.V.C., gone ahead and made great strides towards building up that Volunteer Army of the Empire which is known as the Colonial Auxiliary Forces. In this effort we find that the Sultans in protected territories, both Federated and Unfederated, have always been sympathetic towards the movement.

On the 5th August, 1914 a unit known as the Kedah Volunteers was formed in North Kedah by permission of the Kedah State Council, but it was not governed by any Enactment or Regulations. Its affairs were conducted by an annually elected Committee, usually of five members, under a Commandant. Starting with 18 members its strength never exceeded 25 but the keenness of this unit can be gauged by the fact that throughout the War the cost was entirely borne by the members who paid for their own ammunition and uniform which was of the General Service pattern with no special buttons or badges. They were drilled under the Commissioner of Police, being armed with Police Carbines and later with a dozen E.Y. arms (old arms kept for "EmergencY" use) from Singapore.

In Kelantan two Companies of "Special Constables" were enrolled in August 1914, No. 1 Company consisting of about 30 Europeans and No. 2 Company of about 25 Asiatics. Actually they were the Kelantan Volunteer Rifles as by the Kelantan Volunteer Enactment of the 8th August, 1917 they took that title with retrospective effect from the 8th August, 1914. By this Enactment the High Commissioner may accept the offer of services of any British subject in the State and commission officers, and the General Officer Commanding Troops, Malaya, may make Regulations. In these early days the Volunteers in Kelantan were financed from police votes, members of the Corps providing their own uniform and meeting camp expenditure. Webb equipment was on loan from the police until the British Adviser (Captain R.J. Farrar) paid for Webb equipment out of his own pocket.

The Johore Volunteer Rifles followed in October 1914 and the Johore (European) Volunteer Enactment was assented to by His Highness the Sultan on the 18th August, 1915 to provide for the organisation and maintenance of the force. By this Enactment the Governor of the Straits

Settlements had power to accept the services of any European resident in the State and to commission officers, with the concurrence of His Highness the Sultan, and to call out the Corps in case of emergency. His Highness the Sultan could also call out the Corps with the concurrence of the General Adviser, in case of an emergency arising in the State of Johore.

In all three of these newly formed units in the Unfederated States parades were carried on under considerable difficulty owing to the Corps being scattered over wide areas in their respective territories. Motor cars and bicycles were used largely over distances which would be considered a hardship to travel in these days. The F.M.S.R., with free passes, helped in Kedah and Johore while many estates in Kelantan and places where waterways were adjacent to parade centres allowed the use of their launches free of charge. Difficulties such as these, though never experienced by the Singapore Volunteer Corps, existed throughout the mainland of Malaya until the post-war development of mechanical transport and roadways.

At the beginning of the War the Engine Room Section of the Singapore Royal Engineers (v) were immediately employed on defence electric lights at the forts on the islands of Pulo Brani and Pulo Blakan Mati. In a similar capacity to the S.R.E. (v), the Rangoon Electrical Engineer Company provided full details for manning the search lights at their Syriam and Choki Forts.

1915. *The Singapore Mutiny*[1].—In February, 1915, the week-end Saturday 13th to Monday 15th (inclusive) was a public holiday for the usual Chinese New Year festivities. The Chinese Volunteers were relieved from guard duty at Blakan Mati by the Malay Company on the morning of the 13th for 48 hours, to allow them to keep the festival; they had orders to report back for duty at 7 A.M. on the 15th. The rest of Singapore, (Armageddon seeming to be remotely confined to the battlefields of Europe) and those Volunteers of other nationalities who were not on guard duty were also enjoying the holiday. Pleasures for the latter were, however, interrupted on the afternoon of the 15th when the 5th Light Infantry[2], the Indian regiment stationed in Singapore, mutinied. Thirty-five Europeans and five Malays were killed and 11 Europeans wounded.

(1) This account of the Singapore Mutiny has been compiled from a collection of "*Straits Times*" cuttings of the period; Mr. W. Bartley's article in "One Hundred Years of Singapore"; Sir Song Ong Siang's account in "One Hundred Years of the Chinese in Singapore"; the official account in the Annual Report of the Straits Settlements for 1915 by Mr. W.G. Maxwell, Acting Colonial Secretary, and anecdotes received verbally from some of those Europeans who were here at the time, Messrs. V.D. Knowles, A. Robertson and T.C. Hay.

(2) The 5th L.I., an old Indian Regiment of standing, was raised by Lieut. F.M. Johnson at Cawnpore in 1803 and was one of the native regiments which remained loyal during the Indian Mutiny.

A disposition of the troops in Singapore at the time will allow us to follow a description of the mutiny more easily. The 5th Light Infantry, 815 men, commanded by Lieut.-Colonel Martin, were quartered in the barracks at Alexandra, on the other side of the road to and nearly opposite the present Gilman Barracks. This Indian Regiment being under orders to proceed to Hongkong by the troopship *"Nore"* on the 16th February, 200 men of the Johore Forces, under command of Captains Cullimore and Abdul Jaffar, had been sent to Singapore on the 14th February to assist in the garrison duties; they were stationed at Tanglin Barracks. About 100 men of the Malay States Guides and Malay States Volunteer Rifles under Captain Sydney Smith were in a training camp at Normanton, almost adjoining the Alexandra Barracks and near the present Admiralty Fuel Oil Tanks off Ayer Rajah Road. A mountain battery of the Malay States Guides was also stationed at Alexandra Barracks. H.M.S. *"Cadmus"* was lying in port. The Prisoner of War and Enemy Subjects Internment Camp at Tanglin Barracks consisted of a part of the barracks, near the present No. 2 sports ground lying towards Pierce Road, completely fenced in with barbed wire with look-outs on high scaffolding: the guard at the time consisted of a section of the recently reformed Singapore Volunteer Rifles under Second-Lieutenant Love-Montgomerie. A small detachment of the 36th Sikhs was also quartered at Tanglin Barracks. The Singapore Volunteer Corps, under command of Lieut.-Colonel G.A. Derrick, were at call and furnished guards and patrols at the Drill Hall, King's Dock, the Prisoner of War Camp, Pulo Brani and gun manning at Blakan Mati in conjunction with the regular forces, the Royal Garrison Artillery under Lieut.-Colonel C.W. Brownlow, and the Royal Engineers.

The 5th L.I. had spent the morning of the 15th being inspected and preparing for their intended departure for Hong Kong on the 16th February. Machine guns with their ammunition had already been sent to the store and were to have been followed by the small arms ammunition which had been collected at the Quarter Guard. During his inspection of the regiment in the morning H.E. the General Officer Commanding had been favourably impressed with the demeanour of the native officers and men, and there was no reason to expect any trouble.

At about 3 P.M. on Monday the 15th February a shot was fired at the Quarter Guard of the 5th L.I. and the mutiny broke out with startling suddenness. The mutineers took possession of all the ammunition which was being packed into motor lorries under the supervision of Lieut. Elliott

S.V.A. DRILL HALL—FORT FULLERTON SITE
Johnsons Pier and the Singapore Club

S.V.A. DRILL HALL—FORT FULLERTON SITE
from the Padang before Anderson Bridge was built

THE CHINESE VOLUNTEER CLUB, BEACH ROAD
Built in 1907

THE S.V.C. DRILL HALL—BEACH ROAD, 1908-1933
Originally built for the S.V.A. in 1891 on Fort Fullerton Site

for transport to the Store prior to their embarkation, due to take place the next day. Some of the British Officers of the 5th L.I. made their way from their quarters to the Indian Officers' Lines but were persuaded by the latter of the impossibility of any attempt to stop the men. The first victims were Lieut. H.S. Elliott and Captain P. Boyce, 5th L.I. and Captain M.F.A. Maclean, R.G.A., attached to the Mountain Battery of the M.S.G., who, in attempting to quell the disturbance, were shot. Meanwhile the Malay States Volunteer Rifles had been acquainted with the position and they concentrated on the defence of Colonel Martin's bungalow, the party consisting of Colonel Martin, Major Cotton and Captain Ball of the 5th L.I., together with Capt. Sydney Smith, three other Officers and 81 men of the M.S.V.R. The bungalow, in which Mrs. Cotton had also taken refuge, was promptly besieged and the telephone wires cut soon after Col. Martin had managed to acquaint headquarters at Fort Canning of the outbreak, so that further reliable information by telephone was impossible. Fort Canning warned the naval authorities prior to which, however, Admiral Jerram had disembarked a detachment of 90 Officers and men from H.M.S. *"Cadmus"* which advanced along Pasir Panjang Road towards the scene of the outbreak. By this time the Civil Police and the Colonial Secretary had been informed.

The mutineers had divided themselves roughly into three parties, one engaging at Col. Martin's bungalow. The second of about 100 men advanced across country to Tanglin Barracks and the third towards the town by the Pasir Panjang Road. The cross-country force arrived at the Prisoner of War Camp just as a telephone message came through to Lieut. Love-Montgomerie warning him of the émeute and therefore took him, practically, unawares. The Mutineers fired on the guard killing three British Officers and one Malay Officer, seven European Volunteers and Regular N.C.O's and men, two Malay N.C.O's and men and one prisoner of war and wounded three European Volunteers and Regular soldiers and one prisoner of war[1]. Having dispersed the guard the mutineers threw open the gates of the camp and fraternised with the inmates, few of whom showed any signs of taking advantage of their liberty, most of them being interned civilians. Seventeen, however, left the unguarded camp after

---

(1) *Killed*—Capt. P.N. Gerrard (Comdt. P. of W. Camp), 2/Lieut. J. Love-Montgomerie, S.V.R., Capt. H. Cullimore (2nd in Comd. J.M.F.), Capt. Abdul Jaffar, J.M.F., Sergt. E.H. Sexton, A.S.C., Corpl. J.R.V. Beagley, R.G.A., Cpl. J. Lawson, S.V.R., Cpl. Salleh, J.M.F., L/Cpl. J. Harper, S.V.R., Pvte. J. Drysdale, S.V.R., Pvte. A.J.G. Holt, S.V.R., Pvte. B.C. Cameron, S.V.R., Pvte. Yakub, J.M.F., and Prisoner of War E.F. Senftleben.
Wounded—Pvte. R.L.V. Wodehouse, S.V.R., Pvte. J. Robertson, S.V.R., Gunner A. Hind, R.G.A., and Prisoner of War H. Kampf.

dark, four being captured later, while the others made good their escape. Meanwhile two civilians[1] were killed in Alexander Road, presumably by the rebel detachment attacking Col. Martin's bungalow.

The third party committed a number of dastardly murders. They met and killed four Europeans civilians,[2] one a lady, driving their cars along Pasir Panjang Road, after which they entered a house, also in Pasir Panjang Road, and murdered three more European civilians[3].

From Pasir Panjang Road they deployed, some marching towards the Hospital and Sepoy Lines into Outram Road where they met and shot two Officers[4] of the Royal Garrison Artillery who were on their way back to their Units and wounded two Chinese. Another party called upon the native warder at the Central Gaol to surrender the prison keys. Receiving a defiant answer they proceeded along New Bridge Road and held up motor cars and killed four European civilians[5] and a car syce and wounded another European civilian who saved his life by feigning death. Other mutineers of this body advanced towards Keppel Harbour and met the naval force from H.M.S. *Cadmus* who, after an exchange of brisk firing, drove them back towards Alexandra.

That the mutineers murderous attitude was mainly directed against Englishmen and their families was evinced by the fact that when Mr. Scully was held up in a car in Alexandra Road and replied to the challenge "You Ingleesh?" with "No, Irish!" he and his friend got away with their lives. Dutchmen and Frenchmen, also, were similarly spared and Mr. Tan Soo Bin and his family passing some mutineers, taking cover in a drain, thought there was a sham fight going on as the mutineers after bringing their rifles to the present and discovering the car contained Chinese allowed it to pass. By sunset the entire European community had received the alarm and preparations were being organized rapidly. Martial Law was proclaimed at 6.30 P.M. The Sikh police were concentrated at the Central Police Station and the S.V.C. mobilized at the Drill Hall. Parties were despatched to bring in European women and children for whom accommodation was arranged on the steamer *Ipoh*. In response to a telephone message a further 150 men of the Johore Military Forces arrived at Tank Road Station, by the mail train from Penang, under

---

(1) Mr. N.F. Edwards and Mr. H.B. Collins.
(2) Mr. C.V. Dyson, Mr. W.J. Marshall and Mr. and Mrs. G.B. Woolacombe.
(3) Mr. D. McGilvray, Mr. E.O. Butterworth and Mr. J.B. Dunn.
(4) Major R.H. Galwey and Capt. F.V. Izard.
(5) Mr. G. Wald; Mr. C. Smith; Dr. E.D. Whittle, Warder J. Clarke and Hussin Ketchil bin Hussin. *Wounded*—Mr. T.A. Flett.

command of H.H. the Sultan of Johore in person. This serious situation, however, had no effect on the Chinese quarters of the city where the New Year festivities continued with complete unconcern and even Europeans in those parts of the suburbs affected by the mutiny mistook the rifle fire for Chinese crackers until they learnt otherwise.

The night of the 15th February was a restless one throughout Singapore. There was some sniping in the vicinity of Orchard Road Police Station and Paterson Road, where two of the rebels were killed. Colonel Martin's bungalow remained in a state of seige, Mrs. Cotton being still there and administering admirably and cheerfully tea and food for the defenders; it was probably saved from being rushed by the mutineers owing to the searchlight which played on it from Blakan Mati. Its position was precarious, however, the detachment from the *Cadmus*, reinforced by the Volunteers having, as already stated, driven some rebels back along Keppel Road towards their own barracks and no relief arrived from the Tanglin side due to a hold up near Cemetery Hill behind Alexandra Road Police Station where firing took place.

As many men as could be spared from the forts were brought to the P. & O. Wharf which was made the headquarters of the R.G.A. and forces in the South had been considerably strengthened during the night by further details from the S.V.C. and armed civilians.

Early on the morning of the 16th the relief of the party in Col. Martin's house was carried out by Lt.-Col. C.W. Brownlow, R.A., who advanced from Keppel Harbour with a force of 80 men of H.M.S. *"Cadmus"*, 50 men of the Singapore Volunteer Corps, 21 men of the Royal Garrison Artillery and 25 armed civilians, in all about 180.

The mutineers attacked the bungalow at dawn, in typical North-West Frontier style, but Colonel Martin knowing the possibility of this had drawn in his M.S.V.R. pickets and was ready for them. The bungalow party sustained no casualties at all but shot about sixteen of the rebels before the relief force arrived.

Col. Brownlow's force had met with some opposition. The *"Cadmus"* detachment soon came under fire but after support from the S.V.C. both advanced and Alexandra Barracks, which had not been held in strength, were eventually occupied by the armed civilians under Captain E.A. Brown, S.V.I., with Mr. Cooke-Yarborough as his lieutenant. The force then moved towards its final objective, Col. Martin's bungalow, but came under heavy fire from a high ridge on their left. This ridge was attacked and cleared by the *"Cadmus"* and Singapore Volunteer Corps detachments, after which the bungalow was reached without further difficulty. The party was relieved and Mrs. Cotton despatched to Government House. The relief force still being out-numbered by the rebels was not in sufficient strength to hold the position so, with the bungalow party, it retired sweeping the Keppel Golf links on the way to Keppel Harbour. Its losses totalled two killed and four wounded[1], and its gains about ninety prisoners with forty mules.

Over night strong pickets had been sent out to Tanglin cross roads and the end of Cluny Road and during the morning of the 16th the Veteran Company, S.V.C. occupied Tanglin Barracks unopposed and took charge of the Prisoners of War and interned aliens, the former being mainly the fifty prisoners from the *"Emden"* who had been landed at Penang at the end of 1914 and escorted to Singapore by Penang Volunteers, less, of course, those who had made good their escape the previous evening. The Volunteers were divided between the Drill Hall and Keppel Harbour from which detachments were despatched and guards provided for Government House, the General Hospital and Fort Canning. Some S.V.A. were based at Pasir Panjang Police Station under Lieut.-Col. Scott, R.G.A. Fort Silinsing was manned throughout the mutiny by Lieut. W. Murdoch, Corpl. F.E. Dilley and 15 men, while Fort Siloso was manned by a mixed detachment of R.G.A. and S.V.A.

The forces in Singapore were reinforced during the 16th and subsequent days as follows:—

16th February	..	200	European Special Constables.
,, ,,	..	190	Japanese Special Constables raised by the Japanese Consul.
17th ,,	..	190	men and 2 machine guns from the French Cruiser *"Montcalm"*.
18th ,,	..	76	men from the Japanese Cruiser *"Otawa"*.
,, ,,	..	40	men from the Russian Cruiser *"Orel"*.
19th ,,	..	75	men from the Japanese Cruiser *"Tsushima"*.
20th ,,	..	6	Companies of the 1/4th King's Shropshire Light Infantry (Territorial Force) from Rangoon by the *s.s. "Edavana"*.

---

(1) *Killed*—Stoker C.F. Anscombe, H.M.S. *"Cadmus"*, Special Constable F. Geddes; *Wounded*—Sapper W. Flint, S.R.E.(v); Private W. Letts, M.S.V.R.; Private A.S. Gardener, S.V.R., Gunner F.W. Sabey, R.G.A.

HEADQUARTERS "F" MALAY COY., S.V.C., 1910–1937
(The old Gaol, Bras Basah Road)

THE CHINESE COMPANY S.V.I., 1906 AT H.Q. BRAS BASAH ROAD
Centre—2nd/Lieut. E.A. Brown, Major Ellis, 2nd/Lieut. Song Ong Siang

THE S.V.A. 1912—MOUNTING A 6-INCH GUN AT THE DRILL HALL, BEACH ROAD
(Group includes (R to L) Lt. D.T. Lewis & Capt. W. Makepeace)

THE SINGAPORE VOLUNTEER FIELD AMBULANCE COMPANY
*at Tanglin Barracks Military Hospital 1917
Major Norman Black, M.C. (centre)*

During the day of the 16th the Military Authorities armed the European and Japanese Special Constables who were detailed off to various police stations whence they supplied armed patrols in all directions. The removal of women and children to ships in the harbour continued, the Eastern Extension Telegraph Company's s.s. *"Recorder"*, the Peninsular and Oriental Steam Navigation Company's s.s. *"Nile"* and the Straits Steamship Company's s.s. *"Penang"* being placed for the purpose at the Military Authorities' further disposal. Ninety more mutineers surrendered to the forces at Keppel Harbour in the afternoon and by the evening a complete line of posts had been established from the P. & O. Wharf to Cluny Road, thus cutting off the mutineers from the town, and forces with motor transport were ready to move to any threatened point.

The situation was not without its lighter and somewhat amusing moments. On the night of the 16th/17th two sections of the S.V.A. Maxim Company under Capt. Tongue and Lieut. T.C. Hay were instructed to take up a position on Cemetery Hill (behind Alexandra Road Police Station). They arrived there after dusk and while one section under Lieut. Hay remained at the foot of the hill, the other section under Capt. Tongue pushed on to the top, after having encountered thick barbed wire which they crossed twice under the impression it was cattle fencing round the hill. They found to their surprise, next morning, that nothing so formidable existed and they were not "fenced in" but had merely chosen a path straight across a large private Chinese grave site which had recently been enclosed with barbed wire. During the night there were several bursts of fire at the foot of the hill and the men, comfortably secure at the top behind "wire entanglements", believed their comrades below were being attacked by the mutineers. It appears that the sentries below heard heavy rustling in the scrub, and, no replies being received to their challenge, fire was opened with the Maxim. A few bursts seemed to rout the "enemy" but they returned several times before morning to meet the same warm reception. Searching the scrub after daylight the gunners found a number of dead pigs!

Next morning the Gunners on top were reinforced by a number of "armed civilians" and later a party of Japanese who were helping to rout the mutineers mistook the men on the hill for rebels. They opened fire which was returned before the mistake was discovered, fortunately without casualty, though one "armed civilian" put a bullet through the shirt of a man in front of him.

Serious sniping did, however, continue in the whole district, in which Lieut. (Dr.) A.F. Legge of the Singapore Volunteer Medical Company and Gunner J. Barry, R.G.A. both lost their lives near Alexandra Road Police Station.

From the 17th February onwards the arrival of the various Allied Cruisers in response to wireless messages despatched on the afternoon of the 15th, and the landing of the detachments already mentioned, allowed the Military Authorities to make arrangements for rounding up the mutineers still remaining at large on the island.

Some of the rebels having been traced to the Seletar District the 190 men and two machine guns from the *"Montcalm"* proceeded there by motor transport, but the mutineers had crossed the Straits of Johore before their arrival and 61 of them surrendered to His Highness the Sultan of Johore. The eastern side of the island being known to be clear, the French force moved towards the West.

On the 18th Lieut.-Col. Brownlow's force, reinforced by the 76 Japanese from the *"Otawa"*, marched out of Keppel Harbour and retook Alexandra Barracks, occupying them without opposition and capturing six

NOTICE.

Notice is hereby given that the following rewards are offered:

$200 for the marking down of large bodies of mutineers consisting of ten and upwards.

$20 for the capture or surrender of mutineers up to ten in number.

$500 for the recovery of the body of Captain BOYCE, 5th L. I.

$5 for each rifle which can be proved to have been the property of native infantry or the Malay States Guides.

$1,000 for the capture of any German prisoner.

$50 for information leading to the capture of any German prisoner.

A. M. THOMPSON, MAJOR,
Provost-Marshal.
Singapore,
20th February, 1915.

men in the barracks. The Japanese detachment of this force continued to Normanton Camp where it came under fire from snipers but captured 12 men consisting of followers and hospital patients. A considerable part of the residental area being now safe for occupation the Provost-Marshal, Major A.M. Thompson, S.V.C., made a declaration to this effect and the majority of the women and children left the steamers in the harbour for their homes again where they found in most cases their Chinese domestic staffs had carried on as unconcernedly as if their employers had been away for a holiday.

It was now clear that such mutineers as remained at large could be considered as being in the Western part of the island and the various detachments made a 'drive' in this direction on the 19th February. The operation was, however, without success as by this time the mutineers had broken up into small and scattered bands, which hid in the jungle by day and came out in search of food by night. On the 20th the Provost-Marshal issued a public notice (see facsimile in illustrations) offering rewards of:—$200 for the marking down of large bodies of mutineers consisting of ten and upwards: $20 for the capture or surrender of mutineers up to ten in number: $500 for the recovery of the body of Captain Boyce 5th L.I.: $5 for each rifle which could be proved to be the property of the native infantry or Malay States Guides: $1,000 for the capture of any German prisoner and $50 for information leading to the capture of any German prisoner.

The round ups continued and on the 22nd February, one week after the outbreak, 614 of the 5th Light Infantry had surrendered, or been captured, and 52 had been killed, wounded or drowned, making 666 accounted for out of 815.

A Summary General Court Martial commenced on the 23rd February composed of Lt.-Col. Brownlow, R.G.A., Major Edge, 4th K.S.L.I. (T.F.) and Captain Ball 5th L.I., when sentence of death was passed on 41 mutineers and lesser sentences on 125 others.

Executions were carried out at the Gaol at Outram Road on various dates. On the 25th March the S.V.A. Maxim Company and S.V.R., under Capt. H. Tongue, provided a firing party of 110 men for the execution of 22 of the mutineers.

The promulgations were read at the various times by Major A.M. Thompson, Provost-Marshal Singapore, Colonel G.A. Derrick, S.V.C., and Colonel Garratt of the Shropshires who presumably provided the firing party for the last three executions on the 17th May.

In all 126 mutineers were sentenced, 37 were executed; 41 transported for life, 8 for 20 years, 16 for 15 years, 10 for 10 years; and 2 for 7 years; while 12 received various terms of imprisonment from 1 to 5 years[1].

A reconstruction of the mutineers's plans, in the first issue of the M.S.V.R. Corps Magazine, shows how completely they failed. It states that the mutiny had not been planned to start in the afternoon at all but at 8 P.M. in the evening when the Officers of the 5th L.I. and their guests, the Officers of the M.S.V.R., were to have been murdered in cold blood while sitting at dinner in Mess. The mutineers were then to have descended in full strength upon the Volunteer N.C.Os. and men as they sat in their Mess tent at dinner,—unarmed,—their rifles in barracks,—their ammunition, as the mutineers thought, in the Magazine,—and to have massacred them to a man. The intention was then to march to Tanglin under cover of darkness, murder the guard and release the prisoners of war; proceed to Orchard Road Police Station, kill the police and take the station; from there to Government House and after the murder of the Governor, to end up with an orgy of murder and loot in Singapore. But the whole plan was frustrated by their Colonel getting his preparations for embarkation further ahead than they anticipated, with an order to move the ammunition into store on the afternoon of the 15th instead of next morning, and this precipitated matters[2].

It must not be thought that the 5th L.I. contained no loyal members or that the whole regiment mutinied. Soon after the M.S.V.R. occupied Colonel Martin's house a body of 80 men came up and offered to join in the defence but it was considered wiser not to accept their offer and they were directed to surrender at the nearest police station. This they did; in all 91 surrendered during the night of the 15th and day and night of the 16th at the Central Police Station which was as much occupied in accepting surrenders of men of the 5th L.I. as in enrolling Europeans as additional constables.

All the loyal members of the Indian Military forces were naturally anxious not to be mistaken for the mutineers or as having sympathies with them. During the night of the 15th, a total of 138 men of the 5th L.I. arrived at the Bukit Timah Police Station and gave themselves up. The detachment of the 36th Sikhs from Tanglin Barracks reported itself to a picket in Orchard Road at day-break on the 16th and was marched into Orchard Road Police Station from whence it proceeded in lorries to the

---

(1) *See* Chronological Summary of Surrenders, Captures and Sentences Appendix VII (b).
(2) From the M.S.V.R. narrative in the *Singapore Free Press* of the 26th April, 1915.

Drill Hall. All these men were confined on board the s.s. *"Cheang Hock Kian"* in the harbour under a guard of Chinese Volunteers. Meanwhile the Mountain Battery of the Malay States Guides had moved in a body from Alexandra Barracks to Johore, their main idea being to get clear of Singapore and rejoin their regiment in Taiping.

The loyal section of the 5th L.I. left Singapore some months later for the Cameroons and after excellent work there saw active service in other parts of the Empire during the War.

A bronze mural memorial tablet to those officers and N.C.Os. of the S.V.C. who fell in the mutiny was erected in St. Andrews Cathedral.

The Reasons for the Singapore Mutiny are still not quite clear as may be seen by the following extract from a book *"Turmoil and Tragedy in India"* by General Sir George MacMunn, K.C.B., K.C.S.I., D.S.O. published in 1935.

> "This strange fierce outbreak, which might have been so disastrous, was "believed to have been largely due to the influence of German agents but "unconnected, to any great extent, with the wishes of the German residents. "It found, however, a small cell of Moslim fanaticism to work with."

Attempts made by an Unofficial Member of the Legislative Council to effect publication of the official report of the commission of investigation sent from India were unavailing, but it seems clear from outside evidence that it was really and mainly due to general unrest in India which existed in a desultory way before the War and had since its outbreak been fed by German influence. The numerous murders and plots in India prior to the outbreak of the Great War[1] were not considered "isolated or spontaneous crimes, but red beads on the string of an organised and continuous conspiracy"[2]. *"Persistent attempts were made, not without success, to tamper with the Indian troops* in at least a dozen stations in the Punjab and United Provinces" and the Muslim wing of Indian regiments, such as the 5th Light Infantry, were guided into these plots and rebellions through the channels of fanaticism.

The Mutiny emphasised the necessity for all European residents to be trained in the use of arms for local defence and the immediate result was the "Reserve Force and Civil Guard Ordinance" which became law on the 16th August, 1915. It is worthy of note that this was the first law passed in any British Colony imposing compulsory local Military Service.

---

(1) The Kennedy ladies 1908, Mr. Jackson and Sir Curzon Wyllie in 1909, the Howrah Plot 1910, the Dacca Plot 1911, and the attempt on the life of Lord Hardinge in 1912.

(2) See Report of the East India Sedition Committee 1918, over which Mr. Justice Rowlatt presided, for an historical and fully documented account of these underground activities.

Under its provisions all male British Subjects between the ages of eighteen and fifty-five who were not members of His Majesty's Army or Navy or of the Volunteer or Police Forces of the Colony were compelled to undergo military training, those between the ages of eighteen and forty being at any time liable by proclamation to be transferred into the Singapore Volunteer Corps, those above forty being enrolled as a Civil Guard. Including the Reserve Force to the S.V.C. the Corps numbered 1,379 members at the end of 1915.

During the Mutiny a few of the old Volunteer Snider rifles, with their big curved bayonets, were turned out for the Special Constables and the size and weight of cartridge led to a discussion as to whether the objective of the "Specials" was not the Elephant!

The Kelantan Expedition.—On the 29th April, 1915 an abortive rising broke out at Pasir Puteh in the State of Kelantan in consequence of the murder by a native (one To' Janggut) of a Sergeant of Police. A band of rebels headed by To' Janggut and Ungku Besar sacked Pasir Puteh and took complete possession of the district until order was restored by a force from Singapore consisting of 163 men of the 4th K.S.L.I. (T.F.), 50 of the Royal Garrison Artillery and 21 Singapore Volunteer Infantry under Lt. Colonel Brownlow, R.G.A., which arrived in Kelantan on the 5th May, being reinforced on the 13th May by 140 of the Malay States Guides with two machine guns. The expedition met with little or no opposition and with the exception of the M.S.G. was able to be withdrawn ten days later. A detachment from H.M.S. "*Cadmus*" also assisted. When the Malay States Guides were called away for duty in Aden in September they were relieved by one officer and 38 men of the Malay Company, Penang Volunteers and two officers and 24 men of the Singapore Volunteer Infantry. The P.V. and S.V.I. returned to Penang and Singapore in November, 1915 leaving the preservation of order in Kelantan to the Special Constables who were the forerunners of the Kelantan Volunteer Rifles.

Let us return to our contemporaries again. 1915 was a year in which a number of new units was formed to allow for the enrolment of the many Malayans who wished to be trained for Local Defence in case of need during the War. These new War units, with few exceptions, continued, however, to form part of the Auxiliary forces of Malaya after the cessation of hostilities in 1918 and have practically an unbroken record since their formation.

1922 Previously "Rifles" instead of "Corps"

In August 1914 practically every European in Malacca district fit or otherwise offered himself as a Volunteer for local defence and one year later, on the 12th August, 1915, Malacca, which had been without a Volunteer Unit since the disbandment of the Malacca Company of the Singapore Volunteer Corps in 1906, formed its own Corps known, up to the reorganisation of 1921, as The Malacca Volunteer Rifles. Major W.M. Sime whose initiative was largely responsible for the enterprise, said "There was need for such a body and its formation had the immediate effect of allaying the fears of the European population" who, after the Singapore mutiny, expected all kinds of trouble. At the commencement the Corps was armed with the "defective"([1]) rifles and carbines borrowed from the Cadet Corps of the Malacca High School.

In November, three months after its formation, the strength was 163 Europeans all ranks; only two Europeans in the Settlement of Malacca, who were fit and of military age, were not members of the Corps. A Chinese unit of half a double Company was authorized in December, 1915 and was followed immediately by a Field Ambulance Section. In May, 1916 a further unit of half a double Company was formed from the Malay community. All these units were constituted as the results of an expressed desire to volunteer on the part of the various sections of the populace. The total strength of the Malacca Volunteer Corps at the end of 1918 stood at 390 all ranks, of whom 61 were on leave and for the most part serving in the Imperial Forces.

Next we have the formation of the Province Wellesley Volunteer Rifles. Early in 1915 a movement was made by the residents in Province Wellesley towards forming a local Volunteer Corps and in May the Resident Councillor, Penang approached the Colonial Secretary stating that there were 116 Europeans prepared to join. This was followed by a deputation to the G.O.C. in September and a petition to the Governor in October which resulted in the Corps being formally constituted on the 3rd November, 1915. It was confined to Europeans, and its greatest strength of 139 all ranks was attained at the end of 1917 against an establishment of six Officers and 159 other ranks.

Captain W. Duncan, general manager of the Caledonia Group of Rubber Estates, was the first Commanding Officer of the Province Wellesley Volunteer Rifles which, like the

Province Wellesley Volunteer Rifles—1915-1921

---

(1) Known as E.Y. (Emergency) Rifles.

Malacca Volunteer Rifles, remained on a strictly "Volunteer" basis throughout the War, the magnificent response from the European community obviating any necessity to enforce the provisions of the recently passed "Reserve Force and Civil Guard Ordinance".

In Province Wellesley there were, however, similar difficulties to those maintaining in Kedah, Kelantan and Johore, in the conveyance of Volunteers to parade. The railway was of little value since the service did not run late trains and the fact that transport formed a very high charge on the Corps is borne out by the record of one parade at Caledonia: attended by 86 Volunteers, it cost $297.48 or $3.49 per head.

In Labuan, an isolated part of Singapore Settlement, a Defence Corps was formed in 1915 by the few Europeans on the island who felt the need for having some official means of defending themselves in case of necessity. How few there were is indicated by the fact that they could muster only twelve Europeans; to them 12 old single loading Long Enfield Rifles were supplied. This must surely have been the smallest Volunteer Corps in the Empire, but it existed under this name until 1922 when after the reorganization of the Local Forces it was reformed as the Labuan Volunteer Detachment S.V.C. and supplied with 12 new short Lee Enfield Rifles.

The Malayan Volunteer Infantry was formed in the Federated Malay States as follows:—

> The Malayan Volunteer Infantry, Perak, March 1915.
> The Malayan Volunteer Infantry, Selangor, 1915–1916.
> The Malayan Volunteer Infantry, Pahang, April 1916.
> The Malayan Volunteer Infantry, Negri Sembilan, September 1916.

In mid 1915 a Mobile Field Battery was formed from the Rangoon, Moulmein and Madras Artillery Volunteers for service in Mesopotamia, which expanded in 1916 to a Brigade strength manning four guns at Kut, four in Nasairiyeh, and six L of C Post guns. The four gun battery was part of Townshend's force which surrendered and was marched into captivity in Turkey on the 29th April, 1916. Owing to the strategic importance of Singapore and the necessity for having volunteer gunners available for manning the forts on Blakan Mati and Pulau Brani they were not given an opportunity of forming part of this composite Volunteer Mobile Field Battery.

S.V.A. (S.R.A.(v)) TROPHIES—THE OLDEST TROPHIES IN THE S.V.C.
*Sir Cecil Clementi Smith Cup & Shield—The Gunnery Prize—St. Clair Bowl-
Plunket Grenade—McCallum Trophy*

S.V.A. NO. 3 SUB-DIVISION RIFLE TEAM 1906. WINNERS OF
THE FINDLAYSON CARBINE TROPHY
*Standing—Gnr. Bonham, Gnr. Rogers, Gnr. Gill
Sitting—Br. Walker, Lieut. Lermit, Gnr. Wallace, Gnr. Wills*

(1)

(2)

(3)

COLLAR BADGES SHOULDER TITLES AND BUTTONS
(1) Penang Volunteers 1900–1921. (2) Province Wellesley Volunteer Rifles 1914–1921.
(3) Malacca Volunteer Rifles 1914–1921—Penang & Province Wellesley Volunteer Corps
1922—Malacca Volunteer Corps 1922

As Administration Officer of the Chinese Company, S.V.I. Captain Song Ong Siang carried on the strenuous duties connected with the mobilization of the Chinese Volunteers to do guard duty at various strategical posts on Singapore Island. At the outbreak of the War he was one of the leaders in the movement, started under the auspices of the Straits Chinese British Association, to get the Straits born Chinese as British subjects to render whatever services they were capable of to King and Country. He contributed several short articles to the brochure "Duty to the British Empire (being an Elementary guide for Straits Chinese) during the Great War", published in 1915 at the expense of the Association and distributed gratis to the educated section of the Straits Chinese Community. Capt. Song Ong Siang's pamphlet entitled "The Straits Chinese and a Local Patriotic League" was also published in 1915 with the same emphasis on the spirit of patriotism and loyalty to the British Throne.

In December 1915 the "Volunteer Amendment Ordinance, 1915", was passed to make it clear that the Volunteer Forces were subject to certain disciplinary arrangements, whether there were Regular Forces in the Colony or not.

On the 28th October, 1915 Voluntary enlistment for Kitchener's Armies started locally and the first Malayan contingent for the new Armies sailed on the 11th November. On the 23rd November the granting of Commissions locally for the Home Armies was announced.

On the 1st November it was decided to form a Veterans Company of the Singapore Volunteer Corps, and enrolment commenced on the 24th November.

1916. On the 14th April, 1916 "The Reserve Force and Civil Guard Amendment Ordinance" was passed, giving to the General Officer Commanding power to draft to such unit of the Volunteer Forces as he deemed fit all members of the Reserve Force, and all those undergoing military training.

By proclamation dated the 26th April 1916 all such Reservists between the ages of eighteen and forty were transferred to the Singapore Volunteer Corps, helping to bring the Volunteer Forces up to strength and becoming liable as Volunteers to be called up for mobilization.

The Volunteer Amendment Ordinance 1916, of the 18th May, gave a statutory footing to the Cadet Corps by attaching them to the Volunteer Corps.

In March, 1916 S.V.A. Specialists were mobilized at Fort Canning for 6-pounder training.

In this year also, 2nd Lieut. F.E. Dilley, compiled a handbook for the S.V.A. It was of the same size and issued under the same title as the one published in 1912 but contained more information in its 66 pages; it might be said to have been a general improvement on, besides a revision of, the previous issue. Being a war issue it also continued a section headed "S.V.C. Alarm Orders". The alarm consisted of three salvoes of two guns each fired in quick succession from Fort Canning with an internal of 30 seconds between salvoes and upon hearing the "Alarm", whether by day or night, all Volunteers were instructed to proceed with the utmost possible speed to Headquarters, Beach Road, dressed in accordance with a detail which followed.

During the great war 1914–1918 the members of the S.V.A. Maxim Company often did mobilized duty with the members of their old parent unit the S.V.A., manning the guns in the fort batteries and they continued to be designated the S.V.A. Maxim Company until 1922 when under the new Defence Scheme the unit became the Machine Gun Platoon of the S.V.C., S.S.V.F.

A Band composed principally of Chinese was formed early in 1916 and up to 1918 was entirely upkept from private funds.

Regulations for the Malacca Volunteer Rifles and Province Wellesley Volunteer Rifles were drawn up in 1916, but never gazetted as it was subsequently intended (at the beginning of 1917) to replace the old Volunteer Ordinance of 1888 and its attended out-of-date Regulations by a new Defence Force Ordinance with one set of Regulations to guide all the Volunteer Corps in the Straits Settlements. It is interesting to note, however, that the M.V.R. and P. & P.W.V.R. from their inception in 1915 were run satisfactorily throughout the War on common sense methods without any Regulations.

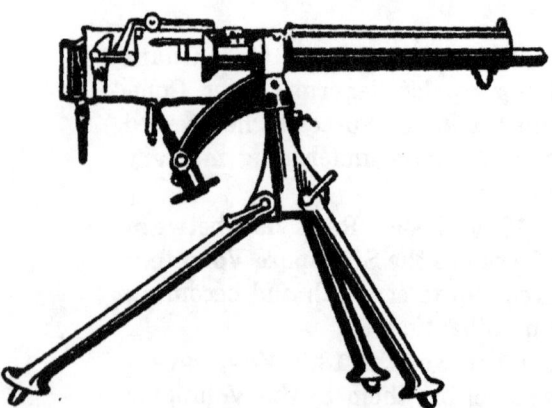

.405 Maxim Machine Gun
S.V.A.—1891–1921

1917. After the entry of the U.S.A. into the War in April, 1917 American subjects resident in Singapore were attached, at their own request, to the S.V.C. for military training.

On the 28th October the Chinese Company, S.V.I., under their Chinese Officers, attended the funeral of Mr. Tan Jiak Kim, C.M.G., one of the most prominent and respected members of the Chinese community, who was largely responsible for founding the Chinese Company S.V.I. in 1901.

([1]) The Volunteer Amendment Ordinance 1917, was passed on the 14th December to provide for compulsory parades under penalty, and to empower the Commanding Officer to impose certain penalties for disobedience and neglect of duty. A later Amendment provided for notices of such compulsory parades and a penalty for not attending the prescribed number of non-compulsory parades.

The next step towards compulsory foreign service was marked by the passing of the "Registration and Medical Examination Ordinance" on the 8th December, 1917 which allowed for registration and medical examination of all British subjects of pure European descent between the ages of 18 and 41, and their classification for active service; this was not coupled however with any compulsory service.

Boards were established to certify whether a man was indispensable or not; but even if the Tribunal declared that a man could be spared, he was not necessarily subject to compulsory service, nor could he, without the consent of his employer, terminate a contract for the purpose of offering himself to the Military Authorities. It was, in fact, the dying effort of the voluntary system and was succeeded on the 20th July, 1918 by the Military Service Ordinance, 1918, which came too late to be of much practical benefit, but which was a courageous attempt to release men for service in the field.

This 1918 Ordinance, after providing for re-examination of all Europeans between the ages of 18 and 41, enacted that all Class "A" men should be liable for Compulsory Military Services abroad unless they applied to and were exempted by a Tribunal on the ground of Imperial interests or special hardship. This closed temporarily the tale of Volunteer and kindred legislation, and left Singapore with a Compulsory "Volunteer" force, under the same discipline as the regular army, and the nucleus of an overseas force in a fairly advanced state of training. In view of the foregoing it is necessary to realize that, as compared with the Civilian

---

(1) The Sections in 1917 and 1918 on Volunteer legislation have been compiled from an article by Mr. W. Bartley, C.M.G., M.B.E., M.C.S., in "One Hundred Years of Singapore" Vol. I page 419 and the Official Report on the Local Forces of Malaya 1914-1918.

Auxiliary Forces serving in England during the War, those in this Colony suffered a considerable amount of hardship as they had to undergo strenuous training without complete or commensurate relief from their civil activities. They filled in fact a dual role, that of the skeleton European personnel required just to carry on Government or Commerce and that of part of the active garrison of the Colony. Consequently had the units of the Volunteer Forces been drafted overseas, as were the Territorial units in England, it would have been imperative to replace them. But who could have replaced them? What Regular regiment or force would have been able to take on that dual role of soldier and civilian? Unfortunately no Territorial Home Service Medal was ever awarded to those civil servants and commercial men in Malaya, many of whom not only pulled the weight of two men in their offices but in addition carried

THE LION AND THE MOUSE—THE FIRST NIBBLE
What the Straits Settlements has done for the Empire

A facsimile of a cartoon that appeared in the Sydney Bulletin of December 16th, 1915. Calling attention to the fact that the S.S. Government led the Empire in introducing Compulsory Service for all white British subjects between the ages of 18 and 55.

out strenuous volunteering duties. Their sole reward had to be the self-satisfaction of a job well and uncomplainingly done.

The Coast Defence Volunteers.—Under the Coast Defence Volunteer Ordinance (No. II of 1892), a Force known as the Coast Defence Volunteers was constituted by the Governor in May, 1917. This Force consisted for the most part of the personnel employed under the Master Attendant in harbour duties at Singapore and Penang. The strength was 9 Officers (who were permitted to wear a quasi-naval uniform and were given naval ranks) 8 Non-Commissioned Officers and 193 men (Malay, Indian and Chinese) at Singapore, and 4 Officers, 1 N.C.O. and 125 men (Malay and Chinese) at Penang.

The command of the whole Force was entrusted to the Master Attendant (Commander B.A. Cator, R.N.), with Lieutenant W.F. Bennett, R.N.R., as Officer Commanding the Singapore Coast Defence Volunteers and Commander D.C. MacIntyre, M.B.E., R.N.R., in command of the Penang Coast Defence Volunteers. The whole Force, although more on a naval than a military basis, was placed under the general direction of Military Headquarters, who were responsible for the defence of the Ports.

The original idea behind the formation of this unit was to have a body of men accustomed to the sea who would have a recognized status and perform signalling duties in the vicinity of the Ports.

At the outbreak of war the Examination Service was instituted at Singapore and Penang, the duties being performed by the personnel employed under the Master Attendant in Singapore and Harbour Master in Penang. This same personnel formed the main part of the Coast Defence Volunteers, who continued to carry out the Examination Services in addition to anti-submarine patrols, harbour patrols and mine-sweeping service. For the anti-submarine work, men from the Singapore Volunteer Corps and Penang Volunteers were mobilized for a short time to man the guns on board the patrol launches, of which there were three at Singapore and two at Penang.

The anti-submarine patrols worked from April to June, 1917. Mine-sweeping was discontinued at the end of November, 1918. No mines were collected.

1918. The conscriptive tenor of the "Reserve Force and Civil Guard Ordinance", and the wider nature of the duties undertaken, had rendered the term "Volunteer" too narrow in its construction; when, therefore, the Government decided to combine all Corps of Volunteers throughout the

Straits Settlements it was suggested that it would be more appropriate and accurate to designate the force as "The Straits Settlements Defence Force", the Singapore Volunteer Corps becoming the "Singapore Defence Corps" and so on.

New Defence Force Bills were prepared by Military Headquarters, one for the Straits Settlements and another for the Federated Malay States and submitted to Government before the end of 1918. These bills, which were never passed, provided for:—

> (i) the Registration, Medical Examination and Compulsory Enrolment in the Straits Settlements and Federated Malay States Defence Forces of European British Subjects between the ages of 18 and 45;
>
> (ii) the acceptance of voluntary offers of service from non-Europeans (and from Europeans over 45);
>
> (iii) the inauguration of compulsory service for any non-European community, if the Government is so requested by the recognized representatives of that community;
>
> (iv) General Military Service in the Malay Peninsula for Europeans under 41;
>
> (v) Local Military Service in the Settlement or State in which the man resides for Europeans over 41 and for all non-European Volunteers;
>
> (vi) Overseas Service for Class "A" Europeans under 41.

Had these Bills been passed the difficulty of maintaining strength in the Auxiliary Forces, one of the main anxieties of the G.O.C. Troops and of Volunteer Commandants, would have automatically ceased; it was decided however that in Malaya, as generally through the Empire, the question of the strength of the Volunteer Auxiliary Forces must be left to the honour of the Empire's private citizens.

Hongkong V.D.C.

The change of name from "Volunteer Force" to "Defence Force" was similarly never effected, although it was still being discussed in 1920 when it was finally decided that it would be inoperative without a new Defence Force Ordinance to legalize the change. It appears to have been carried through in other Colonies though, as the Hongkong Volunteer Corps became "The Hongkong Defence Corps" in 1917 and on its reorganisation in 1920 "The Hongkong Volunteer Defence Corps".

In this connection it is also interesting to note that the Rangoon Volunteer Rifles became a battalion of the Indian Defence Force on the 1st April, 1917 though later, in October 1920, it received the designation "Rangoon Battalion A.F.I." when the Indian Defence Force became the Auxiliary Force (India). (Subsequently on the 1st April, 1937, when the separation of Burma from India came about, it has become the Rangoon Battalion Burma Auxiliary Force).

It is understood that the S.V.C. was kept on a voluntary basis as the result of a promise of strong support from the Ex-Service Men's Association, a promise that was stoutly kept by those who had already seen much active service but, as the vicissitudes of "B" Company subsequently show, their example was not always followed by the post-war youth arriving in this Colony.

Summarized, the Legislation for Volunteering in Malaya is as follows:—

  (i) Act No. XXIII of 1857 passed by the Legislative Council of India on the 18th July, 1857—"An Act to provide for the good order and discipline of certain Volunteer Corps, and to invest them with certain powers".
  (ii) Ordinance No. XV of 1869. (28th September, 1869) "An Ordinance to provide for the support, good order and discipline of Volunteer Corps";
  (iii) The Volunteers Amendment Ordinance 1880 (15th June, 1880 Ordinance No. I).
  (iv) The Volunteer Ordinance 1888; (S.S.).
  (v) The Volunteer Enactment 1910 (F.M.S.).
  (vi) The Volunteer Enactment 1913 (F.M.S.).
  (vii) The Reserve Force and Civil Guard Ordinance 1915 (and Enactment 1915).
  (viii) The Johore (European) Volunteer Enactment 1915.
  (ix) The Registration and Medical Examination Ordinance, 1917 (and Enactment 1918).

(x) The Military Service Ordinance 1918 (and Enactment 1918).
(xi) The Kelantan Volunteer Enactment 1917 (Retrospective to 8th August, 1914).
(xii) The Volunteer Ordinance XXX of 1921 (13th December, 1921).
(xiii) The Volunteer Ordinance XXXVIII of 1922 (29th December, 1922).
(xiv) The Volunteer Ordinance XXIV of 1923 (30th November, 1923).
(xv) The Volunteer Force Ordinance No. 199 of 1926 (covering 1921-1922 and 1923 Ordinances).
(xvi) The Kedah Volunteer Enactment 1349 (1930).
(xvii) The Naval Volunteer Reserve Ordinance 1934.
(xviii) The Volunteer Air Force Ordinance 1936.

On the 4th July, 1918, on the representation of Dr. Noel L. Clarke and Mr. H.R.S. Zehnder the Eurasian Company was reformed having, after the outbreak of War, more than once petitioned the Government to be allowed to take a place in the Volunteer Corps. The original members of the present Eurasian Company of Infantry were carefully selected. The Company was enrolled under Captain F.S. Clarke, and it is interesting to recall that the Sergeants were the Hon. Dr. Noel Clarke, Mr. W.J. Le Cain (both Queen's Scholars), Mr. H.R.S. Zehnder (of the local legal fraternity) and Mr. J.R. Angus while Mr. W.A. Aeria was a Corporal. In its twenty years of life, the present Company has accredited itself excellently.

At the end of 1918 the S.V.A. had the following qualified Specialists:—24 Gun Layers, 23 Depression Range Finders and 13 Position Finders also many with a good knowledge of the latter two specialists jobs though they were not qualified.

At the outbreak of War in 1914 only three Volunteer Corps existed in Malaya, The Singapore Volunteer Corps, the Penang Volunteers and The Malay States Volunteer Rifles. The war was therefore responsible for the formation of the additional forces in existence in 1918, *i.e.* The Malacca Volunteer Rifles, The Province Wellesley Volunteer Rifles, The Malayan Volunteer Infantry, The Johore Volunteer Rifles, The Labuan Volunteer Defence Detachment and The Kelantan Volunteer Rifles, but it will be noticed that none of these new units were, or included, additional Volunteer Artillery although it would appear that mountain guns with Jungle Transport might have been considered for use in case of necessity in the F.M.S.

M.S.V.R., MAXIM GUN AND DETACHMENT
Kuala Lumpur 1916

M.S.V.R., MAXIM GUN AND DETACHMENT
Ipoh—1916. Carriage presented by the Tin Miners of Perak

SINGAPORE ROYAL ENGINEERS (VOLUNTEER)
With the 41st Coy. Royal Engineers at Pulo Brani, 1918
Centre Sitting—Capt. F.H. Robinson and Major G.R.H. Webb

MALAY COMPANY AND H.Q. STAFF P. & P.W.V.C. IN MALAY MESS DRESS
Sitting—R.S.M., P. Sellick; Lt. Md. Noor; Lt. S.M. Osman; Capt. A.T. Dougall; Major E.A. de Buriatte; Lt.-Col. G.D.A. Fletcher; Capt. D.G.B. Ridout (Adjt.); Capt. Md. Noor b. S. Mohamed; Lt. Md. Hussain; 2nd Lt. B. Pawan; C.S.M., S.M. Husain. Standing—Sgt. Md. Sherrif; Sergt. Md. Zain; L/Sergt. Che Ahmad; L/Sergt. N.M. Noordin; L/Sergt. Md. Ismail Man and other members of the Malay Company.

Courses for Officers in India.—Thanks to the courtesy of India Army Headquarters facilities were offered to officers of the Local Forces to attend Instructional Courses in India. Seven places were allotted in 1918 and nine in 1919.

Three M.S.V.R. officers and one J.V.R. took advantage of the facilities offered. All passed out, one with distinction. The courses taken were: Musketry at Pachmarhi, four weeks' course (two officers). Course of General Instruction at Kirkee, six weeks (two officers).

A bonus of $100 on passing out at the end of these courses was granted by the Local Governments.

Officers of the Local Forces found it extremely difficult to leave the country for these courses and the vacancies allotted for 1919 were not all taken up. No officer of any Corps in the Straits Settlements was able to fill any of these vacancies.

Other officers took the opportunity when on leave in England to undergo courses of training at Instructional Schools or to be attached to different units; one officer went through a Lewis gun course while on leave in Australia.

1919. *Electric Light Section S.R.E.(v).*—Another unit, the Electric Light Section, S.R.E.(v) was added to the Corps. It was composed of Malays and was enrolled for continuous mobilized duty and together with the Defence Electric Light Section of the S.R.E.(v) became the Singapore Fortress Company Royal Engineers (Volunteer) in 1930.

The construction of the present 30 yards Rifle Range at S.V.C. Headquarters in Beach Road was recommended to Government in February, 1917, approved in June, 1918 and constructed in April, 1919 at a cost of $3,600.

1921. At the end of 1921 it was decided to re-organize the volunteer forces of the Straits Settlements and to bring them under one control. For this purpose the existing volunteer ordinances were replaced by a new one, all commissions were called in and the four corps were disbanded. The Volunteer Ordinance 1921 published as Straits Settlements Government Gazette Notification No. 1996 dated 16th December, 1921 came into force on 1st January, 1922. Under it the Singapore Volunteer Corps, the combined Penang and Province Wellesley Volunteer Corps and the Malacca Volunteer Corps were to form the Straits Settlements Volunteer Force.

Each Corps was to consist of Colour Service Volunteers, Reserve Service Volunteers and Auxiliary Service Volunteers. The Reserve Service was to provide trained reserves and the Auxiliary Service to fill non-combatant and administrative appointments.

One of the tenor Drums of the S.V.C.

CHAPTER IV

THE FIFTH CORPS 1922–1937

THE S.V.C. AS PART OF THE S.S.V.F.

With the opening of this last and present day chapter it is felt that most of the past S.V.C. history, which was slipping into obscurity, has been put on record with the help of all those living and the ancient journals of the press, which are fast crumbling but have not yet become dust. The record of the S.V.C. as part of the S.S.V.F. being one of comparatively recent events, the historical frills to these sixteen years of volunteering in Singapore can be added, perhaps at some future date, in a more interesting revised second edition of this book as a result of the criticisms and suggestions of those who read this first edition.

Over the period of years 1921 to 1937 Volunteering in Malaya passed through a phase of continuous reorganization, due mainly to a desire to identify more closely the basis of organization of volunteer and regular units and thereby to facilitate the employment of the Volunteer force in war.

The increase in the size of the Singapore garrison was advantageous from a Volunteer training point of view. The volunteers obtained still more instruction from regular soldiers and were able to take a part in military operations and manoeuvres on a larger scale.

1922. Lieut.-Colonel F.E. Spencer, D.S.O., M.C., R.A. was appointed as the first Commandant, S.S.V.F. He was also appointed O.C., Singapore Volunteer Corps, while Volunteer officers were appointed to command the P. & P.W.V.C. and the M.V.C. Each Corps was allowed a regular Adjutant.

On 1st January recruiting was opened. From the enlistments, which came in well, appointments to non-commissioned rank were soon made. The Officers Commanding the Corps, with the help of the Advisory Committees, then selected officers after a careful scrutiny of their records and capabilities.

The establishments of the three Corps were as follows:—

Singapore Volunteer Corps.—

One Company, Singapore Volunteer Artillery	6 Off.	161 O.R.
One Company, Singapore Royal Engineers (v) (including Signallers)	5 „	87 „
Two Companies, Singapore Volunteer Rifles (European British) Each	5 „	158 „
One Eurasian Company, Singapore Volunteer Infantry	5 „	158 „
One Malay Company, Singapore Volunteer Infantry	5 „	158 „
One Chinese Company, Singapore Volunteer Infantry	5 „	158 „
One Company, Singapore Field Ambulance	2 „	124 „

Attached.—The Johore Volunteer Rifles (European British).
The Labuan Volunteer Detachment.

Malacca Volunteer Rifles.—

One Company Malacca Volunteer Rifles. (European British).
One Malay Company.
One Chinese Company.
One Company, Field Ambulance.

Penang and Province Wellesley Volunteer Corps.—

Two Companies (European British).
One Eurasian Company.
One Chinese Company.
One Malay Company.
One Company, Field Ambulance.
European Companies were to have an extra platoon as Machine Gun Platoon.

The Qualifying Training in all Corps was:—
Infantry and Field Ambulance—18 parades.
R.E. & V.A.—24 parades.
Reserve Service—6 parades.

This was in addition to a musketry course and the G.O.C's Inspection. The training year was divided into four seasons: one was a close season and the qualifying parades were to be spread equally over the other three.

1922

The three Corps were reformed as follows:—

Singapore Volunteer Corps.—
A Composite company of 4 Platoons later separated into units.

1 Platoon Artillery Personnel	24.2.22	2/Lt. (Ag. Major) A.A.A. Paterson, D.S.O., M.C.
1 Platoon Engineer Personnel		
1 Platoon Signal Personnel		
1 Platoon Machine Gun Personnel		
"A" Company (European) ..	24.2.22	2/Lt. (a/Capt.) C.E. Wurtzburg, M.C.
"B" Company (European) ..	24.2.22	2/Lt. (a/Major) G.C. Meredith, M.C.
"C" Company (Scottish) ..	24.2.22	2/Lt. (a/Capt.) C.M. Allport
Eurasian Company (incl. Band)	1.1.22	2/Lt. (a/Capt.) F.S. Clarke
Chinese Company ..	1.1.22	2/Lt. (a/Major) E.A. Brown
Malay Company ..	1.1.22	2/Lt. (a/Capt.) T.C. Hay
S. Field Ambulance Company	24.2.22	2/Lt. (a/Capt.) W.A. Taylor
Labuan Detachment (attached)	3.12.22	2/Lt. H.J. Eley

Malacca Volunteer Rifles.—

Officer Commanding ..	1.1.22	Major A.A. Lermit
"A" (European) Company, M.V.R.	1.1.22	2/Lt. (a/Major) L.M. Haybittel, D.S.O.
"B" (Chinese) Company, M.V.R.	1.1.22	2/Lt. (a/Capt.) V.H. Winson
"C" (Malay) Company, M.V.R.	1.1.22	2/Lt. (a/Capt.) E.E. Colman later 2/Lt. (a/Capt.) J.R. Gildea
M.G. Platoon M.V.R. ..	25.10.22	2/Lt. H.W. Esson, M.C.

Penang and Province Wellesley Volunteer Corps.—

"A" (European) Company, P.V.I.	1.1.22	2/Lt. (a/Major) R.N. Holmes, M.C.
European M.G.Pl., P.V.I. ..	1.1.22	2/Lt. A. Dawbarn
"B" (Eurasian) Company, P.V.I.	1.1.22	2/Lt. (a/Major) W.V.L. Van Someron, D.S.O., M.C.

"C" (Malay) Company, P.V.I.	1.1.22	2/Lt. (a/Capt.) A.C. Baker, M.C.
"D" (Chinese) Company, P.V.I.	1.1.22	2/Lt. (a/Capt.) R.R. Robertson
European Company, P.W.V.I.	1.2.22	2/Lt. (a/Major) G.D.A. Fletcher, M.C.
Field Ambulance	1.1.22	2/Lt. (a/Capt.) J. Gossip.

Each Corps had its reserve and auxiliary personnel.

The formation of a Volunteer Scottish Company in the reorganized S.V.C. brings back to us the impressions of the Malays seeing the first Highland regiment in Singapore in the early seventies of the last century when they asked one another what kind of men these were who were dressed as "perempuan" (women) and some suggested that it must be a body of beings who were neither men nor women, in fact they came to the same conclusion as did the peasants of a French village during the Great War that they must be that regiment called the 'Middle-Sex'!

In early March the European companies at Singapore held their first organization parades and on 31st March the S.V.C. provided a contingent for the ex-Service Mens' Guard of Honour for the visit of H.R.H. The Prince of Wales.

The role of the Volunteer Corps was definitely laid down to be primarily internal security and secondly assistance to or relief of the Regular Garrison in case of external aggression.

Training started almost at once. In April, 17 Officers and N.C.O's. attended a 10-day course of instruction with the 2nd Bn. The Middlesex Regiment in Company Drill, weapon training and bayonet fighting. Tactical Exercises were carried out with and without troops. Musketry was restricted to the 30 yards range.

Many of the old members of the S.V.A. came forward again. Among them was Major D.T. Lewis, the last officer to command the S.V.A. under the old regime. Having resigned his commission in 1921, he joined up again as a gunner and remained so until his retirement from the Colony in 1928. During his service at this time as a Volunteer Gunner he was also, simultaneously, a member of the S.S. Legislative Council and though the S.V.C. Headquarters and the Battery rarely referred to him in orders by his correct title, it should have been on every occasion "The Honourable Gunner D.T. Lewis"! An honourable record in every respect, the opportunity is taken to acknowledge it here together with that of Lieut. T.O.

Mayhew. Tommy Mayhew was an old regular gunner and saw service in Egypt in 1892. On his arrival in Singapore in 1896 he immediately joined the Singapore Volunteer Artillery, becoming Battery Sergeant Major in 1901, which rank he held up to 1917. During the War he was persuaded to take a commission but resigned it at the first opportunity, in 1921, in favour of his job of Battery Sergeant Major, a bill he filled so popularly. On re-enrolling in 1921 he made a special effort to get to the Drill Hall first and by doing so asserted his right, both as the oldest member of the Corps and by virtue of being first comer, to the Regimental No. 1 which he retained until his untimely end in 1932.

On Monday, 24th July, the Composite Company ceased to exist as such, and the platoons became—

The Singapore Volunteer Artillery	Comdr. 2/Lt. (a/Capt.) A. Gordon Lee, M.C.
The Singapore Royal Engineers (v) (including Signal Section)	Comdr. 2/Lt. (a/Major) P.H. Keys, D.S.O., M.C.
Machine Gun Platoon	Comdr. 2/Lt. L.H. Chidson, M.B.E.

2/Lt. (a/Major) A.A.A. Paterson, D.S.O., M.C. then took command of "A" Company vice 2/Lt. Wurtzburg transferred to Penang.

Arms.—

All units had S.M.L.E. Rifles (latest pattern) except the P. & P.W.V.C. who had 118 old rifles.

The S.V.C. had 6 Vickers and 20 Lewis Guns: P. & P.W.V.C. 4 Vickers and 12 Lewis Guns: M.V.R. 2 Vickers and 8 Lewis Guns.

Equipment.—

Only leather bandoliers were available in Singapore and Malacca though Penang had the more modern webbing equipment.

Competitions.—

The 30 yards Range (Malcolm) Cup match was inaugurated this year. The S.R.E.(v) won it as well as the Warren Shield and the Inter-Company Swimming Match.

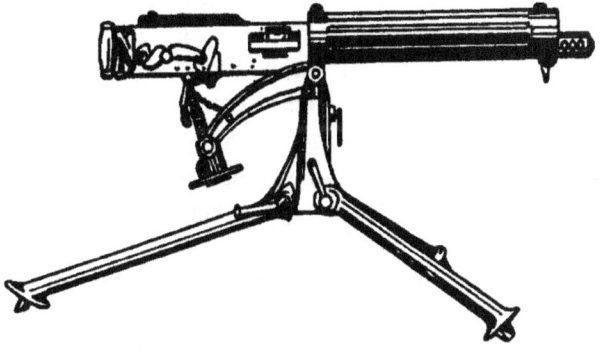

S.V.C. 1922—.303 Vickers Machine Gun

The S.V.A. were very fortunate in this and the succeeding two years in having as Commandant of the Corps a Gunner in the person of Lt. Col. Spencer, D.S.O., M.C., who naturally took especially keen interest in the Volunteer counter part of his own particular branch of the service. As he was an extremely active man he escaped the possible criticism of devoting more of his time to the S.V.A. than to other units. He certainly did do a great deal for the S.V.A. and nearly managed to get them, at a much earlier date than they eventually arrived (1930), four 3.7-inch Mountain Howitzers, the efficient little pieces of ordnance which were so useful in difficult country during the war, instead of the 4.5-inch QF. Field Howitzers with which the S.V.A. was equipped on the re-organisation.

S.V.A. Drills up to the autumn of 1922 were held at Fort Canning after which the four 4.5-inch Howitzers were brought to the Drill Hall and the reclamation opposite Raffles Hotel was used for Gun Drill.

"The Battle of Lavender Street".—On the 16th November, 1922 sections of the Singapore Volunteer Corps were called out to assist the police in capturing a gang of about 20 gang robbers, who, raided at their headquarters during the night, had taken refuge in a house near Lavender Street, close to the Kallang district, which they defended with pistols and revolvers against the efforts of the police to dislodge them.

The affair was known as the "Battle of Lavender Street" owing to its similarity to another of its kind in the East End of London in January, 1911, which the press christened "The Battle of Sydney Street", when two desperadoes also took refuge in a house and fired promiscuously with Mauser pistols, first at the police who tried to arrest them, and then at any one who came along the street. The forces against these two men in London were from 1,000 to 1,500 police partly armed with shot guns and revolvers; 90 men of the Scots Guards with rifles and a machine gun; a section of Horse Artillery with one field gun and a strong reserve of the London Fire Brigade!

In Singapore though the gang comprised 20 men (as against only two men in the London "battle"), the police cordon was small but the seriousness of the resistance is indicated by the fact that the Volunteers were called upon to bring Lewis and machine guns and a section of Artillery on the scene. In London Mr. Churchill, as Home Secretary, was among those present under fire and in Singapore Mr. F.S. James, Colonial Secretary, Captain Chancellor, I.G.P., Mr. Hannigan, C.P.O., and Captain Groves, A.S.P. were all on the spot.

Volunteers of the Lewis Gun sections, Machine Gun and Artillery units were surprised to get telephone calls in their offices, about 8.45 A.M. in the morning, to parade at the Drill Hall for action! The Lewis Gun section got away first and arrived at Lavender Street just as the gang robbers had surrendered after a four hour stand. The Artillery section having just hooked in their guns to the recently arrived lorries, were about to leave the Drill Hall when the Machine Gunners returned bringing the news that there was "No sport—battle all over!" The account of the London "battle" says of the field gun that was called up, "fortunately for everybody in the proposed line of fire it arrived too late to be brought into action" and the chronicler records that the Singapore Volunteer gunners heaved a sigh of relief for similar reasons, when they heard that they were not required!

Of the robbers the leader, a Cantonese, was killed and three were wounded while the police casualties amounted to three in all, two detectives and one police constable being wounded.

An amusing sequel to this affair occurred some months later when the *"Dumfries and Galloway Advertiser"* published a letter from a Singapore Volunteer to his family describing what might have happened had the artillery and Lewis guns really got into action. The fiction was most lurid but unfortunately taken for "gospel" and published as an authentic account. It was read by a Scotsman whose daughter was shortly sailing for Singapore to get married; he was so much disturbed by the thought of his daughter residing in a 'hell spot' of the Far East where such events were more or less the order of the day that he wrote an irate letter to the fiancé telling him that if he wished to marry his daughter he must find a job in a more civilized country! He enclosed a copy of the newspaper cutting......It is believed that the fiancé of the girl and the Volunteer with fictionable abilities met!

Assistance by Volunteers in Quelling Civil Disturbances.—This subject of Volunteers being called out to assist in quelling civil disturbances brings us to an interesting point in the Manual of Military Law Chapter XIII which clearly distinguishes between (i) Unlawful Assembly (ii) Riot and (iii) Insurrection. How many Volunteers, especially the Officers, have, it is wondered, read this Chapter of Military Law and when called out to assist the civil authorities are aware of the extent of their responsibilities, the onus which is upon them, how much force they may use and if and when they may fire. When "unlawful assembly" becomes a "riot" and the difference between "riot" and "insurrection" is dealt with in Military law as far as possible but it is a difficult question, generally one that can only be answered by the man on the spot who must be guided by the general attitude of the assembly. The law emphasises the necessity of using only the "minimum amount of force" to quell such disturbances, and the use of more than that minimum is classed as unnecessary force and may have dire consequences for those in command. In Malaya, where the Volunteers first duty is to help to maintain internal security, every Volunteer should have a clear knowledge of his responsibilities in case of eventuality. There is rarely time for reference to books when the call comes.

1923. The training year was divided into four periods, the dates differing slightly in the three settlements. In Singapore they were:—
 1st February—30th April. Individual and Section Training.
 1st May—31st July. Platoon and Company Training.
 1st August—31st October. Company Training.
 1st November—31st January. No training.

In the first period each unit was allotted one fortnight, in which 6 or 8 qualifying parades had to be done. This saved congestion and allowed training to be progressive without long intervals.

The Seletar Range was taken into use this year for the first time, and the Balestier Range was retained for use as a 30 yards range only.

On the 9th February, Government Gazette No. 9 announced that H.M. The King had approved the grant to the re-organized Artillery and Engineer Units of the title "Royal". He also approved the following designations: Singapore Royal Artillery (Volunteer): Singapore Royal Engineers (Volunteer): Singapore Volunteer Infantry, Singapore Volunteer Field Ambulance.

In March Establishment and Equipment Tables were issued.

During the year the Singapore Volunteer Rifle Association resumed its activities and held monthly spoon shoots. The M.V.C. won the Penang Veteran's and Murray Cups. "C" (Scottish) Company won the Gibbons Cup and the Eurasian Company, S.V.C. the Malcolm Cup.

S.R.A.(v) 1923

In the ranks of Volunteer units in Malaya, both during and after the war, amusing incidents occurred similar to one related by the Hon. W. Best in *"Forest Life in India"*. His story is as follows:—

> A general officer was inspecting the Indian Defence Force detachment at Simla during the war. Passing along the ranks he saw one man of considerable age with many ribbons on his chest.
>
> "Ah!" he said, "That's what I like to see. A stiffening of veterans in the ranks."
>
> Looking closely to identify the ribbons, he remarked: "What are these medals? I don't seem to know them?"
>
> "K.C.I.E., K.C.M.G., C.S.I., sir," replied the man.

At a General's Inspection in 1923 Major N.H.P. Whitley, M.C., (now Mr. Justice Whitley) appeared in the ranks of the S.R.A.(v) with his chest of ribbons including, in addition to the Military Cross and three War Medals, The French Croix de Guerre, The Order of the Crown of Italy and the Order of El Nahda (Hejaz). Many then present will recollect how the G.O.C. stopped and made remarks somewhat similar to those mentioned by Mr. Best's General Officer.

In September the Hon. Mr. A. Gibbons presented a trophy allotted with his approval to the company with the highest musketry figure of merit. In 1923 it was won by "C" (Scottish) Company.

On 7th October the S.R.A.(v) carried out a 4.5 in. Howitzer practice shoot at Blakang Mati. The G.O.C.'s Singapore Inspection on 21st October took the form of a tactical exercise in which half the S.V.C. opposed the other half. At Penang the inspection was a tactical exercise on 23rd September, followed by field firing.

On 31st October it was announced that the Government had decided that charges in the Government hospitals to efficient colour service volunteers, their wives and families should be half only of the fees charged to the general public.

Officers and a certain number of N.C.O's were at about the same time granted exemption from Jury service.

On 6th December a special recruiting day was held for all European Units in Singapore, producing some 60 recruits.

A new Volunteer Ordinance 1923 was published in the Straits Settlements Government Gazette Notification No. 1997 of 21st December, 1923.

The S.S.V.F. Establishment was laid down as:—

S.V.C.—

    One Battery S.R.A.(v).
    One Company, S.R.E.(v), including one Signal Section.

Two (European) Companies, S.V.I.
One (Scottish) Company, S.V.I.
One Eurasian Company, S.V.I.
One Chinese Company, S.V.I.
One Malay Company, S.V.I.
One Singapore Volunteer Field Ambulance (H.Q. and 2 Sections).
One Machine Gun Platoon.
The Labuan Volunteer Detachment.

P. & P.W.V.C.—
One (European) Company, P.V.I.
One (European) Company, P.W.V.I.
One Eurasian Company, P.V.I.
One Chinese Company, P.V.I.
One Malay Company, P.V.I.
One P. & P.W.V. Field Ambulance (H.Q. and 2 Sections).
One Signal Section—One Engineer Section—One M.G. Section.

M.V.C.—
One (European) Company, M.V.I.
One Chinese Company, M.V.I.
One Malay Company, M.V.I.
One Eurasian Company, M.V.I.
One M.V. Field Ambulance (H.Q. and 1 Sec.).
One Signal Section—One M.G. Sub-section.

This Ordinance also increased the duties allotted to Advisory Committees, abolished the reserve service and introduced a Reserve of Officers. The place of the Reserve Service was taken by the First Reinforcement Group of the Auxiliaries.

The S.V.A. and S.R.A.(v) having passed from Garrison Artillery 1888 to 1896 to Mountain Artillery 1896 to 1906 and back to Garrison Artillery from 1906 to 1921 were now Field Artillery, but as such could find no better camping place from which firing practice could be carried out than the regular gunners' domain at Pulo

4.5-inch Howitzer S.V.A.—1922

Blakan Mati. Consequently a repetition of history took place in 1923 when the S.R.A.(v) camped over Easter at Blakan Mati with their 4.5 Howitzers where the first S.V.A. camp was held on the 7 inch. M.L. gun in 1888 and with this revival it once again became the custom for the S.R.A.(v) to hold a camp each year at Blakan Mati over the Easter holidays.

With the introduction of the new Volunteer Ordinance 1923, the Reserve Service was abolished and in 1923 the following classes constituted the Force:—

    Colour Service.
    Auxiliary Service.
    Reserve of Officers.

A group of the Auxiliary Service consisting of trained men was styled "First Reinforcement" and they were expected to attend six parades and musketry annually and thus maintain a standard of efficiency fitting them for taking their place with the Colour Service on mobilization.

1924. The 1924 efficiency qualification was laid down as:—

    Artillery, Engineers, Signallers, Machine Gunners .. 24 parades.
    Infantry and Field Ambulance .. .. 18 ,,

For all, an approved standard in musketry course and attendance at G.O.C's inspection.

The system of training was the same as in 1923, except that company camps were introduced. Officers' and N.C.O's camps were held at Lumut (Dindings) and Siglap for P. & P.W.V.C. and S.V.C. plus M.V.C. respectively with vacancies allotted to the other corps so as to promote esprit-de-corps. An Officers' Revolver Course was also introduced. The S.R.E.(v) held their camp at Pulau Brani in conjunction with the 41st Fortress Company, R.E. and a second one at Siglap. The S.R.A.(v) camped at Blakang Mati.

Bukit Timah Range was first available for use on 21st June. The name of the Seletar Range was altered to Farrer Range. At Penang a site was obtained for a new H.Q. The Malacca H.Q. was completed during the year.

On the 11th February, "C" (Scottish) Company provided a guard of honour at Government House on the occasion of the landing of the Vice Admiral Commanding the Special Service Squadron.

On the 2nd June a special recruiting day was held in Singapore for European units.

The First Reinforcement Group of Auxiliaries was started this year to cater for those who wished to do a certain amount of training without being active service volunteers. Their training was laid down as six drills yearly, a musketry course, and all mobilization parades. Other Auxiliary Groups had to attend mobilization parades and any lectures ordered.

The Penang Veterans' Shield was won by the P. & P.W.V.C., the Gibbons Cup by the S.R.E.(v) and the Command M.G. Cup by the M.G. Platoon, M.V.C.

1925. In this year rubber and tin came into their own and there commenced an era of great commercial prosperity.

Training was carried out on the same lines as before, the instruction being given mainly by the permanent staff. The Commandant was responsible for tactics and officers' instruction classes and the Adjutants and W.O's for drill and weapon training. Six day camps were held in Singapore and Penang for officers and N.C.O's. These were poorly attended by Europeans for business reasons. The Malacca Volunteers attended the Singapore or Penang camps. The M.G. camp at Singapore was held on Pulau Brani with Field Firing on Blakang Mati.

The Command Rifle Meeting was held in Penang for the first time on record.

For some time the Labuan Volunteer Detachment was reduced to four Colour Service Volunteers.

A considerable amount of special expenditure was approved; at Singapore for the Eurasian Volunteer Club; at Penang the Chinese Volunteer Club was completed, and at Malacca the Chinese Volunteer Club was finished and the Malay Club changed. A certain amount of building was uncompleted, both at Singapore and Penang.

1926. Rubber and tin were still prospering and volunteers found less time to spare for volunteering. Training continued on the same lines but in place of six-day courses for officers and N.C.O's a system of two long week-end (2½ days) camps was tried out. This proved successful and 67 Europeans, in place of 26 in 1925, were able to attend. Company training was carried out in week-end camps and individual training in evening drills. Camps were held this year at Malacca for volunteers other than Malays, who attended the Singapore camp. For weapon training reliance was placed on regular instructors. The M.G. camp at Pulau Brani, with field firing, was repeated.

In the Command Rifle Meeting, the Singapore Eurasian Company won the Straits Trading Company's Lewis Gun Shield and the Falling Plate and Superiority of Fire Competitions. The S.V.C. team won the Knockout Revolver Competition. Of the S.S.V.F. and S.V.C. trophies, the Eurasian Company, S.V.C. again won the Murray Cup and also the Penang Veterans' Shield, while the S.R.E.(v) won the Gibbons Cup for the best Musketry Unit in the Corps for the 3rd year in succession.

During the year Major L.H. Chidson, M.B.E. was appointed Machine Gun Officer, S.S.V.F.

The S.V.C. took a prominent part in the 1926 semi-military Pageant, being entirely responsible for "the attack on the Desert Mail" and for Highland Dancing.

Several changes took place in the S.V.C. composition during the year. "B" Company, always rather low in numbers, as the first war emigrants to the Colony, for whose enrolment it had been formed in 1922 did not volunteer in sufficient numbers, was merged into "A" company in 1926. At one time, containing as it did volunteers of all nationalities, "B" Company was known by members of the Corps as "the Foreign Legion".

The Motor Cyclist Platoon was brought up to full strength and from it was formed the Intelligence Platoon of the S.V.C.; with the increasing popularity of the small car, however, it was difficult to find members with motor cycles and the Corps eventually had to provide motor cycles on the establishment for despatch and intelligence work.

Two new Asiatic units were formed, namely the Defence Electric Light Unit (Auxiliaries), which was recruited in the summer, and the S.R.A.(v) Asiatic Signal Unit, formed at the beginning of the year, from trained G.P.O. operators (12 O.Rs.). A special recruiting day, held in December, brought the total of recruits obtained in that month to 100.

All European Units, except S.R.A.(v) and the Motor Cyclist Platoon, were completely equipped with webbing in place of bandoliers. Two more Vickers Guns were obtained, bringing the S.V.C. total to eight, and the formation of an ammunition reserve was commenced.

As regards buildings and other work, the Singapore Eurasian Club was finished and taken into occupation. The parade ground was metalled and the short road up to Bukit Timah Range was made passable for cars. At Penang, the Eurasian Club was completed and the new Headquarters well under way.

1927. Early in the year Singapore was disturbed by Chinese agitators. This had little effect on volunteer training, in fact a healthier attitude was manifest among the younger men towards volunteering. The year was less prosperous than 1926 but was a busy one.

1927 saw the departure of H.E. Sir Laurence Guillemard, the Governor, and of H.E. Sir Theodore Fraser, the G.O.C., and ceremonial parades were held on both occasions. A Guard of Honour was also provided by the S.V.C. for the arrival of the new Governor, Sir Hugh Clifford.

In the Command Rifle Meeting, held at Kuala Lumpur, the Eurasian Company, S.V.C., again won the Falling Plate Competition and the S.V.C. were first in the Revolver Team event and second in the Vickers Gun and Lewis Gun Competitions. "A" Company P. & P.W.V.C. won the Superiority of Fire Competition. The Eurasian Company, S.V.C. again won the Murray Cup; the Chinese Company, M.V.C. the Penang Veterans' Shield and the Eurasian Company, P. & P.W.V.C. the Bromhead Matthews Shield. The Malay Company won the Iroquois Cup which was presented this year by H.M.S. *"Iroquois"*.

Recruiting this year, except in the case of one company, was carried out by individual effort and on the whole the quality improved though quantity suffered.

The replacement of bandoliers by webbing equipment proceeded in all three Corps. As regards clothing, flannel shirts were gradually replaced by cotton ones and a superior and better fitting kilt for the Scottish Company was obtained.

Experiments were made this year in converting a Morris six wheeler into an armoured car.

The gun shed was extended by an open shelter for housing timber and R.E. material. At Penang the new Headquarters, though not quite finished, were opened by the G.O.C. on the 5th December, the Malay Company H.Q. being still under construction. At Malacca a new building was rented as H.Q. for the Eurasian Company.

The Bukit Timah Range was improved by the addition of a pavilion and a car park and by repairs to firing point shelters, butts and galleries.

The system of long week-end camps for Officers and N.C.O's. was continued with success. The annual inspections at Penang and Malacca took the form of counter-attacks upon forces which had already landed in the neighbourhood. In Singapore mechanized forces met in an encounter battle. In all cases reconnaissances were carried out beforehand. The

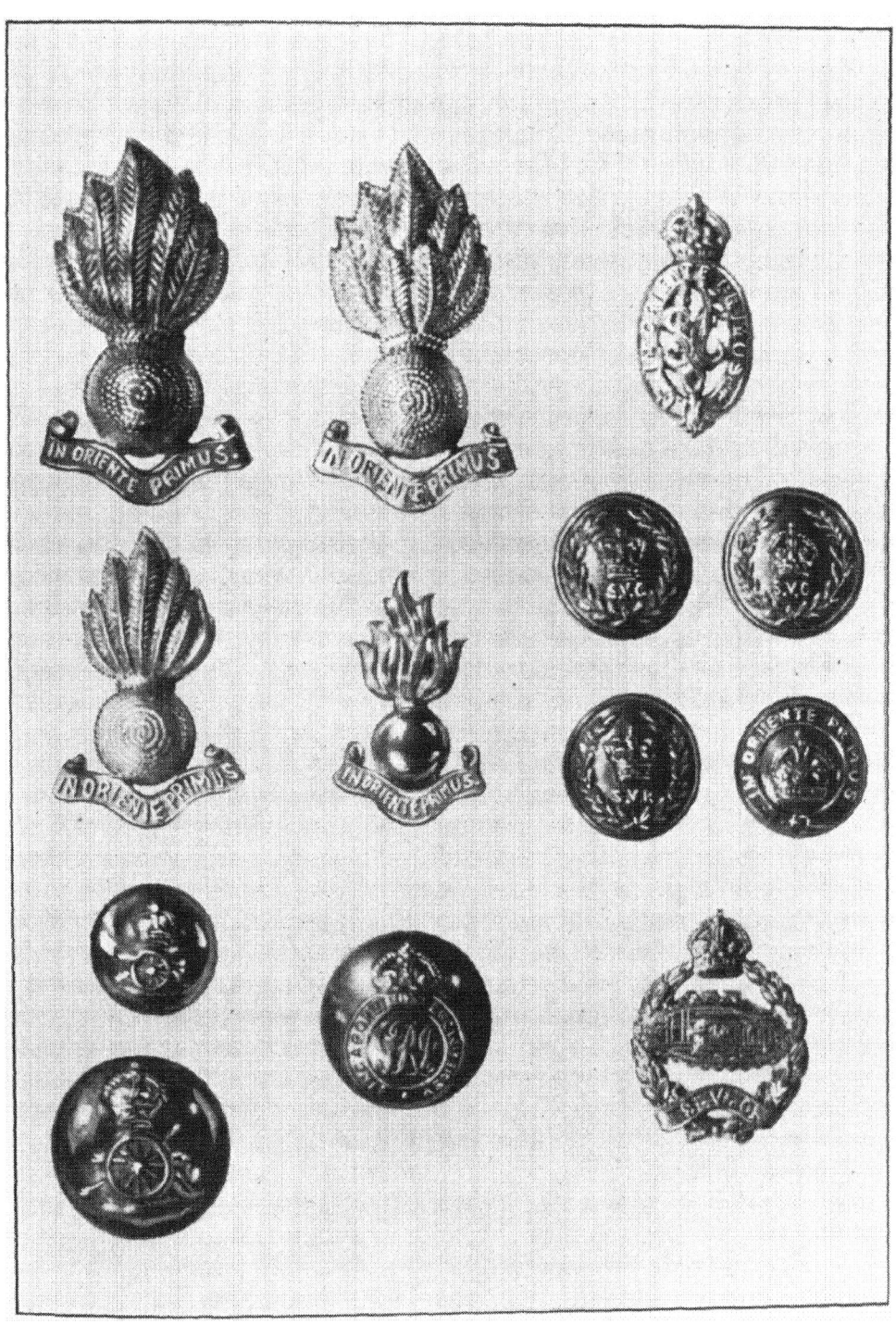

S.V.C. COLLAR BADGES AND BUTTONS

1st Column—S.V.A. & S.R.A.(v) Officers Collar Badge; Other Ranks Collar Badge S.V.A. Gun Button (bullet shape); S.V.A. & S.R.A.(v) Gun Button. *2nd Column*—S.R.E.(v) Officers Collar Badge; Other Ranks Collar Badge; Button. *3rd Column*—S.V.C. Collar Badge, All Ranks; first S.V.C. Button(L); Present S.V.C. Button(R); S.V.R. Button(L); M.V.I. Button(R); Armoured Car Unit Collar Badge.

S.V.C. SHOULDER TITLES
The small titles (s.v.c. & s.v.i.) were worn with white uniform

M.G. camp at Pulau Brani, with field firing, was repeated at Easter and a M.G. demonstration and Field Firing also took place over August bank holiday.

In Singapore there was an increase in numbers instructed and exercised in Vickers and Lewis Guns. Ten Officers and N.C.Os. attended courses at home, six from the S.V.C. three from the P. & P.W.V.C. and one from the M.V.C.

Early in the year the Commandant visited Labuan where the volunteer detachment was revived. The Adjutant visited the island in November and gave lectures and instruction in the Lewis Gun.

The Eurasian Volunteer Headquarters and Club were opened in the S.V.C. Headquarters domain in Beach Road on the 2nd February, 1927 by the G.O.C. Troops Malaya (Major General Sir Theodore Fraser). This building was of a fine modern design, the Eurasian Company Headquarter offices being below, the Club Rooms above. It was mainly due to the efforts of Major General Sir Neil Malcolm and Lt. Col. F.E. Spenser that the Government provided the funds to erect this edifice.

The Club part of it was held to be a recognition by the Government of the excellent work of the Eurasian Company during recent years. This work was in a large measure due to Lieutenant H.R.S. Zehnder, and his services in this respect were recognised in 1928 when he had conferred on him the O.B.E. (Military Division) after promotion to Captain. The Company Officers at the time were Captain E.A. Stringer, M.C. (Commanding), Lieutenants H.R.S. Zehnder, J.R. Angus, W.A. Aeria and E.G. Wheatley.

The S.R.A.(v) Year Book was first instituted by 2nd Lieut. J. Lee in this year and has proved a most useful medium for conveying to all Volunteer Gunners a Programme of the Year's Training, a general knowledge of the working of the Battery together with a resume of the previous year's training, promotions, appointments, news and photographs. In 1935 while commanding the Battery Captain Lee was so overwhelmed with work that he omitted to publish the Year Book; its popularity, however, was amply demonstrated as Captain Lee was made to produce a double number for 1936! This little booklet was in truth the inspiration for the present S.S.V.F. Year Book which, first published in 1931/2 as the 1st Battalion Year Book, has however in no way superceded the Gunners Year Book now in its tenth year.

Referring to the matter of policy, His Excellency the General Officer Commanding, in his Annual Progress Report for 1927, said "The establishment of the Naval Base at Singapore has necessarily altered the strategical situation of Malaya as a whole and of Singapore in particular. This, in its turn, has influenced the Volunteer forces and it is now necessary to demand from them a higher standard". He continued by referring to the drop in efficiency figures of 1927 as compared with 1926 and concluded that the falling off was due to the fact that, with increased responsibilities, the general standard had been raised.

1928. A new Corps Badge was issued in 1928. The Badge in use up to this time was the cypher "S.V.C." encircled with a garter, on which the motto "In Oriente Primus" was inscribed and surmounted by the Royal Crown (similar in general appearance to the old S.V.A. Badge, which was of the same design but with the "S.V.A." cypher, and a grenade instead of a crown surmounting the garter). It was, however, considered that the badge of the Corps should have some connection with the Public Arms of the City of Singapore and it was therefore obvious that a Lion must be included. In designing the new badge there was a choice of three types of lion: (1) the demi-lion "rampant guardant" ("supporting in the paws a staff proper thereon plying to the sinister a banner azure charged with three imperial crowns") as used in the Crest of the Colony Arms: (2) the lion "passant guardant" as used over a tower representing the Settlement of Singapore in the first quarter of the Coat of Arms of the Colony granted in 1911: (3) the lion "statant" in front of a Coconut Palm tree proper, as used in the Crest of the Singapore Municipal Commission.

S.V.C. 1928

It is assumed that the demi-lion was vetoed as being only half a lion and a decision was made in favour of the lion "statant" of the Municipal Crest, presumably because it assumes a more militant appearance than the lion "passant and guardant" of the Singapore Coat of Arms, though since it is a volunteer's first duty to guard, the guardant position of the head would appear to have been more in keeping with the Corps' aims. This apart, however, the result is artistically pleasing to the eye and incorporates the required features.

To the casual observer the main outline of the new badge is much the same as the old one. A Royal Crown still surmounts the whole, the garter has given place to a circle or band with a double spray of oak leaves in the place where the garter buckle used to be; the words "Singapore Volunteer

Corps" take that position in the upper part of the circle which in the case of the old garter used to bear the motto now appearing in the scroll, under the circle, to balance the crown. In the centre of the circle the S.V.C. cypher has been replaced by the lion and palm but, instead of being a relief in brass, the centre has been clean cut leaving a combined shape for the lion and palm which have been superimposed thereon in white metal.

At the same time Collar Badges, hitherto only worn by Officers of the S.R.A.(v) and S.R.E.(v), were instituted for wear by all ranks throughout the Corps. A Corps collar badge was designed in the form of an oval garter surmounted by a Royal Crown with the S.V.C. cypher, in script, superimposed in white metal in the centre, the cut out design having been maintained.

The S.R.A.(v) and the S.R.E.(v) continued to wear their own cap and collar badges, other ranks being allowed to follow their Officers as regards the latter, which were similar to those of the respective units of the regular army but with the local titles and the Corps motto.

Machine Gun Sections and Companies provide one further exception, a badge which might be described as semi-official since it is only worn in the helmet flash; it consists of a pair of crossed machine guns with the intertwined cypher "S.V.C." below the centre.

The S.V.A. buttons for Non-Commissioned ranks have been practically unchanged since the formation of the unit; they were reliefed with a gun and crown while the Officers wore a "bullet" button also reliefed with a gun and crown but shaped like those worn by the Royal Horse Artillery. The latter were worn by the Officers up to 1915 when the open tunic was adopted, and the ordinary Royal Artillery half round button, similar to that used by other ranks, was issued.

The Singapore Volunteer Engineers on their formation in 1900 adopted a button similar to the Royal Engineers, the Royal cypher "V.R.I." in a circlet bearing the words "Singapore Engineers" and surmounted with a crown, the whole in relief. The design exists to the present day, and the wording was not altered to "Singapore Royal Engineers" after the receipt of the Royal Warrant in 1902 although the cap badge and shoulder titles were corrected.

S.V.C. "M.G." Companies Helmet Badge

In 1900 the buttons for Corps staff use and those for the Singapore Volunteer Rifles were of the same design, being reliefed with a St. Edwards Crown under which was the lettering S.V.C. or S.V.R. on a lined background or surface, the whole encircled by a wreath of laurels. The special S.V.R. button was subsequently discontinued and later the St. Edward's Crown([1]) in the S.V.C. button gave place to a Royal Crown which is the Corps general button of the present day. Regiments were originally known by their Colonels' names and it was not until about 1768 that special buttons with numbers or regimental designs were adopted. Before this date the colour of the facings was the distinguishing mark of the regiment.

The Singapore Volunteer Infantry Cap Badge and Buttons were of one design, circular and reliefed with a Royal Crown encircled by a garter bearing the motto "In Oriente Primus". These buttons were also worn by the S.V.A. Maxim Company and S.V.A. Bearer Section.

In 1931 when the Armoured Car Section was formed, a separate badge, similar to that of the Royal Tank Corps, was adopted for this unit; a badge in white metal consisting of a wreath of laurels surmounted by a crown with the cut out reproduction of a tank in the centre over a scroll bearing the letters "S.V.C.". Small replicas of the same badge are worn as collar badges of this unit.

The end of 1928 saw a re-arrangement of the infantry units in the S.S.V.F. as follows:—

1st Battalion S.S.V.F.—Singapore Volunteer Corps.—

1st Battalion Signal Section	By transfer of the S.R.E.(v) Signal Section formed on 24.2.1922.
"A" (M.G.) Company (European)	Amalgamating "A" (European) Company and the Machine Gun Platoon (European) both formed in 1922.
"B" Company (European)	Re-formed after being moribund since 1926.
"C" (Scottish) Company	Formed 24th February, 1922.
"D" (Eurasian) Company	Formed 4th July, 1918.

---

(1) In the heraldic representation of St. Edward's Crown, when for state or official purposes the crown is represented over the Royal Arms or other insignia, the fleur-de-lis upon the rim are only half Fleur-de-lis. This detail was scrupulously adhered to, but during the reign of Queen Victoria many of the other details were very much "at the mercy" of the artist. In the reign of King Edward VII, however, a War Office Sealed Pattern of the Royal Crown and Cypher was issued for use in the army, and this has since been adopted for all official purposes.

2nd Battalion S.S.V.F.—Singapore Volunteer Corps. (less one Coy. and 3 M.G. Sections).—

"E" (Chinese) Company .. Formed 1902.
"F" (Malay) Company .. Formed 1910.
M.G. (Eurasian) Platoon .. Formed 1928.
2nd Battalion Signal Section .. Formed 1929.

3rd Battalion S.S.V.F.—Penang and Province Wellesley Volunteer Corps. (less 2 M.G. Sections).

4th Battalion S.S.V.F.—Malacca Volunteer Corps. (less two M.G. Sections).

Lewis Guns were increased in numbers and a decision was made to arm Asiatic companies with these weapons, when they were fit to use them. The 4.5 Hows. of the S.R.A.(v) were marked for replacement in 1929 with 3.7 Hows.

As regards clothing, experiments were made in Singapore-made boots; it was also decided to revert to the flannel shirt as the cotton ones were found to be unsatisfactory.

This year a course for Officers was held at Tanglin Barracks. Only two S.S.V.F. Officers were able to attend the full course but in all four were able to be present at times.

At Singapore the G.O.C. opened the new Bukit Timah Range Pavilion on 17th March. Temporary improvements were effected at Siglap Camp.

As regards training, the following rulings were made by the G.O.C. at the beginning of the year.

(i) Musketry Courses to be fired as early as possible.
(ii) A "close season" to exist from 1st November to 1st February except for a few schemes and lectures.
(iii) For the time being training was to be limited to platoon training.

These were tried out this year and, except for the first where range accommodation made it impossible to finish very early in the season, were successful. In training a speciality was made of T.Es.W.T. (Tactical Exercises Without Troops). During Easter a combined S.S.V.F. machine gun camp was held at Port Dickson.

The Labuan Defence Corps formed in 1915 was disbanded in 1920. It was reformed as a European defence unit to commence training in 1923, in which year it received one Lewis gun and twelve short rifles. It was then styled the Labuan Defence Detachment of the Singapore Volunteer

Corps and wore the S.V.C. cap badge. During the few years it existed it was visited by the Commandant, S.S.V.F. on two or three occasions. Such visits on account of the distance of Labuan from Singapore proved, for an enrolment of 12 members, too expensive and instruction by N.C.O. instructors was equally difficult for the same reason. In 1926 and 1927 it passed through a period of considerable apathy among the small population of European residents, and, as practically no work was done, it was disbanded in August, 1928 as being too small a unit to continue. The rifles were left, however, for the purpose of a Rifle Club.

The Johore Volunteer Rifles were reorganised in 1927 and as from the 1st January, 1928 became the Johore Volunteer Engineers. A case for the change was put up early in 1927 on the grounds that, owing to the very scattered nature of the unit and the fact that there were no Sappers on the mainland, an Engineer unit would be a much more practicable proposition and provide a form of training that could be carried out by small numbers of Volunteers in many centres. The Advisory Committee unanimously agreed and the change, after having been tried out for four years, was eventually ratified in Johore Government Gazette No. 220 of 1932. The Cap Badge of the new unit was exactly the same as the old one except the word "Engineers" instead of "Rifles", but Collar Badges and Buttons were quite different.

An Artillery Unit in the F.M.S. was instigated by Major-General C.C. van Straubenzee in July, 1928 and received the approval of the Secretary of State in November. It was recruited from the M.S.V.R. and they were armed with four 3.7-inch Mountain Howitzers, the first to arrive in this country. One section of two guns was stationed in Ipoh and the other, together with the Battery Headquarters, at Kuala Lumpur. In

S.V.C. Armoured
Car Section 1933

1928
Previously "Rifles"
in place of "Engineers"

1929

February, 1929 it was suggested that the title should be the Malayan Light Battery and that the unit should function as part of the Volunteer Artillery of Singapore. This idea was not carried through and it was decided to maintain the two Batteries as separate units so that in May, 1929 the two Sections of Artillery in the F.M.S. received the title of "The F.M.S. Light Battery".

About this time there was an epidemic of piracy on the high seas between Singapore and Hongkong by Chinese pirates, of the famous Bias Bay stronghold, mostly carried out against ships that transported Chinese coolies between China and the Straits. The pirates used to try to smuggle their own men in among the coolies, and consequently guards of one officer and twelve other ranks were later provided for the ships by the regular regiment (The Duke of Wellingtons) stationed at Singapore and the S.V.C. Altogether four guards were furnished by the S.V.C. late in 1928 and early in 1929 consisting of those members of the Corps who wanted a sea voyage and could manage to get away from their business. The first guard went up under command of Lieut. F.J.L. Mayger, M.C. in October, 1928. The second in November, 1928 under command of Lieut. W.T. Cherry was the only one to experience any trouble and that only of minor character, near Swatow. Owing to questions in the Press and Legislative Council regarding the Government's liabilities in the case of casualities to the Volunteers, the provision of guards by the S.V.C. ceased sometime before the piracies were stopped and the Bias Bay stronghold destroyed.

1929. Several ceremonial parades were held this year, including Guards of Honour for H.R.H. the Duke of Gloucester both at Penang and Singapore and also a review in honour of the King and Queen of Siam.

Training was carried a step further as compared to the previous year in that platoons were exercised in company schemes. Several demonstrations were given by the Welch Regiment and much help received from them in connection with camps, lectures, etc.

Emphasis was laid this year on the importance of home courses for volunteer N.C.Os. and men, for which allowances were sanctioned. One S.R.A.(v) Officer (Capt. T.M. Winsley) qualified at a Territorial Course at the School of Gunnery at Larkhill, England.

"A" (M.G.) Coy. camp was held at R.A.F. base with Field Firing.

Recruiting improved, partly owing to a special recruiting effort in January.

The appointment of a Brigade Major, S.S.V.F. was sanctioned and was filled by Captain V.C. Russell, D.S.O., M.C., The Suffolk Regiment, who arrived out in August.

1930. In Penang an experiment, started rather late in the year (September), was made in enrolling two permanent Malay instructors. During the year with the co-operation of the various clubs, who agreed to offer no counter-attractions, it was arranged that "Monday night is Volunteer night" and notices in these words were hung in all clubs. As a result Penang units were able to rely on large attendances every Monday. In Singapore great strides were made by Volunteers doing their own instructing, the permanent staff being mainly responsible for teaching them how to instruct. This method was also followed in the other Settlements. A field firing demonstration, including M.G. overhead and flanking fire in co-operation with "B." Coy., was held at the R.A.F. base.

Promotion examinations for Officers were held with encouraging success. Tactical training was based on section leading and platoon training. Exercises without troops, sand model schemes and, at Penang, war games were held and training with mechanical transport was a special feature in all three Corps.

In Singapore, "D" (Eurasian) Company found a guard of honour on the arrival of the new Governor, Sir Cecil Clementi, K.C.M.G. and at Penang and Malacca mixed guards were formed.

The 1st and 2nd Battalions S.S.V.F. began to work properly as battalions with volunteer Commanding Officers, Adjutants, and Quartermasters. In all three Settlements new mobilization stores added to the efficiency and ease of storekeeping.

The 1st Bn. was made up to establishment by the revival of "B" Company as "B" (English) Company. The S.V.F.A. increased remarkably in strength and efficiency. Arrangements were completed for the formation of the Singapore Fortress Company, R.E.(v) and for the enrolment in certain units of European foreigners.

A Traffic Control Section (previously the Traffic Section) was revived during this year. It had been a most useful unit at all big parades such as the King's Birthday and G.O.C's inspection parades and had proved the necessity for such a section in a time of mobilization. This unit subsequently became the Provost Section in 1937.

In Penang a Scottish platoon was successfully formed and the band was trained in ambulance work. The P. & P.W.V.C. strength reached a figure of 70 Officers and 761 O.R.

In Malacca a Field Ambulance Section was started successfully near Tampin.

Malay long camps were held in Singapore, Penang and Malacca. These were of one fortnight's duration each, though few volunteers were able to stay for more than a week.

Promotion examinations for officers were commenced again in 1930, during which year six Captains passed for promotion to Major and 27 Subalterns for promotion to Captain.

1931. The training season this year was divided into three periods for individual training, section and platoon training and company and battalion training: the system being adopted for other arms. Weapon training was spread over all three, every effort being made to complete it early. At the beginning of the third period a "cadre" carried out the instruction of Officers, N.C.Os. and Specialists, while the permanent staff formed classes for recruits.

Major L.H. Chidson, M.B.E. was re-appointed M.G.O., S.S.V.F. in order to co-ordinate the machine gun training of all three Settlements. Experiments were begun in regard to a mono-wheel and also a pack-carrier for carrying machine guns into action.

An Armoured Car Section.—The Corps' first Armoured Car was delivered this year *via* the Singapore Harbour Board, who built the body on to a 4-ton, six-wheel Albion lorry, with armoured plating obtained from England. Recruiting was opened for the new Armoured Car Company in September, but, owing to one car only being available one section only was raised, under 2nd-Lieutenant C.E. Collinge, and trained as part of "A" (Machine Gun) Company, with a strength of two officers and seven other ranks. During their leave in Europe in

S.V.C. Malay Coy. Cap with old S.V.I. Badge

The Armoured Car Beret

1932 both 2nd-Lieutenant Collinge and Lance Corporal S.D. Taylor attended a course in Mechanized Vehicles at the Tank Corps Central School.

S.R.E.(v) Fortress Company.—It is perhaps a very late date to record for the first time the history of the Fortress Company, S.R.E.(v), but the fact that they became a separate unit in this year makes the time suitable. Their forerunners go back to pre-war days, when they were the Engine Room Section of the Singapore Royal Engineers (Volunteer); their work in connection with Defence Electric Lights was, for the most part, performed in co-operation with the Artillery, to cope with which our Volunteer contemporaries in Burma formed, in 1902, an Electrical Engineer Company. In 1912 the Overseas Defence Committee made some highly complimentary allusions to the handling, by the Engine Room Section of the S.R.E.(v), of the lights both in the emplacements and in the directing station; they further remarked that the unit would undoubtedly be in a position to afford considerable assistance to the Royal Engineers during war—a prophetic allusion to the most useful and silent work which they did in Singapore during the years 1914 to 1918, sweeping the coasts with their lights. The continuous hard work performed by this small unit was acknowledged in 1918 when, on the 1st February, an Electric Light Section of thirty-six Malays was formed "in order to relieve the strain on the European Unit". After the war, however, the S.R.E.(v) were busy reorganising their Field Company and it was not until 1926 that serious attention was again given to the Volunteers usefulness in connection with Defence Electric Lights. In April of that year a small unit, under Captain F.H. Robinson, was formed from Auxiliary Volunteers and provisionally called the Defence Electric Light Unit. The establishment strength was then four officers and sixty other ranks.

In their first year as a Colour Service Unit the Fortress Company was, Captain Robinson being absent from the Colony, commanded by Lieutenant (Acting Captain) F. Bedford.

The S.R.E.(v) were changed from a Field Park Company into a Field Company and its establishment was altered in consequence.

A change in organization was tried out, the Brigade Major being relieved of all administrative work by the Adjutant, S.V.C., who in reality acted as Staff Captain, S.S.V.F. In consequence the Brigade Major was able to pay more attention to tactical exercises, sand model schemes and camps. This re-allotment of duties was made possible by the fact that each Battalion possessed a volunteer Adjutant and the scheme worked well throughout the year. Stress was laid on the competitive spirit in all forms of training.

Great advantage was taken of the availability of two barrack blocks at Changi and the 1st Battn. held a battalion camp there in order to promote *esprit-de-bataillon*.

The G.O.C.'s Inspection took the form of a landing from H.M.S. "*Kent*", the Gloucestershire Regiment acting as defenders. Further promotion examinations were held in Penang and Singapore. In the latter place "E" (Chinese) Company furnished a guard of honour to H.E. the Governor on his return from England and on the 14th June a ceremonial parade was held by him on the Padang.

In Penang the 3rd Battn. carried on their training without help from the regular battalion. A cadre was formed and instruction afterwards carried on by volunteers. The system of non-European permanent staff instructors was discontinued. The strength of the 3rd Battn. further increased to 73 Officers and 842 O.R.

In Malacca "A" (European) M.G. Coy. shewed improvement but "B" (Chinese) Coy. was so weak that its disbandment was seriously considered as a possibility should no improvement take place in the next year.

All Singapore companies held rifle meetings. In the Command Meeting "A" (M.G.) Coy., S.V.C. were 2nd to the Gloucestershire Regt. by 7 points in the M.G. competition. Lewis Gun classification results shewed great improvement.

1915

At the end of this year the G.O.C. approved that the time limit for the command of volunteer battalions should be fixed at 4 years, yearly extensions being possible, with special approval, in exceptional cases.

Owing to the "slump" a large cut in the expenditure estimates for 1931 and 1932 had to be made, but fortunately with no appreciable loss of efficiency. As regards equipment and stores, the appointment of a quartermaster led to marked improvement in organization and system.

The enlistment of European foreigners did not come up to expectation; only 38, comprising

Present Day "Rifles" in place of *Previously* "Regiment"

nationals of 13 different countries, joining. They were absorbed into "B" Company and S.R.E.(v). The Singapore Fortress Coy., R.E.(v) commenced training this year.

In 1931 the volunteers of the Federated Malay States were brigaded on similar lines to the S.S.V.F. The Malayan Volunteer Infantry, who were State troops, combined with the Malay States Volunteer Regiment to form the Federated Malay States Volunteer Force, but even then the former were State—as opposed to Federal—troops. In 1936, however, the final re-organisation took place and the whole of the volunteers in the Federated Malay States, known as the F.M.S.V.F., are now Federal.

1932. On the 8th March, H.E. The Governor, Sir Cecil Clementi, laid the foundation stone of the new Headquarters at Singapore, "A" (M.G.) Coy. providing the Guard of Honour. Pile-driving and preliminary work had been going on for over a year. The Headquarters were actually completed in October and, though not officially opened, were taken into use so as to allow the demolition of the old Drill Hall which had been in use since 1890. The first official parade in the new Headquarters was the conference held on the 18th October after the G.O.C.'s Inspection scheme.

Training followed the same general lines as in 1931, as much advantage as possible being gained from exercises on the ground. Inspection by the G.O.C. took the form of attack schemes in all three Settlements. The narratives were in all cases issued some time beforehand and T. Es. W.T. and reconnaissances carried out by all commanders down to platoon commanders. Training in mob control and street fighting was also carried out. At Singapore H.E. The Governor was present throughout the G.O.C.'s Inspection Scheme. The Royal Singapore Flying Club also co-operated in it.

Further experiments were carried out with machine gun carriers, a standardized system for packing M.G. equipment into light lorries was laid down and in Penang a satisfactory type of mobile Signal set was contrived and approved. A Machine Gun Field Firing demonstration was carried out at Bedok.

Twelve Officers and O.Rs. attended courses at home. Promotion Examinations for Officers and N.C.Os. were held at Singapore, and for Officers at Penang. A course was also run at Singapore for range takers.

Each unit was allotted a special evening for parade and this evened out the nightly activities at Headquarters. At Penang and Malacca it was still possible to have one evening a week allotted to volunteering activities.

Camps were well attended and use was again made of the barrack blocks at Changi. At Penang camps were held at Headquarters and at Malacca great value was obtained from the new permanent camp at Tanjong Bruas. "A" (European) M.G. Coy. and "B" (Chinese) Coy., M.V.C. registered special improvement during the year.

Company Rifle Meetings at Singapore and Battalion meetings at Penang and Malacca were held as usual but a big economy was effected in ammunition without undue loss of efficiency. At the Command Rifle Meeting at Kuala Lumpur, P. & P.W.V.C. won the M.G. Competition, the Lewis Gun Shield, the Knockout Falling Plate, Rifle Team Match and Revolver Team Match and were second in the Superiority of Fire Competition. "A" (M.G.) Coy., S.V.C. were second in the M.G. match.

A revised machine gun course was found more satisfactory than the previous one. Lewis Gun training again improved. A number of competitions, both in shooting and other sports were held with the 1st Bn. The Gloucester Regt., who on their departure presented the S.V.C. with the Back Badge Cup. This cup was allotted to the best shooting company or unit of the S.V.C., the Gibbons Cup being revived and allotted to the runner-up.

Opportunity was taken this year to place the administration of the three Corps on identical lines and the advantages were at once apparent. This has been one of the results of the new H.Q. Staff organization, which received War Office approval. Major H.L. Graham, M.C., was confirmed in the appointment of Staff Officer, S.S.V.F.

The S.S.V.F. vote in 1932 was reduced to $374,463 as compared with $809,941 in 1931. In spite of this a substantial saving was made.

In the interests of economy it was decided at the end of the year to amalgamate the Adjutancy, M.V.C. with the adjutancy of the Negri Sembilan Bn., F.M.S.V.F. and Captain W.J. Irwin, R.U.R. Adjutant N.S. Bn. relieved Captain Exham, who was appointed from Malacca to the new Malay Regiment.

1933. On Saturday the 4th March, His Excellency The Governor, Sir Cecil Clementi, G.C.M.G., officially opened the new S.S.V.F. Headquarters in Beach Road. H.E. was received by a Guard of Honour of "B" Company, 1st Bn., S.S.V.F., which he inspected. He was then challenged by the Quarter Guard found from "C" (Scottish) Company, 1st Bn. S.S.V.F. who presented him with the special golden key. The Governor then opened the gate and proceeded to the Main Hall where a large and distinguished company was present. Here, at the request of H.E. the G.O.C., Major-General L.C.L. Oldfield, he formally declared the Headquarters open. Lieut.-Colonel M.J.T. Reilly proposed a vote of thanks. After inspecting the buildings, the Governor watched a display of Drill by "F" (Malay) Coy., 2nd Bn., S.S.V.F. under Captain C.A. Scott, and an Artillery display by the S.R.A.(v) under Captain J. Lee.

The ceremony was followed by a 'Pahit Party' and Dance which was very popular with some 2,000 guests.

In October a communication was received that H.M. The King had been graciously pleased to approve of the three Corps of the S.S.V.F. being permitted to carry Colours, and also of the proposed designs for the King's and Regimental Colours.

In the case of the S.V.C. and the P. & P.W.V.C. these stands of Colours were most generously presented by the Municipalities. At Malacca, the M.V.C. raised the required sum by Volunteer and private subscriptions.

During the year, for reasons of economy, all Asiatic Companies were limited to a strength of 100.

In addition to this decrease of 204 members the S.S.V.F. suffered a loss of 140 Europeans from retirement or transfer.

Training continued on the same lines as in the previous year. Standards of training were drawn up for guidance in the future. Intelligence Sections were formed in each Battalion, in addition to the Intelligence Platoon which had become an H.Q. unit.

Battalion and Company Camps were held in all three Settlements. The 1st Bn. held their camp over August Bank holiday, at Changi, and the 2nd Bn. were concentrated during one week-end at Siglap.

At Penang an experimental European M.G. Camp was successfully held on Penang Hill during August week-end.

Malay and Chinese Companies in all Settlements held camps of one week's duration.

Difficulties were found at Singapore and Malacca in securing a good attendance of Chinese for such a long camp, but the results justified a repetition of an experiment, which has since become a regular part of the years training.

H.E. The Governor was once again an interested spectator at the G.O.C.'s Annual Inspection at Singapore. This took the form of an attack in the Jurong area, against the 1st Bn. The Wiltshire Regiment and the J.M.F. The Royal Singapore Flying Club again co-operated with the S.V.C.

At Penang and Malacca the inspection schemes were in the forms of attacks carried out by one portion of the Corps against another portion, and in each case the Resident Councillors attended. All these schemes were preceded by Tactical Exercises without Troops, and reconnaissances.

At Penang a successful Night Operation (the defence of Prai Station) was carried out by the European Companies. All camps were well attended.

At Malacca the absence of a full time Adjutant had an adverse effect on the training of the Companies. An experiment was made in substituting monthly week-end camps for weekly parade nights. This was most successful but had later to be abandoned on account of expense.

The Command Rifle Matches were this year, for reasons of economy, decentralized and fired on local ranges. P. & P.W.V.C. repeated their successes of 1932 and "swept the board". Besides Winning The Grand Aggregate, the Officers, Warrant Officers, and Sergeants Matches, the Company Team Rifle and L.G. Match, the Platoon Team Rifle Match, the Individual Revolver Match and the Platoon L.G. Match, they were second in the Warren Shield, Platoon Team M.G. Match and the Team Revolver Match. The only remaining match, the Malcolm Cup for the 30 yards Range was won by the M.V.C.

P. & P.W.V.C. also won the Bromhead Matthews Cup, the Penang Veterans Shield, and the Murray Cup, which were awarded this year for various features in the Classification Courses.

In Singapore all Companies held Rifle Meetings in addition to the S.V.R.A. Meeting, and Corps Meetings were also held at Penang and Malacca.

The Classification results showed an improvement with a decrease in the percentage of 3rd Class shots. Suggestions were put forward for the revision of the Classification Courses on the lines of those in use at home.

The Miniature Range was opened on 7th February by the Colonial Secretary, Sir John Scott. All recruits now commence with the Empire Test on this range.

An Anti-Aircraft Course was fired by a few Lewis gunners.

Machine gun training continued to improve.

The M.G. monowheel carrier, known as the "Chidwheel", having been originally invented by Major L.H. Chidson, M.B.E., Brigade Machine Gun Officer, S.S.V.F., was thoroughly tested and approved and additional ones were ordered. This device has also been adopted in modified form by the F.M.S.V.F. Subsequently the Johore Military Forces and the Regular garrison adopted the device of the S.S.V.F.

"A" (M.G.) Coy. staged a successful demonstration at Bukit Timah.

3.7 in. Howitzer Ammunition being available only in alternate years, the S.R.A.(v) undertook training with the 3-in. 20 cwt. A.A. Gun. Great keenness was displayed, attendances averaged little under 100% and the results of the half charge and full charge shoots carried out in October were excellent, earning the special praise of the G.O.C. and the C.R.A.

Instruction was carried out by Officers and W.O.'s of the 7th A.A. Battery. The R.A.F. and the R.S.F.C. co-operated throughout the training.

The Armoured Car Section was able to have its second car in use for its Annual Camp and the G.O.C.'s inspection; at other times the chassis of the second car was in use by the P.W.D. while the Armoured body was stored by the Singapore Harbour Board. The Section ceased to be a part of "A" (M.G.) Coy. and was constituted a separate unit in August and transferred together with Captain C.E. Collinge to come directly under Corps H.Q.

An experiment was tried of enlisting a few Europeans as operators in the Brigade Signal Section.

Whilst on leave, three Officers and two other ranks attended courses in England at their own expense, the Government having ceased, as a "Slump" economy, to provide for this type of training out of the Volunteer Vote.

Promotion examinations for Officers and N.C.O.'s were again held in all Settlements.

To turn to Kedah for a moment. At the end of the War the Volunteer units in Kedah were disbanded, but the movement was revived in 1933 with the formation of the Kedah Volunteer Force which started with one European and two Malay platoons and has since been expanded to a complete battalion of three Companies and an H.Q. Wing, with headquarters

S.R.A.(v)—1933
3-inch (20 cwt.) Anti-Aircraft Gun

in Alor Star and Company headquarters at Sungei Patani and Kulim. The Unit is commanded by a Volunteer with the rank of Lieut.-Colonel who is assisted by a regular Adjutant and two Regular Company Sergts.-Major and Instructors.

Mr. Peh Wah Kok, Chief Clerk, S.S.V.F. completed 21 years service in Headquarters.

A saving of about $40,000 was made on the 1932 expenditure. This was done by reducing the strength of certain units, cutting down transport and ammunition, and reducing messing expenditure. There was little or no loss in efficiency but the upkeep of ranges and arms could not be fully maintained.

The 1933 season ended with the first S.V.C. Pantomime, six performances being given before X'mas. The third edition of the 1st Battalion, S.S.V.F. Annual appeared and it was decided to produce the 1934 magazine as a Corps magazine. On 31st December the S.S.V.F. defeated the F.M.S.V.F. 22 points to 8 in the first Inter-Force "Rugger" match.

1934. Up to this date the Volunteer forces of Malaya had been represented by the Military arm only, but at the beginning of 1934 The Straits Settlements Royal Naval Volunteer Reserve was constituted under the "Naval Volunteer Reserve Ordinance 1934". Commander L.A.W. Johnson, M.V.O., R.N.V.R. (R.N. retired) was appointed first Commanding Officer with an establishment of 50 officers and 200 Malay ratings.

In May and July ceremonies of Presentation of Colours[1] took place in all three Settlements.

Penang.—On Whit Monday 21st May, in the absence of H.E. the O.A.G., H.E. the G.O.C., Major-General E.O. Lewin, C.B., C.M.G., D.S.O., presented Colours to the P. & P.W.V.C. The ceremony was followed by a tiffin party to which the Municipal Commissioners were invited.

Singapore.—On Saturday the 26th May, 1934, before a crowd of some 20,000 spectators, H.E. the Officer Administering the Government, Mr. Andrew Caldecott, C.M.G., O.B.E., presented to the S.V.C. their Colours, a gift of the Singapore Municipality. A "Pahit Party" followed the presentation.

(1) *See* Note on Colours Appendix IX.

Malacca.—The Presentation of Colours to the M.V.C. was carried out on Saturday, 7th July, by the O.A.G., H.E. Mr. Andrew Caldecott, C.M.G., C.B.E., accompanied by H.E. the G.O.C., Pahit parties were afterwards held.

The design of the three stands of Colours had been drastically altered, by the Garter King of Arms, from those originally submitted for the three Corps by the S.S.V.F. and taken home by Lieut.-Colonel J.M. MacKenzie in 1930. The Colours were made by Messrs. Hobsons and cost £143 6s. (exclusive of freight etc.) for each stand. The design, which is similar for all three Corps, is as follows:—

King's Colour.—The Union Jack, richly embroidered in gold and silk. In the centre is the Title of the Corps, surmounted by the Imperial Crown. The Flag is fringed with a gold and crimson fringe. It is carried on a polished ash pike with gilt Lion and Crown mount, and gold and crimson cords and tassels.

Regimental Colour.—A Silk Colour, Green for S.V.C., Blue for P. & P.W.V.C., Buff for M.V.C., embroidered on both sides alike. In the centre are the badges of the Straits Settlements encircled by the title "Straits Settlements Volunteer Force", and surrounded by a wreath of Rose, Shamrock and Thistle leaves. In the base is an additional title scroll "Singapore Volunteer Corps" or "Penang & Province Wellesley Volunteer Corps" or "Malacca Volunteer Corps", the whole surmounted by the Imperial Crown. The Flag is carried on a polished ash pike, with gilt Lion and Crown mount, and gold and crimson cords and tassels.

The training for these ceremonial parades necessarily broke into the normal annual training. In Singapore the season commenced with a cadre course during which classes were held on five nights a week in weapon training, drill and bayonet fighting. The same squads attended twice weekly or 9 or 10 times in all. This was followed by a N.C.Os. week-end at H.Q. when 100 N.C.Os. attended and received instruction from those who had been through the cadre course. An officers tactical week-end was attended by 44 officers.

In all three Settlements the training year worked gradually up to the G.O.C.'s inspection, weapon training continuing until July. Special attention was paid to Battalion Intelligence Sections and to Anti-Aircraft training. In Singapore, Siglap Camp was used by S.R.E.(v) (5 times), "A" and "D" Companies 1st Bn., 2nd Bn. (one week each Company) and S.V.F.A. "B" and "C" Companies 1st Bn. held camps at H.Q. and the

A History of the Singapore Volunteer Corps.

Penang and Province Wellesley Volunteer Corps Colours

Malacca Volunteer Corps Colours

[*Colour plate printed & presented by
The Straits Times Press Ltd.*]

S.R.A.(v) at Changi. The attendance of "E" (Chinese) Coy. showed great improvement. At Malacca all companies made use of Tg. Bruas Camp and at Penang of H.Q. while "B" (M.G.) Coy., P. & P.W.V.C. repeated their 1933 experiment of a camp at Easter up Penang Hill.

The following alterations in establishments were made:—

    S.R.A.(v) remained an A.A. Bty. and did no 3.7 How. training. They carried out A.A. shoots in September with very good results.

    P.W. European Rifle Company was reorganised into the P.W. M.G. Platoon of "B" (M.G.) Coy., P. & P.W.V.C. from January 1934. This change stimulated training considerably.

All non-European Coys. remained limited to 100 strong.

The S.V.C. Armoured Car Unit received their second car for permanent use. Recruitment of European W/T operators for the Brigade Signal Section commenced in September. The establishment was fixed at 3 officers and 63 O.R. of whom not more than 30 were to be recruited in 1934. In December the strength stood at 15.

The S.V.C. inspection by Colonel Dobson, C.B,E., who was acting for H.E. the G.O.C. away under medical orders, took place at Mandai and consisted of an attack on the Wiltshire Regt. The M.V.C. were inspected in a withdrawal scheme near Batang Malaka (23½ miles from Malacca) and the P. & P.W.V.C. in a similar scheme at Penang near Relau and 6 milestone. The latter was held in heavy rain, which did not, however, prevent co-operation by the R.A.F. (100 T.B. Sqn.) who had flown to Taiping for this purpose. On 15th–16th December the S.V.C. took part in a Command exercise in which the Singapore Garrison defended the South part of the Island against an attack by H.M. Ships *"Cumberland"*, *"Terror"*, *"Eagle"* and about 12 destroyers. The exercise lasted from 3 P.M. on the 15th to 6 A.M. on the 16th and S.R.A.(v), S.F.C.R.E.(v), Brigade Signals, Intelligence Platoon and 1st and 2nd Bn. were engaged. Many useful lessons were learnt.

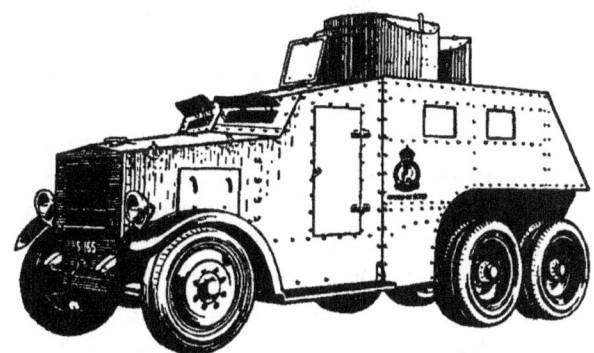

S.V.C.—Armoured Car—1931
Albion Six Wheeler

The Command Rifle Meeting was again decentralized. P. & P.W.V.C. once more cleared the board winning the Grand Aggregate, Officers and W.Os. match, and Platoon Rifle, L.A. and M.G. Competitions. They occupied 3rd, 4th and 5th places in the Warren Shield.

In addition P. & P.W.V.C. won the Bromhead Matthews Shield, Penang Veterans Cup and Murray Cup and the Tong Lao Cup for Chinese Units. "E" (Chinese) Coy., S.V.C. won the Chinese Inter-Port Competition against Shanghai.

Rifle Meetings were held in all Settlements as in past years, but the Singapore Volunteer Rifle Association service shoot was turned into an S.V.C. Rifle Meeting. This was very well attended. The S.V.R.A. took on a fresh lease of life, mainly by devoting more attention to service shooting.

The effect of miniature range shooting was seen in the classification results. "B" and "F" Companies showed the greatest improvement. "B" Coy. advanced from 9th to 1st place in the Back Badge Cup (and won the 1st Bn. Championship Shield) and "F" Coy. from 10th to 5th. "A" (M.G.) Coy. won the Gibbons Cup for 2nd place.

The M.G. units carried out a field firing shoot from the S.W. Coast of Blakang Mati.

Courses and attachments to regular units in England were attended by three officers and six N.C.Os. and one N.C.O. was attached to the Wiltshire Regt. at Tanglin for a fortnight. In Singapore four out of five officers passed the promotion examination for Captain to Major and seven out of eight for Subaltern to Captain. One Captain and two Subalterns passed "Distinguished". Thirteen out of seventeen N.C.Os. also passed for promotion to Sergeant.

Command of "D" (Eurasian) Coy. and "E" (Chinese) Coy. was at the end of this year handed over to Eurasian and Chinese officers and Captains H.R.S. Zehnder and Tan Soo Bin (on his transfer to the Reserve) were promoted to the rank of Major, being the first Volunteers of these two communities to hold this rank, their respective 'Companies having previously been commanded by European Volunteer officers. Captain S.Y. Wong, who succeeded Captain Tan Soo Bin, also received his majority in this year and was, therefore, the first Chinese officer actually to command his unit with this rank.

No changes were made in equipment or clothing, except that the change over to "green" khaki, begun in 1933, was nearly completed. A start was made in issuing khaki "overalls" to units for drill purposes.

S.V.A.—1895

S.R.A (v)—1935

S.R.A.(v), 1927—4.5-IN. HOWITZER
Coming into Camp at Siglap

S.R.A.(v), 1928—4.5-IN. HOWITZERS
Armistice Day Minute Guns

S.R.A.(v), 1931—3.7-IN. MOUNTAIN HOWITZER
The Gun on a Trailer Carriage

S.R.A.(v), 1936—3.7-IN. MOUNTAIN HOWITZERS
Armistice Day Minute Guns

In Singapore the Main Hall was fitted with fans and loud speakers. At Malacca the pump for the Camp Swimming Pool and the Camp parade ground were completed. Permission was received to rent a quarter for the C.S.M. & I. in place of the poor quarters at the Drill Hall. After several months at Mata Kuching the C.S.M. & I. was located in No. 3 Fort Road.

A further reduction of approximately $20,000 was made in S.S.V.F. expenditure, the economies being effected mainly in the clothing, range up-keep and training votes.

The year ended as previously in an S.S.V.F. v. F.M.S.V.F. Rugger Match (won by F.M.S.V.F.), the production of a second Pantomine, which ran for 6 performances, and the production of a Magazine. This Magazine was produced as a S.S.V.F. Annual and was well received throughout the S.S.

1935. At the beginning of the year it was decided that "C" (Scottish) Coy., S.V.C. should become a Machine Gun company and that the Eurasian M.G. Platoon should be turned into "G" (M.G.) Company 2nd Bn., S.S.V.F., consisting of two platoons. With the exception of this "G" Company, all M.G. Companies were in future to consist of three platoons and "A" (Rifle) and "B" (M.G.) Companies, P. & P.W.V.C. were amalgamated to bring "B" (M.G.) Company up to strength.

The establishment of all Non-European Companies was brought back from 100 to 130 and the establishments of both battalions in Singapore were increased to include 22 stretcher bearers, these being permanently attached in peace time to the S.V.F.A.

The year started in Singapore as before with a series of cadre courses in February in M.G., Rifle, L.A. and Drill. Special attention had to be paid to the training of "C" (Scottish) Coy. instructors in M.G. These cadre courses were followed by two N.C.Os. Camps at H.Q. which were each attended by some 60 N.C.Os. Two T.Es.W.T. were also held, one for all officers and one for junior officers and N.C.Os. Penang and Malacca also held cadre courses and T.Es.W.T., the Commandant and S.O.L.F. conducting some of the latter. An Officers' Promotion Examination was held in Penang, five captains and eight subalterns sitting and passing, two captains and two subalterns with special certificates. A small examination for N.C.Os. was held in Singapore.

The S.R.A.(v) trained one section in 3.7" Howitzers for use in aid of the civil power. Otherwise they concentrated on Anti Aircraft; training some men in the Anti Aircraft Lewis Gun. Rifle companies also paid special attention to the A.A.L.G. Training in use of the Anti-Gas respirator was also introduced for the first time into the cadre courses.

An experiment in Musketry was made in Singapore in concentrating the firing of Table 'B' by battalions into battalion week-end camps. The 2nd Bn. camped at their respective Coy. H.Q. and did T.O.E.T. (test of elementary training) and zeroing on Saturday afternoon and classified throughout the greater part of Sunday. The 1st Bn. acted similarly but without camping at H.Q. The experiment was successful, Table 'B' completed earlier in the year than usual and with almost the same amount of preliminary instruction.

A second experiment in Musketry was made with the permanent staff assuming responsibility for those firing Table 'A'. This was not so successful owing to the numbers concerned. The recruits provided a special problem due to the increase in the establishment of companies from 100 to 130. The Permanent Staff were responsible for all these, except "F" Coy.

A M.G. camp was held at Malacca over Whitsun for the S.V.C. and M.V.C. M.G. units. The S.V.C. were taken by Straits Steamship boats and landed at the camp site in open lighters. The disembarkation and subsequent embarkation were most successful in spite of the former being carried out in a very heavy storm. The camp programme comprised work of M.Gs. in the field and in beach defence, including firing out to sea, and over 90 from Singapore and 15 from Malacca attended.

S.R.E. held camp as usual at Siglap and studied the making of Beach Defence M.G. posts.

In Weapon Training the Murray Cup was won by No. 16 Platoon "E" (Eurasian) Coy., P. & P.W.V.C. and the Penang Veterans Shield by No. 5 Platoon "B" (M.G.) Coy., P. & P.W.V.C. The Bromhead Matthews Shield was linked with the Platoon Rifle Match of the Command Meeting owing to the divergence between F.M.S.V.F. and S.S.V.F. range courses. The S.S.V.F. courses remained unaltered except for the exclusion of the grouping score from the Table 'B' total, the addition of two practices to Table 'AA' and several small amendments to Table 'MG'.

On 6/7th July "F" (Malay) Company 2nd Bn., S.S.V.F. celebrated its twenty-fifth anniversary with a Mohamedan religious service at Company Headquarters on the Saturday and an At Home at S.V.C. Headquarters and a "Ronggeng" at Coy. H.Q. on the Sunday. The Malay Company S.V.I., though the initial steps were taken in February 1910, was authorised on the 10th May, 1910, with an establishment of 60, of whom two are still serving. At the At Home, which was attended by Their Excellencies The Governor and The G.O.C. and His Highness the Sultan of Pahang, H.E. The Governor was received by a Guard of Honour of 40 files under Lieut. Mohd. Hassan: Second-Lieut. Kadir carrying the King's Colour.

Being the 25th year of the reign of His Late Majesty King George V, Jubilee Celebrations were held throughout the Empire. In Singapore the town was decorated on May 10th.

Jubilee Medals were struck to commemorate the event and 80,000 distributed throughout the Empire with a generous allotment to the Volunteers of Malaya.(1)

A further development took place during 1935 in the circle of our contemporaries when the Kelantan Volunteer Rifles, which had been in continuous active existence since 1914, were reconstituted and became the Kelantan Volunteer Force. It comprised one European and two Malay Platoons under a Volunteer Captain but unassisted by any regular staff. Captain H.A. Anderson, I.S.O. (a Boer War veteran) continued to command the force, even after his retirement from the post of Chief Police Officer of the State; his twenty odd years connection with the Volunteers in Kelantan, together with his Police experience and knowledge of the Kelantan Malay, were of great value in the reorganisation of the Corps and the maintenance of its traditions.

1936. This year saw the formation of a further arm of the Colony's Volunteer Defences when the Straits Settlements Volunteer Air Force was constituted under the "Volunteer Air Force Ordinance 1936". Squadron Leader D.S.E. Vines, late of the Royal Air Force, was appointed its first commander.

Decorations.—Prior to and during the Great War 1914–1918 the only decorations awarded to Volunteers were the Volunteer Officers Decoration and the Volunteer Long Service Medal or the Colonial Auxiliary Forces Officers Decoration and Colonial Auxiliary Forces Long Service Medal, all necessitating at least twenty-years service to qualify. With the establishment of the Most Excellent Order of the British Empire by King George V in June 1917, however, many Volunteers in Malaya and throughout the Empire have, during recent years,

1935
Previously "Rifles"
in place of "Force"

---

(1) *See* Appendix IV (b) for awards to S.S.V.F.

received the gracious recognition of their Sovereign for their services in the Auxiliary Forces by having had conferred on them one of the five classes of this Order or the Silver Medal of the Order.

In 1930, the Efficiency Decoration and Medal took the place of the Volunteer and Colonial Auxiliary Forces Decorations and Long Service Medals. For the Efficiency Decoration twenty years service is still necessary before an officer becomes eligible for the award but the Efficiency Medal may be awarded to N.C.Os. and men after twelve years service and a bar for each six years service thereafter([1]).

1937. *Dress 1922–1937.*—Since 1922 White Review Order has been a dress of the past, the Corps being equipped, for all occasions, with that khaki uniform with which we became so well acquainted during the Great War. A little colour has, however, been introduced by the adoption:—
(i) in 1922 of flashes of Corps colours on the regulation sun helmet, worn on the left side over the puggaree and under the Corps badge; (ii) in 1928 of hose tops of the colour of the Corps facings—S.V.C., Green—P. & P.W.V.C., Blue—M.V.C., Buff (now Red); (iii) also in 1928 of red sashes for W.Os. Class 2 and sergeants; (iv) in 1932 of forage caps (glengarry style) of red and green.

On the other hand "C" Scottish Company has always had plenty of colour in its uniform, as, since its inception, it has worn the national dress of regulation military style. Under Major D.G. McLeod, O.B.E., (now Lieut.-Colonel commanding 2nd Battalion) whose one hobby was the efficiency and smartness of his Company, many improvements in the Scottish Company's dress took place. In 1928 the sporran (purse) of white hair and two long black tassels, mounted with patent leather top, which, like all patent leather in this climate, proved sticky and unserviceable, was changed to a design, exclusive to the S.V.C., of white hair with six small black tassels, mounted with metal top and bells; the officers' "top" was of runic design with three silver knobs. In the same year two green resettes were added to the kilts of Officers, W.Os. and Sergeants.

S.V.C. and P. & P.W.V.C.
Scottish Bonnet

---

(1) *See* Appendix IV (a) for note on Volunteer Decorations and Medals and List of Awards.

1929 saw a change of the Scottish Company's bonnet from the plain blue Glengarry and red toorie to the knitted Balmoral with green and red diced band (Corps colours) and a large red toorie, as opposed to the khaki flat bonnet, issued during the war and absurdly referred to as the "Tam o'Shanter". In 1932 the members of the Company, unanimous in their agreement that the substitution of white spats for the khaki spats would increase the smartness of their appearance, offered to bear the costs of the alteration provided that white spats were officially adopted and issued to recruits. The change was approved by headquarters and effected at the Company's expense. The Scottish Platoon in the P. & P.W.V.C. wear the same uniform as "C" Company, S.V.C., including red and green dicing to their bonnets.

May the 12th, being the Coronation Day of Their Majesties King George VI and Queen Elizabeth, was celebrated throughout the Empire and the town of Singapore was decorated and illuminated for a week even more lavishly than for the Jubilee Celebrations in 1935. All S.V.C. Units were represented in the Coronation parade of Troops on the Padang at 8 a.m. on the 12th; the parade was said to be the largest and one of the finest spectacles ever witnessed in Malaya. The Muslim Community held an historical procession in the afternoon organised by Lieut. Rahmat bin Abbas and strongly supported by Muslim Volunteers. On a later evening in the week the Chinese conducted a lantern procession. Comparing these processions with those in the past, the mechanical age was evident by the amount of motor transport used in place of rickshaws and pony gharries. The Singapore Airport was opened on the 12th June, the S.S. Volunteer Air Force taking part.

In August a Military Search Light Tattoo was held. The assistance of Volunteers was not required on this occasion, many regular troops having arrived in Singapore since the 1926 Pageant. A very fine performance was put up and the Malay Regiment, substituting at the last moment for the Middlesex Regiment who had gone to Hong Kong, impressed with their efficiency, smartness and precision in a Drill Display.

The official contingent sent to England to represent Malayan Volunteers at the Coronation of the King and Queen was composed of the following eleven Officers and Non-Commissioned Officers:—

    Lieut.-Colonel W.A. Gutsell, 3rd (Negri Semilan) Batt., F.M.S.V.F.
    Lieut.-Colonel H.R. Walden, Kedah Volunteer Force.
    Major A.P. Goldman, S.V.C., S.S.V.F.

Captain L.A. Blackwell, M.C., 1st (Perak) Batt., F.M.S.V.F.
Captain E.H.B. Nobbs, M.C., 2nd (Selangor) Batt., F.M.S.V.F.
Captain S. Toolseram, P. & P.W.V.C., S.S.V.F.
Captain Mohd. Ali bin Maidin, M.B.E., M.V.C., S.S.V.F.
A/Captain Syed Shaidali, 1st (Perak) Batt., F.M.S.V.F.
Lieut. M.C.ff. Shepherd, 4th (Pahang) Batt., F.M.S.V.F.
Petty Officer Mohd. bin Haji Eunos, S.S.R.N.V.R.
A/R.S.M. Cheng Kang Nghee, S.V.C., S.S.V.F.

Ninety thousand Coronation Medals were struck in London for distribution at Home and throughout the Empire to commemorate the Coronation: a number were allotted to the Volunteers of Malaya.[1]

The regular troops held another parade and march past on the Singapore Padang on the 9th June, the official celebration of the birthday of H.M. King George VI.

In recent years the S.V.C. has been without a Band, the unit being so sadly lacking in numbers that it is practically non-existant—a fact that was particularly noticeable during the Coronation Celebrations on the Padang when the Corps had to march off the ground and round the town without the encouragement of martial music. In this respect the P. & P.W.V.C. and M.V.C. are lucky in having a working arrangement with their Municipalities whereby most of the members of the town bands are also volunteers and serve in their respective Volunteer Bands.

A new permanent Volunteer Camp, built by the Imperial Government on the coast at Teluk Paku, Singapore, during the early part of the year, supplied a long felt want and superceded the semi-permanent camp at Siglap, the site of which had been so kindly lent by Mr. Julian Frankel since 1927. The new camp was first occupied by Volunteers in May–June 1937.

At the beginning of this, fifth, chapter mention was made of the benefits of extra instruction that the Corps had derived from the increase in the size of the Singapore garrison. The influx of regular troops, combined with additional regular army staff on the headquarters of the various Corps, have gradually made Volunteering more and more interesting. Indeed, in Singapore the year 1937 closed with what were, without a doubt, the most successful manoeuvres yet experienced in the history of the Corps. The occasion was that of the G.O.C's. Annual inspection on the afternoon and night of the 9th/10th October. Three days

---

[1] *See* Appendix IV (b) for awards to S.S.V.F.

KING'S BIRTHDAY PARADE 1935
On the Padang with a Squadron of the R.A.F. overhead

THE OFFICERS SINGAPORE VOLUNTEER CORPS
Group after presentation of Colours 1934

THE STRAITS SETTLEMENTS VOLUNTEER AIR FORCE
Formed 1936

THE STRAITS SETTLEMENTS ROYAL NAVAL VOLUNTEER RESERVE
Patrol Launch "Panglima"—1937

after the sham fight a large gathering of some three hundred Volunteers and Regulars attended the S.V.C. Drill Hall, where the G.O.C. (Major-General W.G.S. Dobbie, C.B., C.M.G., D.S.O.) and his staff reviewed and explained the various points of the "battle", concluding with constructive criticisms and helpful suggestions for coastal defence.

These annual manoeuvres for the G.O.C.'s inspection have, since 1922, been worked up to the present high order by gradual improvement each year so as to give each unit and individual volunteer as much interesting work of the type expected of them as it is possible to include in a twenty hour scheme.

S.V.C. Historical Committee.—During the preparation of this history the Chronicler felt the necessity for the formation of a body to carry on the work of Volunteer historical research in this Settlement and the formation of a S.V.C. Regimental Museum for the housing, labelling and exhibition of relics which he had himself collected and the collection of further historical relics. In May 1937 he put up this suggestion to headquarters and eventually acted as convenor of a committee promulgated in December. A further reason for this suggestion was that he found that the effort required to produce even the present work was more than the average individual, singlehanded, could be expected to allow time for in a hot climate and that the assistance of collaborators of which he had had but few would not only open up a much wider research area but be a great help in reaching decisions on the many knotty points that arise. It would also decentralize secretarial labour in connection with such work.

The idea behind Regimental Museums, which applies equally to Histories, was discussed in the Journal of the Society for Army Historical Research—1937 Summer and Autumn numbers. Condensed and revised to suit local conditions and the present question they are as follow:—

People who consider themselves realists sometimes ask—if they do not put the question in so many words—"What are the uses of Regimental Histories and Museums?" When one comes to think of it, the question and the answer quickly resolve themselves into this: an integral part of a soldier's training is the creation of the subtle quality called *"esprit de corps"*, which is as necessary for him in the long run as any part of his purely technical training. His *"esprit de corps"* consists of a knowledge of the traditions of his unit—what it has done in the past, as an incentive to what it may do in the present and in the future.

Many of the traditions are purely oral, but some are visible, as in the colours, the uniforms and other aspects of the Regimental life; not least in the uniform, which often includes points, obscure to the amateur eye maybe, differentiating it from other corps.

Generally speaking Regimental Histories and Museums have, in the past, been purely concerns of the Regular soldier but if Volunteer and Territorial units follow suit a civic interest is at once aroused and that interest would be greatly extended by the inclusion of all local contributions to national defence in the past. Therefore Volunteer Regimental Histories and Museums become a matter of far wider importance than attaches to a mere piece of volunteer history published in the press from time to time. They appeal to the whole community.

There are various reasons why the contribution of a district or Colony to national defence has not been fully described by the local historians. In part, it is due to the habit of looking at defence as a problem entirely for a centralized War Office, with its equipment of Regular troops, a view that has been gradually broken down by such moves as the Volunteers, the Linked Battalions, and, later, the Territorial system. The net result has been that very few local historians have concerned themselves with the defence activities of the region they describe. Even if they were interested in the subject, most of them have got no idea of how to set about getting the facts, of which many are to be found in Government Archives, usually beyond their reach, while the locally kept records of such contributors as the unpaid Volunteers have in many cases been almost or completely lost.

Another lion in the path is the fact that a purely Regimental History or Museum is largely a personal matter. A volunteer may be found who is enthusiatic on the subject and he may get research and collections going on a working basis, but there is no guarantee that his successor will be equally enthusiastic.

There is no lack of material in certain districts but it is often scattered. Then again, there are the cases of those who have served in this country and eventually return to homes in England or other parts of the world and carry with them, as mementoes, historical relics which, like those kept in the houses of Volunteers while in this country, would willingly be presented to a Historical Committee for their records or museum if such existed as an official body. Volunteer enthusiasts of this kind obviously feel the necessity for Volunteer Regimental Museums and a place where historical souvenirs and data can be left for permanent record.

These are some general ideas by writers in the Journal of the Society for Army Historical Research and the author of this history. It is felt that if Volunteer History could be approached from the angle of a synthesis of local contributions to national defence, it would assume a greater significance for the average citizen, who would begin to take a pride in local patriotism and the repercussions of that in the defence policy of to-day are too obvious to need underlining.

This history of the Corps is naturally dedicated in the main to the Volunteers themselves, but it would be none the less incomplete if it contained no appreciation of the work of the Regular Staff of Officers and N.C.Os., known generally as the "permanent" staff, the mainstay of volunteer training and administration. Nowadays many of the regular officers on the Volunteer Administrative Staffs have after their names the mystic letters "p.s.c." and are chosen from those who have "Passed Staff College". All the permanent staff are selected for their special ability in the sympathetic handling of volunteer organisations.

The following are extracts from an appreciation of their efforts made by a Volunteer Officer some years ago:—

> "It is recognised that however experienced the officers in the Volunteer Corps may be, they are only Volunteers after all, and have most of their days taken up by their civil or commercial duties, so that it is impossible for them to keep abreast of modern thought and development in military matters.
>
> "The duties and responsibilities of the Permanent Staff are therefore, the direction and superintendence of the training, and the organisation of that vast amount of administrative work connected with correspondence, issuing of orders, control of stores and equipment, and all those details great and small which ensure that everything goes smoothly. This may sound simple enough on paper but in practice requires a great deal of hard work and a considerable amount of tact. Especially is this true in regard to training. The highest pitch possible of efficiency must be obtained; at the same time the initiative of the Volunteer must not be cramped, nor the control by the officer of his own unit interfered with."

The junior Volunteer may rarely give any thought to the unobtrusive work of the Permanent Staff, or Corps Headquarters as they are sometimes called to distinguish them from Battalion Headquarters, the personnel of which is entirely composed of Volunteers. As seniority in the unit brings with it the more responsibility, the greater will be the debt of acknowledgment for assistance received from Corps Headquarters, not so much because of the efficiency of that assistance—efficiency is expected from the Regular Army—but because of the cheerful and ungrudging manner in which that assistance is invariably rendered.

CONCLUSION

It would be wrong to refer to these last few words as the close of the last chapter of the History of Volunteering in Singapore for, as history is still being made, it is merely the last chapter of the first volume.

The Chronicler opened his preface with a quotation from Washington Irving, brought to his notice by it having been chosen by Buckley, in his *Anecdotal History of Old Times in Singapore*, to indicate that an historian can rarely be original, excepting in the lay-out of his volume. It will not then be inappropriate to conclude by repeating the following lines which appeared in the first pages of *"One Hundred Years of Singapore"* since they seem to form as suitable a conclusion to this history of Volunteering as they were a beginning to the wider Civil work:—

> "The Merchants and the Factors and the long-forgotten Writers
> "Who sowed the seed of Empire in a rudely furrowed sod;
> "The race of trader-statesmen and the clan of trader-fighters
> "Who laid the lines of order by the grace and will of God,
> "The sons from these descended, with the peoples in their keeping,
> "The men who bear the burden of this heritage today,
> "Each toiler in the noonday with his heart amid the reaping,
> "To these and those that watch them do I dedicate this lay."

J.A.N.

The Colony Arms & Crest
(Granted to the
Straits Settlements 1911)

APPENDICES

APPENDIX I (a)
SINGAPORE VOLUNTEER RIFLES
RULES AND REGULATIONS

(Printed at the Commercial Press, Singapore by J.A. Rebeiro 1857)

PROPOSED AT A GENERAL MEETING OF THE CORPS HELD ON THE 24TH JUNE, 1857; AND FURTHER CONSIDERED, AMENDED, AND ADOPTED, AT SUBSEQUENT MEETINGS HELD ON 15TH JULY, 22ND AUGUST, AND 28TH SEPTEMBER, 1857.

I. The Singapore Volunteer Rifle Corps shall consist of, a Commandant; a Captain; an Adjutant, who shall also act as Quarter Master; Four Lieutenants; Four Sub-Officers; Four Corporals; and as many of the inhabitants as may be disposed to enrol themselves as Members under the provisions of these Rules.

II. The Senior Subaltern present with the Corps shall have the rank of Captain.

III. The Officers, Sub-Officers and Corporals of the Corps, shall be elected when vacancies occur in their respective ranks, by a majority of the votes of the members, at a time and place to be fixed by the Committee, and under the following regulations:—

1. Officers shall be elected from the Sub-Officers.
2. Sub-Officers shall be elected from the Corporals.
3. Voting Tickets, signed by the Adjutant, shall be forwarded to the members of the Corps at least seven days before the day appointed for the election.
4. As soon as the election is completed, the Committee shall ascertain the number of votes given for each person, and the result of the election shall be notified to the Corps in the Order Book on the day following.

IV. The Officers, Sub-Officers, Corporals, and Four Privates elected by ballot, shall form a Committee for the management of the general business of the Corps, and for the consideration of all matters requiring to be submitted for decision of the Members generally.

V. Every Candidate desirous to join the Corps shall make a written application to the Adjutant, who shall submit the name of the applicant for the approval of the Committee, when, if the consent of three-fourths of the Committee appear, the Candidate shall be declared to be admitted as a member of the Corps, and his name shall be published in the Regimental Order Book accordingly.

VI. The Corps shall not be liable to any call for actual service except in cases of emergency, such as an attack on the Town from without by foreign enemies, or a disturbance on the part of our own population, when the Police Force may be found insufficient to secure the maintenance of the Public Peace.

VII. A parade of the Corps shall take place once a month, or oftener if necessary, for the inspection of Arms and Accoutrements, and Ball Practice when practicable; and, to give proper efficiency to the Corps, a regular Drill of three or more alternate days, Monday, Wednesday, and Friday, shall be attended every Quarter, in the months of February, May, August and November, and shall take place in the morning or evening as the Committee may find to be most generally convenient to the members. These Drills are to be exclusive of those which Recruits will have to undergo on first joining, until they are, in the opinion of the Commanding Officer, fit to join the ranks.

VIII. Any member who shall absent himself from Drill, or other duty, without accounting satisfactorily to the Commanding Officer for such absence, shall be liable to a Fine, not exceeding Five Dollars, as may be deemed by the Committee sufficient to secure regular attendance; such sum to be carried to the credit of the contingent expenses of the Corps, and to be levied by the Committee.

IX. At Full Dress Parades the members shall wear a Green Uniform of the material and pattern originally agreed upon; and at all other times they shall appear, when called on duty, in White Jackets, White Trousers and Cap-covers, Black Neck Ties and Black Shoes.

X. Any member about to leave the Settlement shall give timely notice thereof to the Sub-Officer in charge of the section to which he belongs; and shall at the same time deliver up his Arms and Accoutrements—it being distinctly understood that no member of the Corps has a right to take away from the Settlement the property of Government entrusted to his charge especially and exclusively for its defence and protection.

XI. Any member guilty of flagrant misconduct shall be liable to expulsion from the Corps on the charge being proved against him to the satisfaction of the Committee.

XII. In order to establish a Regimental Fund for the Contingent Expenses of the Corps, and for any outlay which may be considered necessary or desirable by the Committee, subject to the approval of a majority of the members, the following scale of subscriptions has been agreed to, viz.:—

A Captain	Dollars 10	
A Lieutenant	„ 5	On taking rank in their
A Sub-Officer	„ 4	respective grades.
A Corporal	„ 3	

And a Monthly Subscription of Half a Dollar from every Member.

I (a)　　　　　　　　　　APPENDICES

XIII. A Book shall be kept for the registration of members, in which each member entering, shall pledge himself to pay strict obedience, while on duty, to the Officers placed over him; to the foregoing Rules and Regulations; and to all orders touching the discipline of the Corps, which may from time to time be issued by the officer in command.

(Signed)	J. Purvis	Captain
"	J.C. Smith	Lieut. & Adjutant
"	C.H. Harrison	Lieutenant
"	M.F. Davidson	Lieutenant
"	H.T. Marshall	Sub-Officer
"	F.M. Goss	Sub-Officer
"	T. Scott	Sub-Officer
"	J. Watson	Corporal
"	A. Coxon	Corporal
"	G. Cramer	Corporal
"	A.B. Brown	Corporal
"	J.W. Armstrong	Private
"	J.F. Davidson	Private
"	T.O. Crane	Private
"	J. Harvey	Private

} Committee of the Singapore Volunteer Rifles.

By Order,
J.C. SMITH,
Lieutenant and Adjutant.

SINGAPORE, 17th November, 1857.

APPENDIX I (b)

Free Press September 23rd, 1887.

Proposed Volunteer Artillery Corps for Singapore

It has long been felt that something should be done towards the formation of a Volunteer Artillery Corps as a contribution towards the defence of Singapore. It is nothing short of a scandal that of all the important British Sea Ports in the East, Singapore alone should be unprovided with any organization of this nature. And yet there is no place whose necessities are greater, and no place with such advantages and facilities for creating and maintaining an effective corps of this arm of the service. But the attitude of the Local Government towards the movement is the vital question. If the residents of Singapore find the men, they will have done their duty, and there is every reason to expect that the Local Government will be no less ready to perform their share.

But in order to give the Government some definite ground to go upon, it is proposed to take a tentative step. The men whose names appear below are prepared to receive the names of others resident in Singapore, who may have served either in the Volunteer Service at Home, in India or in the Colonies, and in the case of residents not of British Nationality, who have been in the Military Service of their own country. The object being that of colonial defence alone, service in such a corps as is contemplated, would not probably interfere with any obligations under which foreign residents here might be to their own Governments. When a sufficient number of names of those who have already served, has been received, a private meeting will be held, to which all those whose names have been sent in will be invited. The matter will be discussed, and if it is thought advisable the scheme will be further proceeded with as may be determined upon. Gentlemen who are in favour of the idea and who have already served, will be good enough to give their names and the name of the Corps to which they have belonged, to any one of the undersigned. Any suggestions will be gladly received by the pro. tem. Secretary.

E. Scott Russell	London Scottish.
R. Kennedy	2nd Perth Highlanders.
H. Itzel	81st Hessian Regt. German Army.
T.P. Kerr	Mounted Coy. Madras Volunteer Guards.
M. Bean	2nd Brigade Lancashire Artillery Volunteers.
G. Bruce-Webster	London Scottish; Mounted Coy. Rangoon Volunteer Rifles.
J. Lanz	Ceylon Light Infantry Volunteers.
A. Morrison	5th Midlothian Coast Artillery Volunteers.
R. Dunman	5th Lancashire (L.R.B.); Shanghai Volunteer Rifles.
W. Thomson	1st Edinburgh Artillery Volunteers.
T.G. Scott	2nd Batt. Highland Light Infantry Volunteers.
W.G. St. Clair *(Secretary Pro. Tem.)*	Moulmein Volunteer Rifles.

APPENDIX I (c)

CORRESPONDENCE AND OTHER PAPERS CONNECTED WITH A PROPOSAL
FOR THE RAISING OF A VOLUNTEER ARTILLERY BATTERY
FOR SINGAPORE

SINGAPORE, 12th *November*, 1887.

To Capt. Taylor, R.A., A.D.C.

Dear Sir,

Enclosed with this note is a slip which explains my object in now writing to you as A.D.C. to His Excellency the Governor.

A private meeting has been held of a number of those interested in the subject of the possible formation of a Volunteer Artillery Corps for Singapore. The question has been discussed and a general understanding has been arrived at (1) that such a Corps would be of service as a contribution towards the defence of Singapore, (2) that a provisional Sub-Committee be appointed from those present at the meeting to approach Government with a view of ascertaining whether or on what lines the local Government would be willing to aid in the formation and maintenance of the proposed Corps.

The Sub-Committee have no authority to come before the Government with a detailed scheme, but, having sounded others on the subject, they think they have good grounds for saying that, provided the military authorities and the local Government furnish adequate facilities for training and sufficient support of a material nature, a large enough number of men, many of whom have already served, could be got together to form an efficient Volunteer Battery for local defence.

With the object indicated the Sub-Committee would be pleased to be favoured with a personal interview with His Excellency whose practical knowledge of and sympathy with the Volunteer Service is well known.

Yours faithfully,
W.G. ST. CLAIR,
Pro. Tem. Secretary of Committee.

GOVERNMENT HOUSE,
SINGAPORE, *November* 14*th.*

Dear Sir,

In reply to your letter of the 12th instant I am directed by His Excellency to inform you that he will have great pleasure in receiving the Sub-Committee, but he thinks it better to postpone the interview until the arrival of General Cameron at the close of the month, as he proposes to invite him to be present at the meeting.

His Excellency also desires me to say that he has noted with great satisfaction the movement to establish a Volunteer Artillery Corps for Singapore and that it will receive his warmest support.

Yours truly,
P.B. TAYLOR.

I will communicate with you later on as to a suitable day for the interview.

P.B.T.

GOVERNMENT HOUSE,
SINGAPORE, *Monday.*

Dear St. Clair,

His Excellency desires me to inform you that he will be pleased to see the deputation about the proposed Volunteer Corps on Thursday, the 1st December, at noon.

General Cameron proposes to be present.

Yours truly,
P.B. TAYLOR.

SINGAPORE, 28th *November,* 1887.

Dear Taylor,

Many thanks for your note. We shall be very happy to wait on His Excellency at the time you mention and I shall have your letter at once circulated for the information of the deputation. We are deeply sensible of the great interest the Governor has taken in the matter, and we shall be very glad if we can arrive at some practical result as regards the formation of some form of an Auxiliary Artillery force as a contribution to the defence of this Colony.

Yours faithfully,
W.G. ST. CLAIR.

SINGAPORE, 8th *December,* 1887.

To H.E. Sir Cecil Smith, K.C.M.G.

Your Excellency,

I have the honour to forward for your perusal and revision the draft report of the deputation to the Provisional Committee who are promoting the scheme of an auxiliary Volunteer Artillery Battery, laid before you at our interview of the 1st December.

It is so important there should be no doubt whatever as to the result of that interview, whether upon the side of those who are willing to offer their services, or upon the side of the Government who may accept them, that it seems essential that our draft report be subjected to the examination of Your Excellency, and, should you desire it, also of Major-General Cameron, and receive from your hand such modification or alteration as will bring it into harmony with what passed at the interview.

With such revision and sanction the report becomes an authoritative document, as expressing the desires and intentions of the Government with regard to the proposals in question, and it will besides give those who will consent to serve a clear idea of the conditions and obligations connected with the acceptance of their services.

I have the honour to be,
Your Excellency's Most Obedient Servant,
(for the deputation)
W.G. ST. CLAIR.

REPORT OF DEPUTATION

(To Provisional Committee Singapore Volunteer Artillery)

1. Your deputation, consisting of Messrs. Bean, Bruce-Webster, and St. Clair, after correspondence with Capt. Taylor, A.D.C., as to a date convenient to His Excellency the Governor, had the honour of an interview with H.E. Sir Cecil Smith at Government House on Thursday the 1st December, at noon precisely.

2. Major-General Cameron, C.B., Commanding the Forces in China and the Straits Settlements, Colonel Cardew, 82nd Regiment, commanding Singapore, and Major Davies, Military Secretary to General Cameron, were present by desire of H.E. the Governor.

3. Mr. W.G. St. Clair, as spokesman of the deputation, introduced the object in furtherance of which they had sought the interview with His Excellency,—the question whether it would be possible to bring about the formation of a Volunteer Artillery Battery, which should be a useful contribution on behalf of the European residents of Singapore to the military defence of this Colony, and which should at the same time be placed, with the co-operation of the local Government, upon a basis promising, as far as possible, efficiency and permanence.

4. At the conclusion of the remarks of the spokesman of the deputation, His Excellency conveyed to the deputation his great gratification at the movement that had just been brought to his notice, and his earnest desire to do all that he could in support of such a scheme as that submitted to him for approval.

5. Upon invitation from the Governor, Major-General Cameron, from a more purely military point of view, spoke at length upon the proposals in question, and gave them an emphatic approval, which, coming from an Officer of such distinction and experience, afforded your deputation the utmost pleasure and satisfaction.

6. A general discussion followed upon details, in which your deputation indicated as far as possible the main points upon which the success of the scheme seemed to hang, and pointed out the difficulties and dangers which militated so much against the efficiency and even the continued existence of Volunteer Corps in the East, and in what ways these might be avoided or greatly diminished in the case of the proposals now laid before the Governor.

7. Colonel Cardew also spoke strongly in favour of the scheme, and supported the suggestion of the deputation which referred to the place most convenient for the training of the Battery in gun-drill.

8. Your deputation submitted to His Excellency the Governor a nominal roll of those men who have already signified a general approval of the scheme and are understood to be willing to become members of the proposed Volunteer Artillery Battery, upon the condition that such material support will be afforded by the Colonial Government, as will guarantee that the scheme will be placed upon a solid and substantial basis.

9. Your deputation also submitted to His Excellency the Governor the rules and Regulations of several Volunteer Artillery Corps in the East, for His Excellency's inspection.

10. The Governor in bringing the interview to a conclusion again expressed his extreme satisfaction at the practical nature of the scheme which had been laid before him in outline. He alluded to the fortunate circumstance that Major-General Cameron was present to aid him with his opinion in the consideration of the subject they had discussed. Speaking on behalf of the Government he would be happy to take such steps as might be necessary for the establishment and maintenance of the proposed Force. He also signified his readiness to procure the necessary authority for meeting the expenditure requisite for the due carrying out of the object laid before him by the deputation. He desired that the deputation would not hesitate to come directly to himself whenever occasion should arise where his advice or aid could be of service.

11. The deputation then withdrew, after thanking His Excellency for the favour of the interview, which lasted for an hour and a quarter.

12. The general conclusion drawn from the tenor of the whole interview is that your deputation are enabled to state formally that, on every essential point brought up for consideration, H.E. the Governor is in agreement with the views of the deputation, and that on behalf of the Government H.E. the Governor will promote all necessary legislation (if any is necessary), and afford all material aid requisite for the due carrying out of the proposed scheme.

13. The General Commanding, as a military expert, has given his full approval to the various suggestions of the deputation, and, should it be necessary, will approach the Imperial Government with any recommendations that may be required.

14. The absolute condition, clearly understood on both sides, and strongly enforced by His Excellency the Governor as well as by General Cameron, is that the men who enrol themselves undertake the full responsibility of making themselves efficient in accordance with such regulations as may hereafter be adopted.

15. There will be provision made for the attainment of "extra-efficiency," for those who may be able to give the extra time to fulfil the usual conditions attaching to "extra-efficiency."

16. It is agreed that the proposed Battery is to be in its constitution more intimately associated with the Colonial Government and the Military Authorities than ordinary Volunteer Corps are by the usual regulations, and may be looked upon as a reserve to the Royal Artillery in garrison in this Colony.

17. The appointment of the Commanding Officer as well as of all Commissioned Officers of the Battery will lie with the Governor, who will therefore exercise a direct control over the management of the affairs of the Corps, and be directly interested in its efficiency and permanence.

18. The Adjutant of the Royal Artillery stationed at Fort Canning is to be, as far as practicable, also the Adjutant of the Singapore Volunteer Artillery Battery. The Royal Artillery will, it is believed, also furnish the necessary Sergeant-Instructors.

19. A building to be used as a Drill-Shed, Head-quarters, and Armoury, with suitable heavy gun mounted therein, and such other guns and appliances as may be found requisite and necessary, will be provided as close as conveniently possible to the business part of the town of Singapore.

(Probably either on Fort Fullerton or on Teluk Ayer; the former, if possible, to be preferred.)

20. The heavy gun in the Drill-Shed will probably be of the same pattern as that in some portion of the Defences to be placed in charge of the Battery whenever occasion should arise.

21. Every care will be taken by the Government and the Military Authorities to facilitate the training of the men composing the Battery with as little inconvenience as possible as regards time and place. Time being so important a consideration, the work of the Battery is to be as far as possible given more exclusively to gunnery work, so as to attain the highest artillery efficiency possible in proportion to the number of drills attended.

22. The principle is accepted that the efficiency guaranteed by each member of the Battery is all that is required as an equivalent for the necessary Government expenditure.

23. For general purposes the rules to be adopted will be similar to those of other Volunteer Artillery Corps in Her Majesty's Eastern Dominions, due regard being had to the special circumstances connected with the constitution of this Corps.

24. It is proposed that the rules as regards admission to membership of the Battery be assimilated to those in force in Rangoon and elsewhere, and that the names of all candidates for admission be duly proposed, seconded and ballotted for. This practice will tend greatly to maintain the tone of the Battery at a high level, and will indirectly conduce greatly to its military efficiency.

W.G. St. Clair ..
G. Bruce Webster
M. Bean ..
} Members of Deputation from Provisional Committee to H.E. the Governor.

(N.B.—This Report has been revised by H.E. the Governor, and by Major-General Cameron, C.B. All the statements made herein are therefore to be accepted as having the approval and sanction of the Governor.)

Note to (14)—It is so necessary to have a clear understanding before men undertake any obligations in the matter that it is as well to define what is meant by efficiency. "Efficiency," as generally defined, consists in performing a certain minimum number of drills (to be hereafter settled) and in being present at an annual inspection of the Battery, or failing such presence, to be absent only with the full consent of the C.O.

A man failing to fulfil this obligation is liable to make good the capitation grant receivable by the Battery in the event of making himself an efficient of the year. This grant is expended by the Battery upon the members under the head of uniforms, conveyance to ranges, and other heads of expenditure, and members recoup the Battery by earning the capitation grant through making themselves efficient. A man leaving this Colony or failing to make himself efficient for a reason satisfactory to the Commanding Officer is freed from liability in this respect.

As to the time occupied by the drills required to constitute efficiency it will probably amount to a comparatively insignificant number of hours per annum, the work required being less than from members of ordinary Volunteer Artillery Corps, and the facilities to be afforded being, it is hoped, considerably greater. Roughly speaking, from 35 to 50 hours per annum ought to ensure the minimum degree of efficiency.

The above note, though not a part of the report of the Deputation, was however enclosed with it and read by H.E. the Governor and General Cameron. It is intended to give, to those who have not before served, a general idea of what is implied by the term "efficiency," but at the same time the precise details cannot as yet be fixed until the rules under which the Corps is to work shall be drawn up. It may be taken for granted that there will be little material alteration from the terms on the above note. Along with this note Paras. 21 and 22 of the Report should be read.

GOVERNMENT HOUSE,
SINGAPORE, 9 December, 1887.

My dear Sir,

I now return you the draft Report you were good enough to send me. I have made a few pencil corrections and General Cameron has been good enough to write the letter I enclose, which you can make use of. Please return it.

Yours faithfully,
CECIL C. SMITH.

SINGAPORE VOLUNTEER ARTILLERY

The Major-General Commanding,
  I shall be obliged by your making any remarks on these papers.
    See letter within.   C.C.S.
                                                    8.12.7.

GOVERNMENT HOUSE,
SINGAPORE, 9th December, 1887.

H.E. Sir Cecil Clementi Smith, K.C.M.G.,
  Governor, Straits Settlements.
Sir,
  The report of the "Deputation to the Provisional Committee, Singapore Volunteer Artillery" fairly and briefly represents what took place at the meeting at which I was present and the terms agreed upon, under existing Ordinance, for the formation of an Artillery Volunteer Corps which would be of real service to the Colony, and deserving therefore of the liberal support of the Government if worked entirely in accordance with the spirit of all that was said by the promoters of the movement.

As I informed them, in matters Military whatever is done must be done thoroughly,—nothing is so mischievous or fruitful of dangerous delusions as playing at soldiers,—and it is consequently very necessary, if the Colony is to have its money's worth, that the conditions imposed according to agreement should be strictly adhered to, all useless material being quickly eliminated from the Corps.

Until I have had submitted to me the proposed Rules for the Corps, based on the principles set forth by the Deputation—it is unnecessary for me to say more at present, excepting to impress on the Government the all important necessity, as regards efficiency, of a good foundation being laid by the Recruit being thoroughly well grounded before he is allowed to rank as an efficient.

It is also very necessary that there should be a proper form of Inspection Report (Clause 16 of Ordinance 15 of 1869) for the information of the Governor, so that the Inspection should be a reality and not an empty form.

Finally I would suggest the Ordinance being so far amended as to establish the same connection between the Volunteers and the General Officer Commanding and the Commandant, as is the case at Home between the Volunteers, the General and the Officer Commanding the Regimental District, with such modifications however as local considerations may require and as long as the same principles are maintained as prevail at home.

I have the honour to be,
Your Excellency's obedient servant,
W.G. CAMERON,
Major-General
Commanding in China and S.S.

SINGAPORE VOLUNTEER ARTILLERY

A general meeting was held in the Exchange Rooms on Friday the 10th February, 1888 at 5 p.m., which was attended by a large number of those gentlemen who have expressed themselves as favourable to the project of forming a Volunteer Artillery Corps for Singapore.

Among those present were Messrs. Talbot, Presgrave, Kerr, Bruce Webster, St. Clair, Penney, Rowan, Morrison, Dunman, Wade Gard'ner, Cameron, Somerville, Donaldson, Raeburn, Alexander, Brown, Birch, M. Bean, Derrick, Fittock, Paterson, Dennys, Harrison, Mackay, C.P. Derrick, Bagley, Fraser, Fowke, J.P. Ker, Davies, Brinkworth, Barker, Coutts, McKie, Jago, White, Moffat, Thomson, Webbe, Bradbery, Suter, Benjafield, Paterson, A. Bean, Murray, Makepeace, &c.

Mr. A.P. Talbot took the chair, upon the motion of Mr. Bruce Webster, seconded by Mr. St. Clair.

The Chairman said that they were all aware of the excellent object of the meeting from the full information afforded by the printed papers that had been circulated, and which told them what the Provisional Committee had been doing. Any further information would be given by the movers of the various resolutions of which he would call on Mr. Birch to move the first.

Mr. Birch:—Gentlemen, I do not think that it will require much from me to urge upon you the necessity for the first resolution. The question of the defences of Singapore has been for several years a prominent one to those who are or have been connected with the Colony and whose personal interests are associated with the welfare of the place, as are those of all at this meeting. It is one which crops up periodically whenever we receive those alarming telegrams of Reuter, stating that the situation of Europe is rather obscure and which is as soon allayed on the receipt of the Home papers to tell us that the telegrams really meant nothing. But it is never allowed to rest long before being again mooted, not only by the residents of this colony but by the people at home and by Englishmen in every part and possession of the Empire. It is one which has seriously engaged the attention of some of the greatest and most statesmanlike men in charge of the government of British Colonies, and I may especially mention the very able articles and letters of Lord Carnarvon upon the subject of the defences of the Empire. During the last four years the energies of the Government of this Colony have been occupied with it and though the Government has been very often blamed for want of energy in the matter, from correspondence lately come out we know that it has been actively engaged in bringing the armament of the Colony to its present satisfactory condition. Very great strides have been made in building new forts and in sending out the newest equipments from home, and this must be satisfactory to those who live here, and whose interests and those of the place are identical.

Another point which has attracted some attention is the necessity for the presence in the Harbour of a man-of-war. There have been times when the harbour has been absolutely defenceless, but that has been altered by the stationing here of a strong guard-ship for the Colony. Now, gentlemen, if we had only to think of ordinary naval attacks it would not be so very important for us to call upon British subject residents in the place to assist in the protection of the Colony, for the regular troops stationed here would be sufficient for that purpose. But we have it on authority that for any attack in strength it is absolutely necessary to reinforce the regular troops—the number stationed here is not sufficiently large to fully supply all the reliefs for the forts or to keep the place against attacks made by bodies of troops on land. I think you will agree with me that it is necessary, and "necessary" is the word, to call upon British subjects here to give their aid and I am sure it is an aid which will be most cheerfully given by them, knowing that in many cases their little all depends upon it being given, and it is an aid which, I am equally sure looking at the meeting before me and at the class and quality of men who come out to this Colony, will be most valuable. Then in considering the necessity for a local movement look at the distance we are from reinforcements. While we are telegraphing to Hongkong and Ceylon and waiting for reinforcements a time must elapse which may be fraught with the most disastrous consequences to the Colony. It is absolutely necessary that we should, at a moment's notice, be able to obtain competent men to assist in taking charge of the armaments which have been put up here at enormous expense. A point which has been noticed by the paper that has so very usefully and ably advocated the establishment of a volunteer force, is that it would neither be proper nor possible to depend upon residents and citizens to come forward entirely of their own accord and provide the wherewithal for the formation of an Artillery Corps, but this point and other suggestions made by that paper, have been, I venture to say, cordially received by the Government which will do what it can to further the object. I am perfectly certain and you, I am sure, are equally certain, that the Government will not go back from what it has promised. As long as the force proves itself an efficient and capable body, I think the Government will go further than its promise and do what it can to improve and enlarge it. I have had some experience of the formation of different societies and movements in Singapore, how cordially they were taken up and carried on till, from different causes such as the initiators being removed from the Colony, excess of hard work, and the fact that we are only able to take active bodily exercise for a few hours per day, these different projects fell to the ground. But this cause is one which does not appeal to us as residents of this Colony merely, it appeals to us as men born of our own old mother country—as British subjects, and taken up as it is now by men of influence and position, is one which they will not allow to fall to the ground. Even if they leave the Colony, other men of the same stamp will step in and carry on the work, now begun. I beg to move:—

> That it is expedient and advisable to form a Volunteer Artillery Corps for Singapore with the object of aiding the Regular Troops in the Permanent Defence and Security of this Settlement against Foreign Attack and Local Disturbances.

Mr. R. Dunman seconded the resolution, which was carried unanimously.

Mr. St. Clair then rose to propose the second resolution as follows:—

> II.—That the Rules as printed and circulated be adopted by this meeting, subject to such alterations as may be suggested by H.E. the Governor.

He said that the rules had been very carefully drawn up and revised by the Provisional Committee, who had consulted the rules of the Calcutta, Bombay, Madras, Rangoon, and Hongkong Corps and who therefore had the best material at hand for compiling those which they now submitted to the meeting. The most important thing was as to how much time it would be necessary to spend. Being all busy men in Singapore, with but little leisure, that point had been the subject of a consultation between the Committee and Colonel Cardew, the result of which was that the minimum time required would be about 35 hours per annum, which would represent the sacrifice of their leisure they had to make for this purpose. At the same time the succeeding rule gave every inducement and encouragement to do more than the minimum, and those who took an interest in, and had the leisure for further work, would find abundant employment. Some might take unnecessary alarm at the term of service; he would say that the usual period of service at home was for three years whereas they had chosen two years. It simply meant that they undertook to serve for two years, say a minimum of less than seventy hours, failing which they bound themselves to reimburse the Corps for the loss which it would thereby incur. He could not say exactly what it would amount to, but he should think about $20 per annum. Of course, if members left the Colony their liability ceased.

Asked by Mr. Wade Gard'ner as to the meaning of "Commanding Officer's Parade," Mr. St. Clair explained that it simply signified a drill of the whole Battery together under the Commanding Officer which might take place in the Drill-Shed or at one of the forts. The Annual Inspection was perhaps the only one which it might be found necessary to have in public.

Mr. Graham thought that balloting for admission to the corps was unnecessary and undignified; the selection of candidates should be left in the hands of the General Committee. He proposed an amendment to that effect, which, however, was lost.

Mr. Bruce Webster, in moving the third resolution said that he could add nothing to what had been said as to the advisability and necessity of forming an Artillery Corps.

He hoped that they had come prepared to sign the preliminary form of enrolment, to show the Government that there were men ready and willing to work hard and make the Corps a success. He moved:—

> III.—That those present who approve of the scheme and are willing to serve under the proposed Rules, do now sign a Preliminary form of Enrolment, so as to guide the Government in affording the material aid requisite for the due carrying out of the scheme.

Mr. McKie seconded the motion, which was carried nem. con.

Mr. F.G. Penney moved, as a necessary complement to the last resolution, and in order to give the Government reliable statistics of the men who were willing to join, the following resolution:—

> IV.—That H.E. the Governor be asked to make at his convenience arrangements for the embodiment of the Corps, and that a report of these proceedings along with an authenticated list of those who have signified their acceptance of the proposed terms be forwarded forthwith to the Governor for his consideration.

Mr. M. Bean seconded the motion which was also carried unanimously.

Mr. Wade Gard'ner moved and Mr. Moffat seconded the last resolution.

> V.—That the Provisional Committee be asked to continue their duties until the Corps shall have been duly embodied.

The Chairman then drew the attention of the meeting to the sheets lying on the table ready for signature, which bore nearly sixty names at the conclusion of the proceedings. A hearty vote of thanks was accorded to Mr. A.P. Talbot for his services as Chairman, and this very successful meeting then separated.

APPENDIX II (a)

A List of Governors of the Straits Settlements
1826–1937

1826	Mr. R. Fullerton	⎫
1828	Mr. R. Ibbetson	⎪
1833	Mr. K. Murchison	⎪
1837	Mr. S.G. Bonham	⎬ Under the Government of India.
1843	Colonel W.J. Butterworth	⎪
1855	Mr. E.A. Blundell	⎪
1861	Colonel O. Cavenagh	⎭

1867 Major-General Sir Harry St. George Ord, R.E., KNT., C.B.
1873 Colonel Sir Andrew Clarke, R.E., K.C.M.G., C.B.
1875 Colonel Sir William Francis Drummond Jervois, R.E., K.C.M.G., C.B.
1877 Sir William Cleaver Francis Robinson, K.C.M.G.
1880 Sir Frederick Aloysius Weld, G.C.M.G.
1887 Sir Cecil Clementi Smith, K.C.M.G.
1894 Lieutenant-Colonel Sir Charles Bullen Hugh Mitchell, G.C.M.G.
1901 Sir Frank Athelstane Swettenham, K.C.M.G.
1904 Sir John Anderson, G.C.M.G.
1911 Sir Arthur Henderson Young, G.C.M.G., K.B.E.
1920 Sir Lawrence Nunns Guillemard, G.C.M.G., K.C.B.
1927 Sir Hugh Charles Clifford, G.C.M.G., G.B.E.
1930 Sir Cecil Clementi, G.C.M.G.
1934 Sir Shenton Thomas, G.C.M.G., O.B.E.

A List of General Officers Commanding Troops in the Straits
1883–1937

Hongkong and Straits

1883 Major-General J.N. Sargent, C.B.
1887 Major-General W.G. Cameron, C.B.

Straits

1889 Major-General Sir Charles Warren, G.C.M.G., K.C.B.
1894 Major-General H.T. Jones Vaughan, C.B.
1899 Major-General J.B.B. Dickson, C.B.
1904 Major-General Sir A.R.F. Dorward, K.C.B., D.S.O., R.E.
1906 Major-General R. Inigo Jones, C.V.O., C.B.
1907 Major-General T. Perrott, C.B.
1910 Major-General T.E. Stephenson, C.B.
1914 Major-General R.N.R. Reade, C.B.
1915 Major-General Sir D.H. Ridout, K.B.E., C.B., C.M.G.

1921 Major-General Sir J.S. Fowler, K.C.M.G., C.B., D.S.O.
1922 Major-General Sir Neill Malcolm, K.C.B., D.S.O.
1924 Major-General Sir Theodore Fraser, K.C.B.
1927 Major-General Sir C.C. van Straubenzee, K.C.B., C.M.G.
1929 Major-General H.L. Pritchard, C.B.
1931 Major-General L.C.L. Oldfield, C.B., C.M.G., D.S.O.
1933 Major-General E.O. Lewin, C.B., C.M.G., D.S.O.
1936 Major-General W.G.S. Dobbie, C.B., C.M.G., D.S.O.

APPENDIX II (b)

HONORARY COLONELS

S.V.R.C.	1854–1855	Colonel W.J. Butterworth, C.B., Governor S.S.
	1864 ..	Colonel H. Mann.
	1864 ..	Lt.-Colonel R. Macpherson.
	1867–1872	Major-General Sir Harry St. George Ord, Kt.C.B.
S.V.A.	1890–1916	Sir Cecil Clementi-Smith, G.C.M.C.
S.V.C.	1935 ..	Sir Thomas Shenton Whitelegge Thomas, G.C.M.G., O.B.E., Governor S.S.

COMMANDANTS

S.V.R.C.
- 1854–1856 .. Captain R. Macpherson, Madras Artillery.
- 1857–1864 .. Captain W.H. Read, S.V.R.C.
- 1865–1866 .. Captain J. Murray.
- 1867–1868 .. Captain H.E. Wilsone, S.V.R.C.
- 1869–1874 .. The Hon. Captain W.H. Read.
- –1878 .. Lieutenant C.B. Buckley, S.V.R.C.
- 1878–1887 .. Major W.R. Grey, S.V.R.C.

S.V.A.
- 1888–1897 .. Major H.E. McCallum, C.M.G., R.E.
- 1897–1899 .. Major R. Dunman, S.V.A.
- 1899–1900 .. The Hon. Major A. Murray, V.D., S.V.A.

S.V.C.
- 1900–1905 .. The Hon. Lt.-Colonel A. Murray, V.D., S.V.C.
- 1905–1910 .. Major (later Lt.-Col.) E.G. Broadrick, S.V.C.
- 1911–1919 .. Lt.-Colonel (later Colonel) G.A. Derrick, C.B.E., V.D. S.V.C.
- 1919–1919 .. Lt.-Colonel J.A.R. Glennie, S.V.C.
- 1919–1921 .. Lt.-Colonel R.C.F. Schomberg, D.S.O., The Seaforth Highlanders.
- 1921–1921 .. Captain E.A. Brown, S.V.C.

S.S.V.F. and S.V.C.
- 1922–1925 .. Lt.-Colonel F.E. Spencer, D.S.O., M.C., R.A.
- 1925–1928 .. Lt.-Colonel F.J.M. Postlethwaite, O.B.E., K.O.Y.L.I.
- 1928–1930 .. Lt.-Colonel J.M. Mackenzie, D.S.O., The Royal Scots.
- 1930–1933 .. Lt.-Colonel M.J.T. Reilly, M.C., The Royal Inniskilling Fusiliers.
- 1933–1936 .. Lt.-Colonel R.H.L. Fink, O.B.E., M.C., The Royal Scots.
- 1936– .. Lt.-Colonel V.G. Stokes, M.C., The Royal Berkshire Regiment.

HEADQUARTERS STAFF

Adjutants, S.V.C.

1902–1906	..	Captain H.R. Baker, 13th M.I. (Acting until 1903).
1906–1906	..	Captain H.H. Stockley, R.M.L.I.
1906–1909	..	Captain B.B. Colbeck, R.G.A., also S.O.L.F.
1909–1909	..	Lieut. W.B.P. Thring, R.G.A. (Acting) do.
1909–1913	..	Captain C.N. Ewart, R.A. do.
1913–1913	..	Lieut. H.F.G. Carter, K.O.Y.L.I. (Acting) S.O.L.F.
1913–1915	..	Captain G. Badham-Thornhill, R.G.A. do.
1915–1915	..	Major J.A.R. Glennie, S.V.C. (Acting).
1915–1916	..	Captain H.R. Llewellyn, S.V.I. (Acting).
1916–1916	..	Captain F.Y. Blair, S.V.A. (Acting).
1916–1918	..	Captain G.G. Wace, 1/4th K.S.L.I. (Acting).
1919–1919	..	Captain G. Day, M.C., S.V.C. (Acting).
1919–1921	..	Second-Lieut. R.C. Smith, S.V.C. (Acting).
1920–1923	..	Capt. D.M. Noyes Lewis, M.C., S.W.B. Also S.O.L.F. and Adjt. M.V.C.
1921–1921	..	Lieut. S.S. Turner, S.V.C. (Acting)
1922–1922	..	Lieut. W.H.V. Jones, 2nd Middlesex Regt. (Acting).
1923–1927	..	Captain G.A. Stephenson, The Middlesex Regt.
1927–1930	..	Capt. J. Chatterton, M.C., Duke of Wellington's Regt.
1930–1930	..	Captain E.C. Prattley, The Norfolk Regt. (Acting).
1930–1931	..	Captain H.L. Graham, M.C., The Scots Guards.

After this see Volunteer Battalion Adjutants.

Brigade-Majors, S.S.V.F.

1929–1932	..	Captain V.C. Russell, D.S.O., M.C., The Suffolk Regt.
1932–1935	..	Captain E. Foster Hall, M.C., The Buffs.
1935–	..	Bt.-Major E.W. Milford, M.C., The Lincolnshire Regt.

Staff Officers, S.S.V.F.

1932–1933	..	Major H.L. Graham, M.C., The Scots Guards.
1933–1933	..	Captain H.N. Sowden, R.A. (Acting).
1933–1936	..	Captain J.O. Knight, The Worcestershire Regt.
1936–	..	Captain E.L. Percival, The Northamptonshire Regt.

Quartermasters, S.S.V.F.

1928–	..	Capt. A.J. Pharaoh, (late The Royal Sussex Regt.).

Inspector of Small Arms, S.S.V.F.
(Up to 1937—Armourer, S.S.V.F.)

1935–	..	Lieut. C.G. Woodward, (late R.A.O.C.).

II (b) APPENDICES

SERGEANT-MAJORS AND INSTRUCTORS, S.V.C.

1922–1923	..	R.S.M. H.E. Wootten, The Hampshire Regt.
1923–1926	..	R.S.M. F. Powell, M.C., The Royal Welch Fusiliers.
1923–1928	..	C.S.M. A.J. Pharaoh, The Royal Sussex Regt.
1926–1929	..	C.S.M. H. Ensor, K.O.R.R. (Lancaster).
1928–1931	..	R.S.M. J. Imm, The South Staffordshire Regt.
1929–1932	..	C.S.M. J. Weston, Royal Scots Greys.
1931–1933	..	C.S.M. T. Cusack, The Lancashire Fusiliers (to M.V.C.).
1932–1935	..	B.S.M. F. Pugh, R.A.
1932–1935	..	C.S.M. C. Constable, The South Staffordshire Regt.
1933–1934	..	C.S.M. J. Tungate, The Middlesex Regiment (from M.V.C.).
1934–1936	..	C.S.M. G. Moule, The Royal Sussex Regiment (from M.V.C.).
1934–1937	..	B.S.M. B. Frith, R.A.
1935–	..	C.S.M. F. Hardman, The Scots Guards.
1937–	..	C.S.M. C. Constable, The South Staffordshire Regt.
1937–	..	B.S.M. J. Sinatt, R.A.

SINGAPORE VOLUNTEER ARTILLERY
LATER
SINGAPORE ROYAL ARTILLERY (VOLUNTEER)

Commanders.

1888–1897	..	Major H.E. McCallum, R.E., C.M.G.,	S.V.A.
1897–1899	..	Major R. Dunman,	do.
1899–1901	..	The Hon. Major A. Murray,	do.
1901–1903	..	Major W.G. St. Clair,	do.
1904–1906	..	Major C.J. Davies,	do.
1907–1912	..	Major G.A. Derrick, V.D.,	do.
1912–1914	..	Major W. Makepeace,	do.
1914–1915	..	Captain F.Y. Blair,	do.
1915–1920	..	Major D.T. Lewis,	do.
1920–1922	..	Captain J.G. Campbell,	do.
1922–1922	..	Major A.A.A. Paterson, D.S.O., M.C.,	S.V.A.
1922–1933	..	Major A. Gordon Lee, O.B.E., M.C., S.V.A. & S.R.A. (v).	
1933–1937	..	Major J. Lee, S.R.A. (v).	
1937–	..	Major R.B. Henly, S.R.A.(v).	

Acting Adjutants, S.V.A.

1888–1890	..	Major W. Brooke-Hoggan, R.A.
1890–1891	..	Major R.S. Watson, R.A.
1891–1895	..	Lieutenant W. Jennings, R.A.
1895–1898	..	Lieutenant N.D. Cockrane, R.A.

Acting Adjutants, S.V.A.—continued.

1898–	..	Captain P.R. Simmonds, R.A.
1898–1900	..	Captain G. Tyacke, R.G.A.
1900–	..	Second-Lieutenant J.F. Reid, R.G.A.
1900–1902	..	Captain H.G. Sargeant, R.G.A.
1902–	..	Lieutenant J. Thompson.
1902–1903	..	Captain H.R. Baker, 13th M.I. (Adjt. S.V.C. tempy.).
1903–	..	Lieutenant R.H.B. Clark, R.G.A.
1903–1906	..	Second-Lieutenant I.A.J. Pask, R.G.A.

Afterwards Adjutants, S.V.C.

SINGAPORE VOLUNTEER ENGINEERS
LATER
SINGAPORE ROYAL ENGINEERS (VOLUNTEER)

Commanders.

1901–1906	..	Captain R. Peirce, S.V.E. & S.R.E. (v).
1906–1908	..	Captain V.A. Flower, S.R.E. (v).
1908–1914	..	Captain (Hon. Major) A.M. Thompson, S.R.E. (v).
1914–1919	..	Major G.R.H. Webb, S.R.E. (v).
1919–1921	..	Major A.M. Thompson, do.
1921–1921	..	Captain W.L. Kemp, do.
1922–1927	..	Major P.H. Keys, D.S.O., M.C., S.R.E. (v).
1927–	..	Major C.G. Burt, O.B.E., do.

Acting Adjutants, S.R.E. (v).

–1904	..	Lieutenant A.M. Carden, R.E.
1905–1907	..	Captain M.M. Payne, R.E.
1908–1908	..	Lieutenant A. St. J. Yates, R.E.
1909–1911	..	Lieutenant M. Stagg, R.E.
1911–1913	..	Lieutenant C. Preedy, R.E.
1913–1914	..	Lieutenant J.E. Chippendall, R.E.

SINGAPORE VOLUNTEER RIFLES.

Commanders.

1900–1901	..	Major W.G. St. Clair, S.V.A.
1902–1903	..	Captain E.G. Broadrick, S.V.R.

Disbanded 1904 Re-formed 1914.

1914–1919	..	Major C.W. Darbishire, (late 6th R.W.F.).
1919–1921	..	Captain C. Bazell, S.V.C.

Adjutants.

1901–1902	..	Lieutenant R.F.A. Butterworth, R.E.

Later Adjutants, S.V.C.

APPENDICES

SINGAPORE VOLUNTEER INFANTRY.

Commanders.

1903–1905	..	Major E.G. Broadrick, S.V.C.
1905–1909	..	Major E.C. Ellis, S.V.C.

S.V.C.—1ST BATTALION S.S.V.F.

Commanding Officers.

1928–1929	..	Lt.-Col. J.M. Mackenzie, D.S.O., Comdt. S.V.C.
1929–1935	..	Lt.-Col. G.C. Meredith, O.B.E., M.C., S.V.C.
1935–1936	..	Lt.-Col. G.A. Potts, O.B.E., M.C., S.V.C.
1936–	..	Lt.-Col. A. Chamier, O.B.E., S.V.C.

Adjutants.

1928–1929	..	Adjutant, S.V.C.
1930–1930	..	Major A. Chamier, O.B.E.
1930–	..	Captain W. Rose.

S.V.C.—2ND BATTALION S.S.V.F.

Commanding Officers.

1928–1931	..	Major R.R. Robertson, S.V.C.
1931–1931	..	Major T.C. Hay, V.D., S.V.C.
1932–1935	..	Lt.-Col. G.A. Potts, M.C., S.V.C.
1935–1937	..	Lt.-Col. L.H. Chidson, M.B.E., S.V.C.
1937–	..	Lt.-Col. D.G. MacLeod, O.B.E., S.V.C.

Adjutants.

1928–1929	..	Lieutenant E.A. Stringer, M.C., S.V.C.
1929–1930	..	Captain J.S. Miller, S.V.C.
1930–1935	..	Major B.E. Ablitt, M.C., S.V.C.
1935–1936	..	Captain T.H. Newey, S.V.C.
1936–1937	..	Captain W. Penrice, S.V.C.
1937–	..	Captain D.C. Watherston, S.V.C.

P. & P.W.V.C.—3RD BATTALION S.S.V.F.

Officers Commanding.

1899–	..	Lieutenant J.Y. Kennedy (did not assume command. invalided home).
1899–1919	..	Lt.-Col. Sir A.R. Adams, K.B.E., V.D., P.V.
–1924	..	Lt.-Col. W.H. Whyte, D.S.O., R. of O.
1924–1925	..	Major R.R. Robertson, P. & P.W.V.C.
1925–1931	..	Lt.-Col. J.J. Saunders, O.B.E., V.D., P. & P.W.V.C.
1932–1937	..	Lt.-Col. G.D.A. Fletcher, M.C., P. & P.W.V.C.
1938–	..	Lt.-Col. E.A. de Buriatte, P. & P.W.V.C.

Adjutants.

1899–1903	..	Lieut. G.M. Dundas Mouat, 1st London Regt.
1922–1923	..	Lieut. C.E. Wurtzburg, S.V.C.
1923–1924	..	Lieut. A.J.L. Donaldson, S.V.C.
1924–1924	..	Capt. H.A.A. Howell, Middlesex Regt. (A.S.O.L.F.) (temporary).
1924–1927	..	Captain I.R. Lovell, R.W. Kent Regt.
1924–1930	..	Captain E.C. Prattley, Norfolk Regt.
1930–1933	..	Captain G.H. Gilmore, D.S.O., M.C., The Cameronians.
1933–1936	..	Captain D.G. B. Ridout, K.O.Y.L.I.
1936–	..	Captain D.E.M. Fielding, The Y. & L. Regt.

Sergeant-Majors and Instructors, P. & P.W.V.C.

–1924	..	R.S.M. T. Groggins, D.C.M.	P.
1922–1923	..	C.S.M. P. Ingate	P.W.
1924–1925	..	C.S.M. J. McLarty, K.O.S.B. (injured)	P.
1923–1926	..	C.S.M. L.H.S. Taylor, K.S.L.I.	P.W.
1926–1929	..	C.S.M. C. Jeffries, R. Sussex	P.
1926–1927	..	C.S.M. E.J. Goldsmith, Middlesex Regt.	P.W.
1927–1929	..	C.S.M. S.A. Woosey, D.C.L.I.	P.W.
1929–1932	..	C.S.M. E. Field, Oxford & Bucks. L.I.	P.
1929–1932	..	C.S.M. W. Grinter, Rifle Brigade	P.W.
1932–1935	..	C.S.M. H. Farrow, M.B.E., Middlesex Regt.	P.
1932–1935	..	C.S.M. A.W. Foster, Dorset Regt.	P.W.
1932–1933	..	C.S.M. J. Leaney, R. Sussex	P.
1935–	..	C.S.M. P. Sellick, Coldstream Gds. (later P.)	P.W.
1935–	..	C.S.M. S.P. Peyton, R. Sussex Regt.	P.W.

M.V.C.—4TH BATTALION S.S.V.F.

Officers Commanding.

1902–1906	..	Captain R.N. Bland.
1915–1921	..	Major W.M. Sime, O.B.E.
1922–1936	..	Lt.-Col. A.A. Lermit, O.B.E., V.D.
1936–1936	..	Lt.-Col. L.H. Chidson, M.B.E.
1936–	..	Major W.J. Curran Sharp.

Adjutants.

1920–1921	..	Capt. A.H.C. Allen, M.V.R. (acting).
–1921	..	Capt. D.M. Noyes Lewis, M.C., S.W.B., Adjt., S.V.C.
1922–1922	..	Capt. H.A.J. Woodfall, late 6th East Surrey Regt.
1922–1925	..	Capt. K. Horan, Oxford & Bucks L. Inf.
1925–1928	..	Capt. H.P. Mackay, M.C., Gordon Highlanders.
1928–1931	..	Capt. P.J. Gething, M.C., R. Warwick Regt.
1931–1932	..	Capt. K.G. Exham, Duke of Wellington's Regt.
1932–1933	..	Capt. W.J. Irwin, R.U.R., Adjt., N.S.Bn.
1933–1934	..	Capt. J.C.M. Balders, Worcestershire Regt., Adjt., N.S.Bn.

Adjutants—continued.

1934–1934	..	Capt. S.M.C. Theyre, Wiltshire Regt. (acting).
1934–1937	..	Capt. D. Colville, M.B.E., K.S.L.I.
1937–	..	Capt. W.H. Jackson, The Royal Warickshire Regt.

Sergeant-Major Instructors, M.V.C.

1925–1927	..	C.S.M. F. Gould, Devonshire Regt.
1927–1929	..	C.S.M. D. MacDonald, M.M., The Royal Scots.
1929–1932	..	C.S.M. C. Ashurst, The Welch Regt.
1932–1933	..	C.S.M. J. Tungate, The Middlesex Regt. (to S.V.C.).
1933–1934	..	C.S.M. T. Cusack, The Lancashire Fusiliers (from S.V.C.).
1933–1934	..	C.S.M. G.A.F. Moule, The Royal Sussex Regt. (to S.V.C.).
1934–1937	..	C.S.M. T. Cusack, M.B.E., The Lancashire Fusiliers.

HONORARY (VOLUNTEER) A's.D.C. TO H.E. THE GOVERNOR.

1911–1914	..	Captain G.S. Carver, S.V.C.
1916–1917	..	Second-Lieutenant G. Day, S.V.C.
1922–1924	..	Captain C.E. Wurtzburg, M.C., S.V.C.
1924–1925	..	Captain A. Chamier, O.B.E., S.V.C.
1925–1927	..	Captain E.C. Martin, M.C., S.V.C.
1930–1934	..	Captain A.C. Gilbert, S.V.C.
1933–1934	..	Captain R.B. Henly, S.R.A. (v).

APPENDIX III (a)

A LIST OF OFFICERS
of the
SINGAPORE VOLUNTEER RIFLE CORPS
1856–1887

Date	Colonels Commandant and Honorary Colonels	Captains Commandant and Captains	Lieutenants	Ensigns Sub-Lieutenants 2nd Lieutenants
1856	—	R. Macpherson, Madras Artillery (Capt. Comdt.) Robert Church, 47th, M.N.I. (Adjutant)	W. H. Read C. H. Harrison	—
1857	Brigadier McLeod, M.N.I.	W. H. Read, (Capt. Comdt.) J. Purvis, (2nd Capt.) R. Little, (Surgeon)	C. H. Harrison M. F. Davidson J. C. Smith	—
1858	Brigadier McLeod, M.N.I.	W. H. Read, (Capt. Comdt.) J. Purvis, (2nd Capt.) W. J. Thompson, (Actg. Surgeon)	C. H. Harrison M. F. Davidson (Adjt.) J. C. Smith (Q.Master)	—
1859	Colonel George Burn, 14th Rgt., M.N.I. (Col. Comdt.—July 1859)	W. H. Read, (Capt. Comdt.) M. F. Davidson, (2nd Capt.) W. J. Thompson, (Actg. Surgeon)	C. H. Harrison, (Adjt.) J. C. Smith, (Q.Master) J. Guthrie	—
1860	Colonel George Burn, 14th Rgt., M.N.I. (Col. Comdt.)	W. H. Read, (Capt. Comdt.) M. F. Davidson, (2nd Capt.) R. Little, M.D., (Surgeon)	C. H. Harrison, (Adjt.) J. C. Smith, (Q.Master) J. Guthrie	—
1861	Capt. and Bt. Colonel W. Orfeur Cavenagh Bengal Staff Corps (Col. Comdt.)	W. H. Read, (Capt. Comdt.) M. F. Davidson, (2nd Capt.) R. Little, M.D., (Surgeon)	C. H. Harrison, (Adjt.) J. C. Smith, (Q.Master) J. Guthrie	—
1862	Major and Bt. Colonel W. Orfeur Cavenagh Bengal Staff Corps (Col. Comdt.)	W. H. Read, (Capt. Comdt.) M. F. Davidson, (2nd Capt.) R. Little, M.D., (Surgeon)	C. H. Harrison, (Adjt. & Actg. Q.M.) J. C. Smith	—
1863 1864	Colonel Sir W. Orfeur Cavenagh K.C.S.I. (Governor, S.S.) (Col. Comdt.) The Hon. Colonel H. Mann, (Hon. Col.) The Hon. Lt. Colonel R. Macpherson, (Hon. Col.)	W. H. Read, (Capt. Comdt.) Resigned M. F. Davidson, (Capt. Comdt.) C. H. Harrison, (2nd Capt.) R. Little, M.D., (Surgeon)	T. Scott, (Adjt. & Actg. Q.M.) J. Murray	—

III (a) APPENDICES 155

Date	Colonels Commandant and Honorary Colonels	Captains Commandant and Captains	Lieutenants	Ensigns Sub-Lieutenants and Lieutenants
1865	Colonel Sir W. Orfeur Cavenagh, K.C.S.I. (Col. Comdt.)	R. Little, M.D., (Surgeon)	J. Murray, (Commanding) (Adjt. & Q.M. Vacant)	—
1866	Major-General Sir W. Orfeur Cavenagh, (Col. Comdt.)	J. Murray, (Capt. Comdt.) C. H. H. Wilsone, (2nd Capt. & Adjt.) R. Little, M.D., (Surgeon)	J. W. Armstrong D. Rodger, (Q.Master)	—
1867	H.E. Sir Harry St. George Ord, Kt.C.B. (Hon. Colonel)	C. H. H. Wilsone, (Capt. Comdt.) F. von der Heyde, (2nd Capt.) R. Little, M.D., (Surgeon)	A. Duff A. D. Forbes	—
1868	H.E. Sir Harry St. George Ord, Kt.C.B. (Hon. Colonel)	C. H. H. Wilsone, (Capt. Comdt.) F. von der Heyde, (2nd Capt.) H. T. Carmichael R. Little, M.D., (Surgeon)	A. Duff E. B. Souper E. Engel	C. Dunlop, (Ensign)
1869	Major-General Sir Harry St. George Ord, Kt.C.B. Royal Engineers (Hon. Colonel)	W. H. Read, (Re-appointed Capt. Comdt., 4-8-68) A. T. Carmichael, (2nd Capt.) R. Little, M.D., (Surgeon)	Nil	Nil
1870	Major-General Sir Harry St. George Ord, Kt.C.B. (Hon. Colonel)	W. H. Read, (Capt. Comdt.) A. T. Carmichael, (2nd Capt.) R. Little, M.D., (Surgeon)	G. Bushell	J. McE. Angus, (Ensign)
1871	Major-General Sir Harry St. George Ord, Kt.C.B. (Hon. Colonel)	W. H. M. Read, (Capt. Comdt.) A. T. Carmichael, (2nd Capt.) R. Little, M.D., (Surgeon)	G. Bushell	C. B. Buckley, (Ensign) R. Dunman, (Ensign)
1872	Major-General Sir Harry St. George Ord, Kt.C.B (Hon. Colonel)	W. H. M. Read, (Capt. Comdt.) R. Little, M.D., (Surgeon)	C. B. Buckley	R. Dunman, (Sub-Lieut.) C. H. Harrison, Jr. (Sub-Lieut.)
1873	—	W. H. Read, (Capt. Comdt.) R. Little, M.D., (Surgeon)	C. B. Buckley	R. Dunman, (Sub-Lieut.) C. H. Harrison, Jr. (Sub-Lieut.)
1874	—	W. H. Read, (Capt. Comdt.) R. Little, M.D., (Surgeon)	C. B. Buckley	C. H. Harrison, Jr. (Sub-Lieut.) Wm. Dunman, (Sub-Lieut.)
1875 to 1883		No records	--	—
1884 1885 1886		Major W. R. Grey, (Capt. Comdt.)	—	—

SINGAPORE VOLUNTEER RIFLE CORPS

Members—January 1864

Allen, J., Penang
Allen, W.
Almeida, E.D.
Anderson, W.
Armstrong, J.W., Sergeant
Armstrong, F.
Baker, R.
Baumgarten, Alex.
Baumgarten, Augt.
Berwick, Jas.
Bland, J., Corporal
Bremer, C.
Buchanan, H.
Bushell, G.
Cameron, J.
Canters, J.
Cork, F.T.
Cramer, R.
Crane, C.A.
Davidson, J.G.
De la Feuillade, G.
Dickson, A.
Dreyer, H.
Duff, A.
Dunlop, C. (Europe)
Emmerson, G.
Frohlich, H.
Gilfillan, S. (M.C.)
Goldschmid, L.
Gottschalck, F.H.
Greenshields, J.J. (Europe)
Greig, J.
Hannay, M.
Haupt
Helbing, C.J.
Heyde, F. Von der (Europe)
Kendall, F.R. (China)
Kirby, J.L.
Leisk, W.R.
Le Cerf, G.W.
Leveson, E.J. (M.C.)
Lipscombe, G.
Little, M.
Lyall, J., Corporal
Macdonald, J.E. (Europe)
Manford, W.
Martin, A.
McAlister, A.
McClelland, G.C. (Europe)
Moss, M.
Meyer, A.O.
Mulholland, W.
Niven, J.P.
Niven, L.
Oldham, W.
Padday, R. (M.C.)
Purvis, Jos. M.
Read, W.H. (Europe)
Read, R.B. (M.C.)
Reme, G.A. (Europe)
Riedtmann, J.R.
Rodger, David, Corporal
Scott, W.R.
Schmidt, A.E. (Europe)
Smith, J.K.
Smith, W.B.
Spottiswode, A.J.
Staehelin, G.E.
Stark, R., Sergeant
Stevenson, W.F.
Sturzenegger, C.
Taylor, M.W.
Thomson, W.R.
Velge, A.
Walker, E. (Bombay)
Watson, J., Sergeant
Watson, N.B.
Weir, J.
Wilsone, C.H.H., Corporal
Young, J.

List of the Names of the 96 Gentlemen
who enrolled in the
Singapore Volunteer Artillery
on its formation 22nd February 1888

Name	Address	Former Corps (if any)
Alexander, E.M.	Paterson Simons & Co.	1st Lanark R.V.
Almeida, H.d'	Almeida & Son	Singapore Volunteers.
Ayre, A.F.	P.W.D.	2nd Durham, A.V.
Bagley, H.P.	Paterson Simons & Co.	—
Baker, L.J.	P.W.D.	—
Banks, C.W.	John Little & Co.	—
Barker, F.W.	Gilfillan, Wood & Co.	1st Manchester, R.V.
Barker, A.	23, Raffles Place	—
Bean, A.W.	Robinson & Co.	—
Bean, M.	Syme & Co.	2nd Lancashire, A.V.
Benskin, J.W.	Raffles Institution	2nd South Middlesex.
Benjafield, F.J.	Barugh & Benjafield	—
Birch, E.W.	Colonial Secretary's Office	—
Bradbury, W.	Raffles Institution	1st Cheshire & Canarvon, A.
Brett, H.	A.L. Johnson & Co.	—
Brinkworth, G.	Kelly & Walsh	Shanghai Volunteers.
Broadrick, E.G.	Colonial Secretary's Office	—
Brown, G.S.	Raffles Institution	—
Cameron, E.	Singapore Insurance	—
Cooper, F.W.	John Little & Co.	—
Coutts, W.S.	Gilfillan, Wood & Co.	2nd Punjab, V.R.
Crane, C.S.	Guthrie & Co.	—
Davidson, J.G.	Rodyk & Davidson	Singapore Volunteers.
Davison, W.	Raffles Museum	Nilgiri, V.R.
Davies, C.J.	Guthrie & Co.	—
Davies, D.P.	Tanjong Pagar Dock Co.	—
Dennys, A.H.	Boustead & Co.	—
Derrick, C.P.	Raffles Place	—
Derrick, G.A.	Raffles Place	—
Dunman, R.	Raffles Place	3rd Kents, 5th Lancs. Singapore Volunteers. Shanghai Volunteers.
Donaldson, D.	Singapore Insurance	1st Lanark Engineers.
Dick, J.N.	S.Y. "Sea Belle"	—
Durnford, F.D.	Durnford & Co.	—
Earle, T.E.	Gilfillan, Wood & Co.	—
Evatt, P.T.	Chartered Mercantile Bank	2nd Surrey, R.V. Calcutta, V.R.

Name	Address	Former Corps (if any)
Evans, W.	Chinese Protectorate	2nd Cambridgshire, R.V.
Firth, F.N.	Hongkong & Shanghai Bank	
Fox, F.	Cross Street School	Robin Hoods (Notts.).
Fittock, C.	Battery Road	12th Devon Artillery. / 1st Durham Engineers.
Gardener, J.P. Wade	Hongkong & Shanghai Bank	Shanghai Miholoongs. / Bombay, R.V.
Graham, J.	Battery Road	Queens Edinburgh, R.V.B.
Gutcher, W.	Singapore Oil Mills	Singapore Volunteers.
Harrison, C.R.	Straits Dispensary	—
Haughton, H.T.	Land Office	—
Hill, V.	Savings Bank	—
Howell, J.	Malay College	—
Hutton, J.	John Little & Co.	Queens Edinburgh, R.V.B.
Jago, F.E.	Boustead & Co.	
Jones, T.	Chartered Bank of I.A. & C.	—
Jones, J.H.D.	E.E. Telegraph Co.	Singapore Volunteers.
Kerr, J.P.	Syme & Co.	Madras Vol. Guards (Mount).
Kershaw, T.N.	Registry of Deeds	1st Shropshire, R.V.
Laurie, J.	Govt. Engineer Surveyor	—
Little, R.	John Little & Co.	—
Mackay, A.	The Dispensary	Singapore Volunteers.
Macbean, W.	Straits Insurance Co., Ltd.	London Rifle Bde.
Makepeace, W.	Singapore Free Press	2nd Warwick, R.V.
Marshall, J.	E.E. Telegraph Co.	
Martin, W.	John Little & Co.	
McArthur, C.	Gilfillan, Wood & Co.	
McKie, C.F.	New Oriental Bank	1st Fife, R.V., London Scottish. / Hongkong Artillery Volunteers.
McLennan, J.	Hongkong & Shanghai Bank	1st Invernesshire. / Hongkong Volunteers.
Michell, W.G.	Colonial Secretary's Office	—
Morrison, A.	S. & S. Aerated Water Co.	5th Midlothian Coast, A.V.
Moffat, J.	Hongkong & Shanghai Bank	1st Dumfries, R.V. / Hongkong, A.V., Shanghai, A.V.
Maw, D.	John Little & Co.	Singapore Volunteers.
Mouland, H.J.	John Little & Co.	—
Murray, G.	Sayle & Co.	Queens Edinburgh, R.V.B.
Murray, A.	Supreme Court	1st Somersetshire, R.V.
Padday, R.A.	Tanjong Pagar Dock Co.	
Penny, F.G.	Colonial Secretary's Office	Singapore Volunteers.
Presgrave, D.G.	Municipal Offices	Queens Edinburgh, R.V.B.
Raeburn, A.H.	Guthrie & Co.	

III (b) APPENDICES

Name	Address	Former Corps (if any)
Russell, E.S.	John Little & Co.	London Scottish.
Robinson, S.R.	Robinson & Co.	—
Rooke, J.	Sayle & Co., Ltd.	—
Saunders, J.B.	Oriental Telephone Co.	1st Glamorgan, A.V.
Scott, T.G.	Straits Printing Office	5th Lanark, R.V.
Skene, H.M.	Chartered Bank of I.A. & C.	8th Inverness, R.V. / 1st Aberdeen, R.V. / Hongkong, A.V.
Smith, L.S.	Singapore Insurance Co.	—
Somerville, J.	Gilfillan, Wood & Co.	—
St. Clair, W.G.	Singapore Free Press	Moulmein, V.R. / 1st Galloway.
Sturrock, J.S.	McAlister & Co.	—
Suter, C.	Cross Street School	1st Hants, V.R., 3rd Hants, V.R.
Talbot, A.P.	Colonial Secretary's Office	Singapore Volunteers.
Thompson, C.C.	W. Mansfield & Co.	—
Thompson, E.A.	Singapore Dispensary	—
Thompson, W.	The Dispensary	1st Edinburgh, A.V.
Vaughan, G.O.	Raffles Place	Inns of Court, R.V.
Watson, R.G.	Chinese Protectorate	—
Webster, G. Bruce	Chartered Bank of I.A. & C.	London Scottish. / Rangoon, V.R. (mounted).
Webbe, J.T.	Anglo-Chinese School	Royal Artillery & Rangoon, V.R.
Westhorp, W.G.	John Little & Co.	—
White, T.E.	Robinson & Co.	Royal Artillery & Rangoon, V.R.
Wrench, W.T.	Raffles Institution	1st Devon, R.V.
Zeigele, O.	Brinkman & Co.	—

APPENDIX III (c)

A LIST OF OFFICERS
of
THE SINGAPORE VOLUNTEER ARTILLERY
afterwards
THE SINGAPORE ROYAL ARTILLERY (V)
1888 to 1937

Date	Majors	Captains	Lieutenants	2nd Lieutenants
1888	H. E. McCallum, C.M.G., R.E.	G. Bruce Webster	R. Dunman J. P. Wade-Gard'ner W. E. Hooper	—
1889	H. E. McCallum, C.M.G.	G. Bruce Webster R. Dunman	W. E. Hooper A. P. Talbot	—
1890	H. E. McCallum, C.M.G.	G. Bruce Webster R. Dunman	A. P. Talbot W. G. StClair	—
1891	H. E. McCallum, C.M.G.	G. Bruce Webster R. Dunman	A. P. Talbot W. G. StClair	—
1892	H. E. McCallum, C.M.G.	G. Bruce Webster R. Dunman	A. P. Talbot W. G. StClair	J. Fabris E. M. Merewether
1893	H. E. McCallum, C.M.G.	G. Bruce Webster, R. R. Dunman A. P. Talbot *	W. G. StClair C. J. Davies	J. Fabris E. M. Merewether
1894	H. E. McCallum, C.M.G.	R. Dunman A. P. Talbot	W. G. StClair C. J. Davies	J. Fabris E. M. Merewether G. A. Derrick
1895	H. E. McCallum, C.M.G.	R. Dunman A. P. Talbot †	W. G. StClair C. J. Davies E. M. Merewether *	E. M. Merewether G. A. Derrick
1896	H. E. McCallum, C.M.G.† R. Dunman *	W. G. StClair *	C. J. Davies E. M. Merewether	G. A. Derrick A. J. Sisson *† F. Hilton *
1897	R. Dunman	W. G. StClair C. J. Davies *	E. M. Merewether G. A. Derrick *	F. Hilton F. J. Benjafield *
1898	R. Dunman	W. G. StClair C. J. Davies	E. M. Merewether G. A. Derrick	F. Hilton F. J. Benjafield
1899	R. Dunman The Hon. A. Murray	W. G. StClair C. J. Davies	E. M. Merewether G. A. Derrick	F. Hilton F. J. Benjafield
1900	The Hon. A. Murray	W. G. StClair C. J. Davies	E. M. Merewether G. A. Derrick	F. Hilton F. J. Benjafield
1901	The Hon. A. Murray W. G. StClair	C. J. Davies	E. M. Merewether G. A. Derrick F. Hilton * F. J. Benjafield * T.	L. A. M. Johnson *

R. or R.O. = To Reserve.   F.R. = From Reserve.   * Promoted during the year.   † Resigned.

III (c) APPENDICES

Date	Majors	Captains	Lieutenants	2nd Lieutenants
1902	W. G. StClair	C. J. Davies	G. A. Derrick F. Hilton	L. A. M. Johnson P. R. Warren H. A. E. Thomson W. Makepeace
1903	W. G. StClair	C. J. Davies	G. A. Derrick F. Hilton	L. A. M. Johnson P. R. Warren H. A. E. Thomson W. Makepeace
1904	C. J. Davies *	G. A. Derrick * F. Hilton *	H. A. E. Thomson	P. R. Warren † W. Makepeace
1905	C. J. Davies	G. A. Derrick F Hilton	H. A. E. Thomson	W. Makepeace, R.O. D. Robertson
1906	C. J. Davies	G. A. Derrick F. Hilton	H. A. E. Thomson D. Robertson *	A. A. Lermitt G. B. Stratton
1907	G. A. Derrick	F. Hilton	H. A. E. Thomson D. Robertson	A. A. Lermit G. B. Stratton
1908	G. A. Derrick	F Hilton	D. Robertson	A. A. Lermit G. B. Stratton
1909	G. A. Derrick	F. Hilton	D. Robertson G. B. Stratton *	A. A. Lermit W. O. Hildred * J. G. Campbell *
1910	G. A. Derrick	F. Hilton	D. Robertson G. B. Stratton	A. A. Lermit W. O. Hildred J. G. Campbell
1911	G. A. Derrick	F. Hilton W. Makepeace, F.R.	D. Robertson G. B. Stratton W. O. Hildred * J. G. Campbell *	F. Y. Blair *
1912	G. A. Derrick W. Makepeace	—	W. O. Hildred J. G. Campbell	F. Y. Blair D. T. Lewis *
1913	W. Makepeace, R.O.	—	J. G. Campbell F. Y. Blair *	D. T. Lewis J. D. Keay * H. A. Lane
1914	—	F. Hilton, F.R. (1) J. G. Campbell *	F. Y. Blair D. T. Lewis *	H. A. Lane A. A. Lermit W. Murdoch *
1915	—	F. Hilton J. G. Campbell F. Y. Blair * (2) D. T. Lewis * (3)	A. A. Lermit	W. Murdoch S. S. Turner * F. H. Temperley * F. E. Dilley *
1916	—	F. Hilton J. G. Campbell F. Y. Blair (4) D. T. Lewis	W. Murdoch * S. S. Turner *	F. H. Temperley F. E. Dilley
1917	—	F. Hilton J. G. Campbell F. Y. Blair D. T. Lewis	W. Murdoch S. S. Turner	F. H. Temperley F. E. Dilley T. O. Mayhew *
1918	D. T. Lewis	J. G. Campbell	W. Murdoch S. S. Turner	F. H. Temperley F. E. Dilley T. O. Mayhew

(1) Paymaster, S.V.C.—Torpedoed off Plymouth in ss. "Nyanza" and drowned 1917.
(2) O. i/c. S.V.A. end of 1914—16-1-15.
(3) O. i/c. S.V.A. 17-1-15—28-11-16 and O.C. 9-7-17—1-3-20.
(4) Assistant and Acting Adjutant, S.V.C.

Date	Majors	Captains	Lieutenants	2nd Lieutenants
1919	D. T. Lewis	J. G. Campbell	S. S. Turner F. H. Temperley F. E. Dilley T. O. Mayhew	—
1920	D. T. Lewis	J. G. Campbell	W. Murdoch S. S. Turner T. O. Mayhew	—
1921	—	—	W. Murdoch S. S. Turner T. O. Mayhew	—
1922	A. A. A. Patterson, D.S.O., M.C.	A. Gordon Lee, M.C.	—	H. S. A. White T. M. Winsley A. G. Shafe
1923	—	A. Gordon Lee, M.C.	H. S. A. White T. M. Winsley	A. G. Shafe G. B. Adams, M.C.
1924	A. Gordon Lee, M.C.	—	T. M. Winsley A. G. Shafe	G. B. Adams, M.C. O. E. Venables
1925	A. Gordon Lee, M.C.	A. G. Shafe	T. M. Winsley G. B. Adams, M.C.	O. E. Venables
1926	A. Gordon Lee, M.C.	A. G. Shafe	T. M. Winsley G. B. Adams, M.C. O. E. Venables	J. Lee
1927	A. Gordon Lee, M.C.	A. G. Shafe	T. M. Winsley G. B. Adams, M.C.	J. Lee
1928	A. Gordon Lee, M.C.	A. G. Shafe	T. M. Winsley	J. Lee R. B. Henly
1929	A. Gordon Lee, M.C.	T. M. Winsley	J. Lee	R. B. Henly
1930	A. Gordon Lee, M.C.	T. M. Winsley	J. Lee	R. B. Henly H. Scott-Ram T. C. S. Wilkinson
1931	A. Gordon Lee, O.B.E., M.C.	T. M. Winsley	J. Lee R. B. Henly	H. Scott-Ram T. C. S. Wilkinson, (R.) H. J. Rae
1932	A. Gordon Lee, O.B.E., M.C.	T. M. Winsley	J. Lee R. B. Henly	H. Scott-Ram H. J. Rae
1933	—	T. M. Winsley, (R.O.) J. Lee R. B. Henly	H. Scott-Ram H. J. Rae	H. H. Busfield
1934	J. Lee	R. B. Henly	H. Scott-Ram H. J. Rae	H. H. Busfield
1935	J. Lee	R. B. Henly	H. Scott-Ram H. J. Rae H. H. Busfield	
1936	J. Lee	R. B. Henly	H. Scott-Ram (RO) H. J. Rae H. H. Busfield	E. D. Rushworth
1937	R. B. Henly	H. J. Rae	H. H. Busfield	E. D. Rushworth E. G. Vaughton

APPENDIX III (d)

A List of Non-Commissioned Officers
of
THE SINGAPORE VOLUNTEER ARTILLERY
afterwards
THE SINGAPORE ROYAL ARTILLERY (V)
1888 to 1937

Date	Sergeant-Majors and Staff Sergeants	Sergeants	Corporals after 1923 called Bombardiers	Bombardiers after 1923 called Lance-Bombardiers
1888	T. Grimmer, R.A. S.M.I.	W. G. StClair A. Morrison H. F. Ayre S. M. Alexander	W. Hutton M. Bean T. E. White J. Moffat G. Brinkworth H. M. Skene	P. T. Evatt C. F. Mackie H. M. Skene V. Hill G. Brinkworth W. S. Coutts
1889	T. Grimmer, R.A. S.M.I.	W. G. StClair A. Morrison H. F. Ayre S. M. Alexander W. T. Wrench G. Brinkworth	W. Hutton H. M. Skene G. Brinkworth W. T. Wrench	C. F. Mackie W. S. Coutts G. S. Brown H. Brett E. G. Broadrick A. M. Reith J. Graham
1890	T. Grimmer, R.A. S.M.I.	W. G. StClair A. Morrison H. F. Ayre S. M. Alexander W. T. Wrench G. Brinkworth A. M. Reith J. Graham	W. Hutton J. Graham J. M. Fabris G. Murray	G. S. Brown H. Brett A. M. Reith G. A. Derrick A. J. Sisson H. T. Cariss G. Murray R. S. Fry
1891	—	A. Morrison H. F. Ayre W. T. Wrench A. M. Reith J. Graham J. M. Fabris A. J. Sisson	J. Graham J. M. Fabris G. Murray W. Makepeace C. J. Davies A. J. Sisson H. T. Cariss G. A. Derrick L. A. M. Johnstone	G. A. Derrick A. J. Sisson H. T. Cariss R. S. Fry W. J. Caldwell H. Coghlan T. Shields F. J. Benjafield W. R. Scott
1892	—	A. Morrison H. F. Ayre J. Graham A. J. Sisson L. A. M. Johnstone G. A. Derrick F. J. Benjafield W. Makepeace	W. Makepeace H. T. Cariss W. R. Scott F. J. Benjafield W. D. Barnes J. Meikle R. S. Fry	R. S. Fry H. Coghlan T. Shields J. M. Allinson J. Meikle C. Loghan P. Mould D. Fulton H. A. E. Thompson G. T. Batty D. P. Davis D. H. Wade L. J. Jenkins

Date	Sergeant-Majors and Staff Sergeants	Sergeants	Corporals after 1923 called Bombardiers	Bombardiers after 1923 called Lance-Bombardiers
1893	W. Skaw, S.M.I. & Q.M.S.	A. J. Sisson G. A. Derrick F. J. Benjafield W. Makepeace	R. S. Fry H. A. E. Thompson G. T. Batty F. Bruce Norton E Ormiston	C. Logan G. T. Batty D. P. Davies L. J. Jenkins F. Bruce Norton E. Ormiston F. Pearce A. Robertson
1894	W. Skaw, S.M.I. & Q.M.S.	A. J. Sisson G. A. Derrick F. J. Benjafield W. Makepeace A. Morrison G. T. Batty E. Ormiston	R. S. Fry H. A. E. Thompson G. T. Batty E. Ormiston G. Brinkworth A. Robertson F. Nawton F. Hilton	L. J. Jenkins F. Pearce A. Robertson F. Hilton E. Wallace M. Robertson G. E. Mosley W. Fox G. Bruce-Webster
1895	W. Skaw, S.M.I. & Q.M.S.	A. Morrison A. J. Sisson F. J. Benjafield W. Makepeace G. T. Batty	G. Brinkworth H. A. E. Thompson R. S. Fry F. Hilton G. E. Mosley E. F. H. Edlin F. Nawton	M. Robertson G. Bruce-Webster W. C. Suter — Rogers R. Scoular E. F. H. Edlin J. Graham F. Koelle J. Rainnie
1896	W. Skaw, S.M.I. & Q.M.S. H. Muir, Armourer Sgt.	A. Morrison A. J. Sisson F. J. Benjafield W. Makepeace G. T. Batty L. A. M. Johnstone G. Brinkworth F. Hilton F. Nawton H. A. E. Thompson E. F. H. Edlin	H. A. E. Thompson F. Nawton E. F. H. Edlin F. T. Koelle J. Rainnie D. P. MacDougal	F. T. Koelle R. Scoular J. Rainnie M. E. Plumpton W. Cloke E. Wallace
1897	W. Skaw, S.M.I. & Q.M.S.	F. J. Benjafield F. T. Koelle J. Rainnie	F. T. Koelle J. Rainnie M. E. Plumpton W. Cloke	M. E. Plumpton W. Cloke C. A. S. Palmer B. L. Frost A. J. McDonald H. Heaney
1898	—	W. Cloke M. E. Plumpton	M. E. Plumpton W. Cloke B. L. Frost A. J. McDonald H. Heany	B. L. Frost A. J. McDonald H. Heaney R. Risk G. T. Marples S. M. de Montereau J. G. Graves A. R. Linton T. O. Mayhew F. Austess
1890	G. Braun, B.S.M.	B. L. Frost A. J. McDonald T. O. Mayhew	B. L. Frost A. J. McDonald E. Wallace R. Risk J. G. Graves A. R. Linton J. L. Montgomerie C. F. Minnett	J. G. Graves T. O. Mayhew J. L. Montgomerie W. H. R. Allen E. M. Fraser

III (d) APPENDICES

Date	Sergeant-Majors and Staff Sergeants	Sergeants	Corporals after 1923 called Bombardiers	Bombardiers after 1923 called Lance-Bombardiers
1900	A. W. Mugliston, B.S.M. H. L. Coghlan, Q.M.S.	B. L. Frost T. O. Mayhew A. W. Mugliston H. L. Coghlan R. Risk C. F. Minnett	R. Risk C. F. Minnett J. L. Montgomerie W. H. R. Allen A. Ronnald J. B. Harrop P. H. Upton	W. H. R. Allen A. Ronnald J. B. Harrop W. A. Hayward R. Scoular CdeC. Hughes C. N. Brockwell A. E. Passmore F. G. Allen
1901	T. O. Mayhew, B.S.M. W. A. Hayward, a/Q.M.S.	B. L. Frost L. A. M. Johnson E. F. H. Edlin C. F. Minnett W. A. Hayward C. E. Keyworth	J. L. Montgomerie J. B. Harrop W. A. Hayward F. G. Allen H. W. Noon C. E. Keyworth A. E. Baddeley	H. W. Noon C. N. Brockwell W. H. Dark J. L. Hope C. E. Keyworth D. Miller A. E. Baddley A. F. G. Dark
1902	T. O. Mayhew, B.S.M. W. Ryan, Trumpeter Sgt.	W. Makepeace H. A. E. Thompson B. L. Frost W. A. Hayward C. E. Keyworth E. Wallace H. W. Noon	J. L. Montgomerie J. B. Harrop F. G. Allen R. Risk H. W. Noon J. L. Hope A. E. Baddeley	C. N. Brockwell W. H. Dark J. L. Hope D. Miller A. F. G. Dark H. C. Black
1903	T. O. Mayhew, B.S.M. H. C. Black, Q.M.S. J. R. Williams, Sgt. Sig. Instr. W. Ryan, Trumpeter Sgt.	B. L. Frost W. A. Hayward C. E. Keyworth E. Wallace H. W. Noon F. G. Allen R. Risk	J. L. Montgomerie J. B. Harrop F. G. Allen R. Risk J. L. Hope A. E. Baddeley D. Miller J. G. Graves	W. H. Dark D. Miller A. F. G. Dark H. C. Black J. G. Graves F. H. Dark J. R. Williams O. T. Lowe D. Robertson K. S. B. Robertson E. Hodges P. Kitovitz H. C. W. Allen
1904	T. O. Mayhew, B.S.M. H. C. Black, Q.M.S. J. R. Williams, Sgt. Sig. Instr. W. Ryan, Sgt. Trumpeter	W. A. Hayward C. E. Keyworth E. Wallace H. W. Noon F. G. Allen R. Risk D. Miller F. H. Darke D. Robertson	J. L. Hope D. Miller J. G. Graves F. H. Darke D. Robertson E. Hodges P. Kitovitz H. C. W. Allen C. R. Harrison	A. F. G. Darke F. H. Darke O. T. Lowe D. Robertson K. S. B. Robertson E. Hodges P. Kitovitz H. C. W. Allen J. Aitken C. R. Harrison A. A. Lermit J. Henderson C. Baugh D. Munro G. Stockwell J. A. Boyes J. P. Hall B. Thompson H. J. Thicketts A. E. Bailey S. Wooley D. C. Wilkie C. Darke

Date	Sergeant-Majors and Staff Sergeants	Sergeants	Corporals after 1923 called Bombardiers	Bombardiers after 1923 called Lance-Bombardiers
1905	T. O. Mayhew, B.S.M. H. C. Black, Q.M.S. J. R. Williams, Sgt. Sig. Instr.	C. E. Keyworth F. G. Allen D. Miller F. H. Darke D. Robertson E. Hodges P. Kitovitz H. C. W. Allen A. A. Lermit	J. L. Hope E. Hodges P. Kitovitz H. C. W. Allen C. R. Harrison C. Baugh J. A. Boyes B. Thompson H. G. Thicketts A. E. Bailey D. C. Wilkie	K. S. B. Robertson J. Aitken A. A. Lermit J. Henderson C. Baugh G. Stockwell J. A. Boyes B. Thompson H. G. Thicketts A. E. Bailey S. Wooley D. C. Wilkie C. Darke H. J. Murrell J. A. Lindsay J. Hodgins J. F. Fitt
1906	T. O. Mayhew, B.S.M. J. R. Williams, Sgt. Sig. Instr.	F. G. Allen E. Hodges P. Kitovitz H. C. W. Allen A. A. Lermit J. A. Boyes B. Thompson G. Stockwell	C. R. Harrison C. Baugh J. A. Boyes B. Thompson H. G. Thicketts D. C. Wilkie J. A. Lindsay	J. Aitken J. Henderson G. Stockwell S. Wooley J. A. Lindsay J. Hodgins J. F. Fitt D. A. Walker A. D. Livingstone H. Gilmour
1907	T. O. Mayhew, B.S.M. W. King, Sgt. Instr.	E. Hodges J. A. Boyes B. Thompson G. Stockwell C. Baugh	C. Baugh D. C. Wilkie J. Henderson J. F. Fitt D. A. Walker W. O. Hildred	J. Aitken J. Henderson S. Wooley J. F. Fitt D. A. Walker A. D. Livingstone H. Gilmour D. Munro D. A. Bishop C. A. H. Squires E. Gill
1908	T. O. Mayhew, B.S.M. J. A. Boyes, a/B.S.M.	E. Hodges J. A. Boyes C. Baugh W. O. Hildred D. A. Walker J. Henderson J. F. Fitt	W. O. Hildred J. Henderson J. F. Fitt D. A. Walker C. A. H. Squires E. Gill	A. D. Livingstone H. Gilmour D. Munro C. A. H. Squires E. Gill J. Watson E. D. Butler R. W. B. Cochrane E. E. Johnson W. G. Bowman J. G. Rogers G. J. Marshall
1909	W. Careless, Q.M.S.	C. Baugh W. O. Hildred D. A. Walker J. Henderson J. F. Fitt E. Gill	C. A. H. Squires E. Gill E. D. Butler R. W. B. Cochrane E. E. Johnson E. E. Marshall F. G. Campbell	J. Watson E. D. Butler R. W. B. Cochrane E. E. Johnson J. G. Rogers G. J. Marshall D. T. Lewis F. E. Gallimore J. G. Campbell A. E. Beavis F. Stanley N. T. King J. F. Clarke F. J. S. Shaw A. E. Brown F. Y. Blair

III (d) APPENDICES

Date	Sergeant-Majors and Staff Sergeants	Sergeants	Corporals after 1923 called Bombardiers	Bombardiers after 1923 called Lance-Bombardiers
1910	W. Careless, Q.M.S.	C. Baugh D. A. Walker J. F. Fitt E. Gill R. W. B. Cochrane G. J. Marshall F. Y. Blair	R. W. B. Cochrane E. E. Johnson G. J. Marshall D. T. Lewis F. E. Gallimore A. E. Beavis J. W. Williamson F. J. S. Shaw	R. G. Rogers D. T. Lewis F. E. Gallimore A. E. Beavis F. Stanley J. F. Clarke F. J. S. Shaw A. E. Brown F. Y. Blair A. Nunn H. J. Murrell
1911	J. F. Fitt, a/B.S.M. C. Baugh, a/Q.M.S.	J. F. Fitt E. Gill R. W. B. Cochrane G. J. Marshall F. Y. Blair D. T. Lewis J. D. Keay	E. E. Johnson A. E. Beavis J. W. Williamson F. J. S. Shaw J. F. Clarke J. D. Keay B. Sutherland F. W. Howl A. M. Bailey W. P. Miller	R. G. Rogers F. Stanley J. F. Clarke H. J. Murrell J. T. Dawson F. M. Bailey R. H. Anyon W. P. Miller W. H. Threlfall H. Wilkins J. Hook
1912	J. F. Fitt, B.S.M. C. Baugh, Q.M.S.	E. Gill G. J. Marshall D. T. Lewis J. D. Keay E. E. Johnson F. W. Howl	E. E. Johnson A. E. Beavis J. W. Williamson F. J. S. Shaw J. F. Clarke B. Sutherland F. W. Howl A. M. Bailey W. P. Miller J. T. Dawson	F. Stanley H. J. Murrell W. H. Threlfall J. Hook J. T. Dawson R. H. Anyon A. E. W. Freshwater W. Murdoch F. Hilton
1913	J. F. Fitt, B.S.M. T. O. Mayhew, B.S.M. C. Baugh, Q.M.S.	G. H. Marshall J. D. Keay E. E. Johnson F. W. Howl W. B. Sutherland W. Murdoch	A. E. Beavis J. W. Williamson W. B. Sutherland A. M. Bailey W. H. Threlfall	F. Stanley H. J. Murrell W. H. Threlfall J. Hook A. E. W. Freshwater W. Murdoch F. Hilton W. Marsh G. S. Myles G. Achurch S. S. Turner
1914	T. O. Mayhew, B.S.M. C. Baugh, Q.M.S. A. E. Parsons, Sgt. Instr.	E. E. Johnson W. B. Sutherland W. Murdoch W. H. Threlfall S. S. Turner	J. W. Williamson A. M. Bailey S. S. Turner H. W. Burt J. Taylor C. R. Langham F. E. Dilley	F. Stanley H. J. Murrell G. S. Myles G. Achurch H. W. Burt J. Taylor C. R. Langham F. E. Dilley M. Lymberg H. S. A. White E. C. H. Charlwood L. H. Sharpe H. L. Phillips

A HISTORY OF THE SINGAPORE VOLUNTEER CORPS   III (d)

Date	Sergeant-Majors and Staff Sergeants	Sergeants	Corporals after 1923 called Bombardiers	Bombardiers after 1923 called Lance-Bombardiers
1915	T. O. Mayhew, B.S.M. C. Baugh, Q.M.S. A. E. Parsons, Sgt. Instr.	S. S. Turner H. W. Burt F. E. Dilley J. Taylor R. M. Williams	H. W. Burt C. R. Langham F. E. Dilley R. M. Williams C. G. Brown L. H. Sharpe E. C. H. Charlwood J. Taylor	F. Stanley G. Achurch E. C. H. Charlwood L. H. Sharpe F. H. Temperley J. Downes F. L. Robinson R. M. Williams C. G. Brown V. Patterson A. G. Shafe F. S. Gibson J. C. R. Badham K. McMillan
1916	T. O. Mayhew, B.S.M. C. Baugh, Q.M.S. A. E. Parsons, Sgt. Instr.	H. W. Burt J. Taylor R. M. Williams E. C. H. Charlwood	L. H. Sharpe E. C. H. Charlwood F. S. Gibson	V. Patterson C. E. Hughes Davis A. G. Shafe F. S. Gibson J. R. C. Badham E. O. Bruce W. Jones H. C. W. Allen C. Rathborn K. McMillan
1917	T. O. Mayhew, B.S.M. J. Taylor, B.S.M. C. Baugh, Q.M.S. A. E. Parsons, Sgt. Instr.	J. Taylor R. M. Williams E. C. H. Charlwood	L. H. Sharpe F. S. Gibson J. R. C. Badham M. J. B. Watt S. Dunn H. C. W. Allen K. McMillan C. E. D. Warry W. H. Urquart H. J. Fougere	V. Patterson J. R. C. Badham W. Jones H. C. W. Allen C. Rathborn K. McMillan R. Dick M. J. B. Watt H. B. Layton V. M. Grayburn C. E. D. Warry S. Dunn W. H. Urquart H. J. Fougere A. E. Lickfold C. Hewetson W. J. Jamieson
1918	J. Taylor, B.S.M.	R. M. Williams M. J. B. Watt K. McMillan	L. H. Sharpe J. R. C. Badham M. J. B. Watt S. Dunn H. C. W. Allen K. McMillan C. E. D. Warry W. H. Urquart H. J. Fougere	R. Dick H. B. Layton V. M. Grayburn A. E. Lickfold C. Hewetson W. J. Jamieson D. B. Murray J. Hammond
1919	J. Taylor, B.S.M.	R. M. Williams M. J. B. Watt K. McMillan	S. Dunn H. C. W. Allen C. E. D. Warry W. H. Urquart H. J. Fougere	V. M. Grayburn A. E. Lickfold C. Hewetson W. J. Jamieson J. Hammond
1920	J. Taylor, B.S.M.	M. J. B. Watt K. McMillan	H. C. W. Allen C. E. D. Warry H. J. Fougere	J. Hammond
1921	J. Taylor, B.S.M.	K. McMillan	H. C. W. Allen H. J. Fougere	—

III (d) APPENDICES

Date	Sergeant-Majors and Staff Sergeants	Sergeants	Corporals after 1923 called Bombardiers	Bombardiers after 1923 called Lance-Bombardiers
1922	T. O. Mayhew, B.S.M. J. Taylor, B.Q.M.S.	A. Gordon Lee, M.C. E. J. Sutton, M.C. H. S. A. White T. M. Winsley H. Gilmour A. G. Shafe K. McMillan J. Corrie	A. Gordon Lee, M.C. T. O. Mayhew K. McMillan J. Corrie	V. Patterson A. G. Shafe K. McMillan H. Gilmour J. Corrie
1923	T. O. Mayhew, B.S.M. J. Taylor, B.Q.M.S. W. Turner, Wheeler Sgt.	H. Gilmour K. McMillan V. Patterson	V. Patterson G. B. Adams, M.C. A. H. Capel	G. B. Adams, M.C. R. M. Duff A. L. Harrison A. H. Capel W. Jones H. Scott-Ram
1924	T. O. Mayhew, B.S.M. J. Taylor, B.Q.M.S. W. Turner, Wheeler Sgt.	H. Gilmour K. McMillan H. Scott-Ram G. E. Clayton, M.C. H. E. Gubbins A. W. Wallich	H. Scott-Ram A. W. Wallich G. E. Clayton, M.C. A. L. Harrison S. P. Holmes Smith A. H. Capel J. Lee	A. W. Wallich G. E. Clayton, M.C. D. Wilson C. L. Slater O. E. Venables W. Jones
1925	T. O. Mayhew, B.S.M. J Taylor, B.Q.M.S.	H. Gilmour K. McMillan G. E. Clayton, M.C. H. E. Gubbins S. P. Holmes Smith J. Lee	A. L. Harrison S. P. Holmes Smith J. Lee W. Brown W. Turner	C. L. Slater R. M. Williams W. Brown O. E. B. Crowe H. E. Gubbins
1926	T. O. Mayhew, B.S.M. J. Taylor, B.Q.M.S.	K. McMillan G. E. Clayton, M.C. J. Lee S. P. Holmes Smith	A. L. Harrison W. Brown W. Turner O. E. B. Crowe R. B. Henly R. McLeod	R. M. Williams A. L. Harrison F. Stanley G. N. G. Easton H. E. Gubbins
1927	T. O. Mayhew, B.S.M. J. Taylor, B.Q.M.S.	O. E. B. Crowe W. Brown R. B. Henly R. McLeod	R. B. Henly R. McLeod	F. Stanley R. Crawford G. Minto H. J. Rae
1928	T. O. Mayhew, B.S.M. J. Taylor, B.Q.M.S.	O. E. B. Crowe W. Brown R. B. Henly G. Minto H. J. Rae T. C. S. Wilkinson	G. Minto H. J. Rae R. Crawford T. C. S. Wilkinson	F. Stanley R. Crawford T. C. S. Wilkinson H. P. Clarke, M.C. K. G. Wilson H. C. Luetchford H. Busfield
1929	T. O. Mayhew, B.S.M. H. Brett,* B.Q.M.S.	O. E. B. Crowe R. McLeod G. Minto H. J. Rae T. C. S. Wilkinson	R. Crawford	H. P. Clarke, M.C. K. G. Wilson H. C. Luetchford H. H. Busfield
1930	T. O. Mayhew, B.S.M. R. L. Moncrieff, B.Q.M.S.	G. Minto H. J. Rae R. Crawford H. H. Busfield	H. P. Clarke, M.C. H. C. Luetchford	K. G. Wilson F. R. Jones, M.C. N. D. Brooke P. D. Abbott J. H. J. Dredge
1931	T O. Mayhew, M.B.E., B.S.M. R. L. Moncrieff, B.Q.M.S. F. Pugh, R.A., Sgt. Instr.	H. J. Rae R. Crawford H. H. Busfield F. A. Jones, (Sig.)	P. M. Leckie J. I. Miller	H. C. Luetchford F. R. Jones, M.C. W. D. Brooks J. H. J. Dredge

* Bombardier in 1889—1890.

Date	Sergeant-Majors and Staff Sergeants	Sergeants	Corporals after 1923 called Bombardiers	Bombardiers after 1923 called Lance-Bombardiers
1932	T. O. Mayhew, M.B.E., B.S.M. R. L. Moncrieff, B.Q.M.S. J. P. Learney, B.Q.M.S. F. Pugh, R.A., Sgt. Instr.	R. Crawford H. H. Busfield J. I. Miller W. D. Brooks	P. M. Leckie F. R. Jones	J. H. J. Dredge E. D. Rushworth H. Meynell G. M. Coltart A. J. Thursfield P. D. Cork F. H. Bickerdike
1933	F. R. Jones, M.C., Sgt. A/B.S.M. J. P. Learney, B.Q.M.S. F. Pugh, R.A., B.S.M., Instr.	R. Crawford H. H. Busfield J. I. Miller W. D. Brooks E. D. Rushworth	P. M. Leckie A. J. Thursfield G. M. Coltart P. D. Cork J. C. Hosegood W. K. Wilton, M.M. E. G. Farrington	J. H. J. Dredge H. Meynell F. A. Bickerdike H. C. Luetchford E. J. Phillips R. S. MacTier A. H. Wright F. B. Martin E. G. Vaughton
1934	F. R. Jones, M.C., B.S.M. J. P. Learney, B.Q.M.S. F. Pugh, R.A., B.S.M., Instr.	R. Crawford J. I. Miller E. D. Rushworth J. C. Hosegood E. G. Vaughton A. J. Thursfield W. K. Wilton, M.M.	P. D. Cork E. G. Farrington E. J. Phillips R. S. MacTier W. J. McConnell	H. C. Luetchford J. H. J. Dredge D. Wilson H. J. C. K. Toms H. Hunter W. R. S. Perrott I. A. Maclachan, D.C.M.
1935	F. R. Jones, M.C., B.S.M. J. P. Learney, B.Q.M.S. B. Frith, R.A., B.S.M., Instr.	R. Crawford J. I. Miller E. D. Rushworth J. C. Hosegood E. G. Vaughton W. K. Wilton, M.M. R. S. MacTier	P. D. Cork E. G. Farrington E. J. Phillips W. J. McConnell D. Wilson H. J. C. K. Toms W. R. S. Perrott I. A. Maclachan, D.C.M.	H. C. Luetchford J. H. J. Dredge H. Hunter J. K. Gale D. K. Evans W. K. McNeill H. L. King D. A. Johnston H. J. Shuttleworth
1936	F. R. Jones, M.C., B.S.M. J. P. Learney, B.Q.M.S. B. Frith, R.A., B.S.M., Instr.	R. Crawford J. C. Hosegood E. G. Vaughton W. K. Wilton R. S. MacTier D. Wilson E. J. Phillips W. R. S. Perrott	P. D. Cork D. K. Evans H. J. C. K. Toms J. K. Gale I. A. Maclachan, D.C.M. D. A. Johnston H. J. Shuttleworth J. H. J. Dredge E. Kent P. M. Leckie	H. Hunter W. H. McNeill H. L. King L. H. G. Humfrey G. M. Coltart W. S. Hoseason J. E. C. Mitchell
1937	D. Wilson, B.S.M. J. P. Learney, B.Q.M.S. B. Frith, R.A., B.S.M., Instr.	R. Crawford J. C. Hosegood R. S. MacTier E. J. Phillips W. R. S. Perrott I. A. Maclachan, D.C.M. H. J. C. K. Toms D. A. Johnston	P. D. Cork D. K. Evans J. K. Gale E. Kent H. Hunter W. H. McNeill L. H. G. Humfrey W. S. Hoseason G. M. Coltart W. R. Dobbs	A. Kerr Smith D. C. Davey J. D. Hawley R. E. Willgress J. J. Richardson O. L. Bugge G. S. Keyzar H. C. Luetchford J. Phillip E. D. Smith

APPENDIX IV (a)

NOTES ON
VOLUNTEER OFFICERS DECORATIONS
and
VOLUNTEER LONG SERVICE MEDALS

The Volunteer Officers Decoration was instituted in July 1892 for the purpose of rewarding "efficient and capable" officers of the Volunteer Force in Great Britain who had served for twenty years. Two years later (1894) a similar distinction was introduced for officers of Volunteer Forces in India and the Colonies, but in the case of India the qualifying service was reduced to eighteen years. The reward entitled the receipients to use the letters "V.D." after their names. It was awarded, in the Colonies up to 1899, in Great Britain up to 1908 when the Volunteer Forces were disbanded and succeeded by the Territorial Forces, and in India up to 1930.

The Decoration is a badge consisting of an oval oak wreath in silver tied in gold, and having in the centre the Royal or Imperial Cypher surmounted by a Royal Crown, both in gold. It is suspended by a silver ring from a green ribbon 1½ inches wide and has a silver bar brooch with oak leaves on top.

The Volunteer Long Service Medal. This Medal was instituted in 1894 for non-commissioned officers and men of the Volunteer Forces of Great Britain who had completed twenty years meritorious service. In 1896 it was extended to the Indian and Colonial Forces, eighteen years service being the qualification in India, where it was awarded up to 1930. The obverse bore the effigy of the reigning Sovereign with the words "et Imperatrix", or "et Imperator" added to the legend for India and the Colonies, and the reverse bore laurel branches and intertwined scrolls bearing the words "For Long Service in the Volunteer Force".

The Colonial Auxiliary Forces Officers Decoration was established in 1899 and as from that date superceded, for Colonial Officers, the "Volunteer Officers Decoration". The conditions of award were however the same, except that service on the West Coast of Africa and subsequently service in the Great War 1914/1918 counted double. It was, in fact still is, known as the Volunteer Officers Decoration since it also conferred on the recipient the right to use the letters "V.D." after his name. It became obsolete in 1930. It was an oval badge surmounted by an Imperial crown and consisting of the Imperial Cypher "G.R.I. V" surrounded by a band bearing the words "Colonial Auxiliary Forces".

The Colonial Auxiliary Forces Long Service Medal took the place of the Volunteer Long Service Medal in 1908 on the disbandment of the Volunteers in Great Britain and was of the same obverse design as the old "Volunteer" Medal, but with the reverse design altered to bear the words "For Long Service in the Colonial Auxiliary Forces" on a plaque and surrounded by laurel branches surmounted by an Imperial Crown. It became obsolete in 1930.

The Efficiency Decoration was provided for under Royal Warrant of the 23rd September, 1930 for grant to officers who have completed twenty years qualifying service (not necessarily continuous) in the Authorized Auxiliary Forces of the Empire (or their Reserves). It took the place of numerous separate decorations awarded up to that date, and covers the Territorial Army of Great Britain, the Colonial Auxiliary Forces, the Auxiliary Force (India) and similar forces in all other Dominions, Colonies and Territories under His Majesty's protection to which attach similar obligations for training in peace. Recipients of this Decoration are entitled to the letters "E.D." after their names. The brooch of the Decoration having inscribed on it the name of the country in which the recipient is serving at the time of the award (*e.g.* "Malaya").

The Efficiency Medal is the equivalent for N.C.O.'s and men of the Efficiency Decoration and was instituted at the same time, but is granted after twelve years service and a bar is issued for every six years thereafter. The service to be continuous, however, unless under exceptional circumstances as laid down. The word "Malaya" is inscribed on the bar mount of these medals to indicate the place in which the recipient is serving at the time of the award.

There was a seven years discussion on the conditions and titles of these "Efficiency" decorations and medals during which time no awards were made. Eventually, when the first awards were promulgated in this country in October 1937 the conditions were practically the same as those originally gazetted in 1930 without any alteration in the titles to satisfy the opinion of those who held that the award should bear some reference to the Service either Volunteer or Territorial *e.g.* "Volunteer Efficiency Medal".

APPENDIX IV (b)

List of Members of the S.V.C. & S.S.V.F. who have received Decorations & Medals for Volunteering

This List has been compiled with difficulty, there being, apparently, no complete Official List in the country, it is therefore feared that that there are many ommissions, information regarding which will be welcome also dates of award where not stated.

ORDER OF THE BRITISH EMPIRE.

Knight Commander. (K.B.E.).
    Lieut.-Colonel A.R. Adams, V.D., P. &. P.W.V.C., 1919.

Commander. (C.B.E.).
    Colonel G.A. Derrick, V.D., S.V.C., 1919.

Officers. (O.B.E.).
    Major H.R.S. Zehender, "D" (Eurasian) Coy., S.V.C., 1928.
    Lieut.-Colonel A.A. Lermit, V.D., M.V.C., 1929.
    Lieut.-Colonel J.J. Saunders, V.D., P. & P.W.V.C., 1929.
    Major A. Gordon Lee, M.C., S.V.C., S.R.A. (V), 1930.
    Captain E. Newbold, P. & P.W.V.C., 1933.
    Major D.G. MacLeod, "C" (Scottish) Coy., S.V.C., 1933.
    Lieut.-Colonel G.C. Meredith, M.C., 1st Batt., S.V.C., 1934.
    Lieut.-Colonel G.A. Potts, M.C., 1st Batt., S.V.C., 1937.
    Major C.G. Burt, S.R.E. (V), S.V.C., 1937.

Members. (M.B.E.).
    B.S.M. T.O. Mayhew, S.R.A. (V), S.V.C., 1930.
    Lieutenant Syed Salleh Alsagoff, P. & P.W.V.C., 1931.
    Captain R.M. Richards, P. & P.W.V.C.
    Captain Koh Keng Bock, M.V.C., 1931.
    Lieut. A.J. Minjoot, M.V.C., 1934.
    C.S.M. (Instructor) T.A. Cusack, The Lancashire Fusiliers, M.V.C., 1934.
    Captain Abu Bakar bin Haji Arshad, "F" (Malay) Coy., S.V.C., 1935.
    R.S.M. (Instructor) H. Farrow, The Middlesex Regt., P. & P.W.V.C., 1935.
    C.S.M. J.R. Danson, D.C.M., P. & P.W.V.C., 1936.
    Captain Md. Ali bin Maidin, M.V.C., 1936.
    Captain Tan Seng Tee, M.V.C., 1936.
    Captain D. Colville, K.S.L.I., Adjutant, M.V.C., 1937.

Medal of the Order.
    C.Q.M.S. H.A.L. Orchard, "A" Coy., S.V.C., 1937.

COLONIAL AUXILIARY FORCES OFFICERS DECORATION (V.D.).
    The Hon. Major A. Murray, S.V.A., S.V.C.
    Colonel G.A. Derrick, S.V.C.
    Lt.-Col. A.R. Adams, P. & P.W.V.C.
    Lt.-Col. J.A.R. Glennie, S.V.C.
    Major W.R.C. Middleton, S.F.V.A. Coy., S.V.C.
    Major A.M. Thompson, S.V.C.
    Lt.-Col. A.A. Lermit, M.V.C., 1923.
    Lt.-Col. J.J. Saunders, P. & P.W.V.C., 1930.
    Captain J.S. Dawbarn, P. & P.W.V.C., 1930.
    Major T.C. Hay, S.V.C.
    Major E.A. Brown, S.V.C., 1922.
    Lieut. H.R.S. Law, S.V.C., 1933.
    Lieut. G. Ambler, M.C., S.V.C., 1930.
    Captain Song Ong Siang, "E" (Chinese) Coy., S.V.C.

EFFICIENCY DECORATION (E.D.).
    Lt.-Col. L.H. Chidson, M.B.E., S.V.C., 1937.
    Lt.-Col. A. Chamier, O.B.E., S.V.C., 1937.
    Lt.-Col. G.D.A. Fletcher, M.C., P. & P.W.V.C., 1937.

COLONIAL AUXILIARY FORCES LONG SERVICE MEDAL.
    Ager, A.P., Private, S.V.C.
    Abu Bakar bin H. Arshad, Lieutenant, "F" (Malay) Coy., S.V.C., 1931.
    Abdul Aziz bin Masood, Lieutenant, "F" (Malay) Coy., S.V.C., 1931.
    Brown, E.A., Second-Lieut. (a/Major), S.V.C., 1922.
    Baugh, C., Private, S.V.C., 1923.
    Biggs, L.A.C., Private, P. & P.W.V.C.
    Burt, C.G., Captain, S.R.E. (V), S.V.C., 1928.
    Buchannan, A., Private (M.M.), S.V.C., 1930.
    Coveney, A.E.G., Lieutenant & Quartermaster, S.V.C.
    Craik, D. McLeod, Private, P. & P.W.V.C.
    Chan Tiang Seng, Private, "E" (Chinese) Coy., S.V.C., 1923.
    Chater, R.W., C.Q.M.S., S.R.E. (V), S.V.C.
    Cheong Chin Heng, Private "E" (Chinese) Coy., S.V.C., 1927.
    Curran-Sharp, W.J., Second-Lieutenant, 1929.
    Dawbarn, J.S., Captain, P. & P.W.V.C., 1929.
    Danson, J.R., C.S.M. (D.C.M.), P. & P.W.V.C., 1920.
    Dandie, H., Private, S.V.C., 1931.
    De Silva, R.E., Sergeant, "D" (Eurasian) Coy., S.V.C.
    De Buriatte, E.A., Captain, P. & P.W.V.C., 1929.
    Eusof bin Hussain Jewa, Lieut., "F" (Malay) Coy., S.V.C., 1931.
    Fitt, J.F., R.Q.M.S., S.V.C.
    Fulcher, E.W.P., Lieutenant, S.V.C., 1928.
    Gilmour, H., Sergeant, S.R.A. (V), S.V.C., 1923.
    Gallistan, E., Sergeant, "D" (Eurasian) Coy., S.V.C., 1926.
    Gan Hock Chuan, Second-Lieutenant, 1929.
    Grant, J.S., Corporal, P. & P.W.V.C., 1928.

COLONIAL AUXILIARY FORCES LONG SERVICE MEDAL—*continued.*

Hamilton, W., Private, P. & P.W.V.C., 1922.
Hay, T.C., Captain, S.V.C.
Holley, W.H., Private, S.V.C., 1929.
Hodgins, J.F., Private, S.V.C., 1929.
Haji Abas bin Omar, Lieutenant, "F" (Malay) Coy., S.V.C., 1931.
Johnson, E.E., Private, "B" Coy., S.V.C., 1923.
Livingstone, A., Corporal, M.V.R., M.V.C.
Lesslar, T.S., R.Q.M.S., P. & P.W.V.C., 1922.
Lobb, H.R.W., Private, S.V.C., 1927 (late C.S.M., S.V.A. (M.)).
Lim Liang Quee, Private, "E" (Chinese) Coy., S.V.C., 1927.
Lewis, the Hon. Gunner D.T., S.R.A. (V), S.V.C. (late Major, S.V.A.), 1929.
Lee Kiah Wah, C.Q.M.S., "E" (Chinese) Coy., S.V.C.
Mayhew, T.O., Second-Lieutenant, S.V.A., S.V.C., 1917.
Makepeace, W., Captain & Hon. Major, S.V.A., 1913.
McLeod, K.M., Private, P. & P.W.V.C., 1930.
Myles, G.S., Corporal, S.V.C.
Marsh, F.E., Sapper, S.R.E. (V), S.V.C.
Morrell, F.A., Captain, S.V.C.
Mayger, F.J.L., Second-Lieut., (M.C.), "C" (Scottish) Coy., S.V.C., 1930.
Mohamed bin Dol, Sergeant, "F" (Malay) Coy., S.V.C., 1931.
Mukhtar bin H. Hassan, L/Sergeant, "F" (Malay) Coy., S.V.C., 1931.
Moncrieff, R.L., B.Q.M.S., S.R.A. (V), S.V.C., 1931.
Ogle, J.W.B., C.S.M., P. & P.W.V.C., 1921.
Parsons, A.E., Private, S.V.C. Auxiliary, 1936.
Perrott, R.T., L/Corporal, M.V.C., 1932.
Pennefather, R.H., L/Sergeant, "D" (Eurasian) Coy., S.V.C., 1929.
Pennefather, F.J., Bandmaster, S.V.C.
Reutens, J.S., Sergeant, P. & P.W.V.C., 1927.
Ruchwaldy, F., Private, S.V.C., 1927.
Robinson, F.H., Captain, S.R.E. (V), S.V.C., 1930.
Ramat b. Abass, C.M.S., "F" (Malay) Coy., S.V.C., 1931.
Smith, E.E.J., Private, S.V.C.
Song Ong Siang, Captain, "E" (Chinese) Coy., S.V.C., 1923.
Southam, G.B.F., Colour-Sergeant, P. & P.W.V.C., 1919.
Slight, E.W., C.Q.M.S., S.V.C., 1927.
Shaik Ali b. Md. Banamah, C.Q.M.S., "F" (Malay) Coy., S.V.C., 1931.
Shafe, A.G., Captain, R. of O., S.S.V.F. (late S.R.A. (V)), S.V.C., 1931.
Stanley, F., Private, P. & P.W.V.C., 1929.
Samy, S.B., Private, M.V.C. Auxiliary, 1931.
Savage, P.G., Private, M.V.C.
Tan Soo Bin, Captain, "E" (Chinese) Coy., S.V.C., 1927.
Teow Keong Hee, Second-Lieutenant, "E" (Chinese) Coy., S.V.C., 1922.
Tan Piah Eng, C.Q.M.S., "E" (Chinese) Coy., S.V.C., 1922.
Tan Chow Kim, Lieutenant, "E" (Chinese) Coy., S.V.C., 1922.
Tyte, J.H., Private, M.V.R., M.V.C.
Taylor, J., B.Q.M.S., S.R.A. (V), S.V.C.

COLONIAL AUXILIARY FORCES LONG SERVICE MEDAL—*continued.*

Tan Teck Yee, Sergeant, M.V.C.
Teale, F.A., Sergeant, S.V.C., 1927.
Terrell, A.K.aB., Lieutenant, P. & P.W.V.C., 1928.
Wemyss, L.H., Sergeant, P. & P.W.V.C., 1920.
Webb, G.R.H., Major, S.R.E. (V), S.V.C.
Ward, W.H., Sergeant, P. & P.W.V.C., 1919.
Williams, E.S., Sapper, S.R.E. (V), S.V.C.
Webb, C., C.S.M., S.R.E. (V), S.V.C.
Winsley, T.M., Captain, S.R.A. (V), S.V.C., 1931.
Woodfall, H.A.J., Captain, "B" Coy., S.V.C., 1936.

EFFICIENCY MEDALS (1930–1937).

Albuquerque, C.B., Sergt., S.V.C.	Medal & Clasp
Abdullah bin Awang, A/Cpl., S.V.C.	
Abdullah bin Bachik, A/Cpl., S.V.C.	
Abdul Hamid bin Ismail, L/Sergt., S.V.C.	
Abdul Kadir bin Depong, Lieut., S.V.C.	
Abdul Aziz bin Slyman, Private, P. & P.W.V.C.	
Abdul Rahim bin Abass, Sergt., P. & P.W.V.C.	
Abubakar bin H. Musa, C.S.M., P. & P.W.V.C.	Medal & 2 Clasps
Ahmad bin Din, L/Cpl., P. & P.W.V.C.	
Ahmad bin Haji Ismail, L/Cpl., P. & P.W.V.C.	
Abu Bakar bin Ali, L/Sergt., M.V.C.	
Abdul Rahim bin Karim, L/Cpl., S.V.C.	
Ahmad bin Ariff Patail, L/Cpl., S.V.C.	
Baile, C.J., C.S.M., S.V.C.	
Brett, H.C., C.Q.M.S., S.V.C.	Medal & Clasp
Brodie, W.F., Private, S.V.C.	
Bahari bin H. Ismail, Sergt., S.V.C.	Medal & 2 Clasps
Boyle, J.W., Lieut., P. & P.W.V.C.	Medal & Clasp
Beng Eng Lim, Sergt., M.V.C.	
Bowerman, E.H.R., C.S.M., S.V.C.	
Collinge, C.E., Captain, S.V.C.	
Crawford, R., Sergt., S.V.C.	
Chan Teng Toon, Aux., S.V.C.	Medal & Clasp
Cheng Kang Nghee, A/R.S.M., S.V.C.	Medal & 2 Clasps
Che Ahmad bin Mohd. Taib, L/Sergt., P. & P.W.V.C.	
Chembee bin Sekandar, L/Cpl., P. & P.W.V.C.	Medal & Clasp
Chemat bin H. Merican, L/Cpl., P. & P.W.V.C.	Medal & Clasp
Che Ibrahim bin Che Mat, Cpl., P. & P.W.V.C.	
Chan Cheng Kiat, C.S.M., M.V.C.	
Corkill, W.A., Private, S.V.C.	
Danson, J.R., C.S.M. (M.B.E., D.C.M.), P. & P.W.V.C.	
Del Tufo, M.V., Gnr., S.V.C.	

EFFICIENCY MEDALS (1930–1937)—*continued.*

Foe, W.E. de, Private, S.V.C.	
Gardiner, W.R., Sergt., S.V.C.	
Geddes, L.W., Cpl., S.V.C.	
Galistan, I., Private, S.V.C.	
Galistan, J.M., Aux., S.V.C.	
Galistan, J.F., L/Sergt., S.V.C.	Medal & Clasp
Ganno, E.T., Sergt., S.V.C.	
Gomes, A.K., L/Cpl., S.V.C.	
Grosse, F.M., Lieut., S.V.C.	
Hanson, E.H., L/Sergt., S.V.C.	Medal & Clasp
Henderson, A.S., L/Sergt., S.V.C.	
Hogan, N.S., Private, S.V.C.	
Ho Kim Toon, Private, M.V.C.	
Kraal, G.H., Sergt., S.V.C.	
Kellar, G.H.A., Cpl., S.V.C.	Medal & Clasp
Kirwan, H.S., Aux., S.V.C.	Medal & Clasp
Karim bin Mat Latim, Private, P. & P.W.V.C.	
Kruseman, W.M., Sergt., M.V.C.	
Lazaroo, F., Private, S.V.C.	
Lazaroo, R.A., Private, S.V.C.	
Leicester, N., Private, S.V.C.	
Lee Kiah Thong, Sergt., S.V.C.	
Leong Wah Cheong, Aux., S.V.C.	
Lim Hock Siang, Aux., S.V.C.	Medal & Clasp
Lye Nam Hong, C.S.M., S.V.C.	Medal & Clasp
Lim Ah Liat, C.Q.M.S., P. & P.W.V.C.	Medal & Clasp
Leman bin Mamat, C.S.M., M.V.C.	
Maclachlan, I.A., Sergt. (D.C.M.), S.V.C.	Medal & Clasp
Mc Morine, J.B., R.Q.M.S., S.V.C.	Medal & Clasp
Meyer, C.W., Private, S.V.C.	
Mitchell, A., Private, S.V.C.	
Modder, N.F., Private, S.V.C.	
Moore, B.C.W., Aux., S.V.C.	
Mohamed bin Tahir, C.Q.M.S., S.V.C.	Medal & 2 Clasps
Mohamed Yusoff b. Isnin, Private, S.V.C.	
Monteiro, A.C., L/Cpl., S.V.C.	
Monteiro, H.T., Private, S.V.C.	Medal & Clasp
Meah bin Walisah, Cpl., P. & P.W.V.C.	
Mohd. Ismail bin Man, C.Q.M.S., P. & P.W.V.C.	
Mohd. bin Husin Meah, Cpl., P. & P.W.V.C.	Medal & Clasp
Mydin bin Babu, Private, P. & P.W.V.C.	Medal & Clasp
Mohd. Zain bin Haji Mohd. Saman, Sergt., P. & P.W.V.C.	

EFFICIENCY MEDALS (1930–1937)—*continued.*

Nairn, J., C.Q.M.S., S.V.C.	
Naidu Krishnasamy, Aux., S.V.C.	
Neijenhoff, J.V., Private, S.V.C.	
Nyak Puteh bin Tunku Bintang, C.Q.M.S., P. & P.W.V.C.	Medal & Clasp
Orchard, H.A.L., C.Q.M.S. (M.B.E.), S.V.C.	Medal & Clasp
Ong Seng Wee, A/C.Q.M.S., S.V.C.	Medal & Clasp
Orchard, V.A., Private, S.V.C.	
Oliveiro, A.M., C.Q.M.S., P. & P.W.V.C.	Medal & Clasp
Ong Him Tean, Sergt., P. & P.W.V.C.	
Pereira, A., Sergt., S.V.C.	
Perreau, W., Aux., S.V.C.	
Perry, G.C.F., Private, S.V.C.	
Pestana, J.L., Private, S.V.C.	
Philip, J., Gnr., S.V.C.	
Prins, T.W., Sergt., S.V.C.	
Pearson, A.M., Sig., S.V.C.	
Pawan, B., Second-Lieut., P. & P.W.V.C.	
Pennathamby Uthariasamy Peter, Cpl., P. & P.W.V.C.	
Quek Kim Kiat, Cpl., S.V.C.	
Raja Jaffar, Sergt., S.V.C.	Medal & 2 Clasps
Rodrigues, C.M., L/Sergt., S.V.C.	Medal & Clasp
Rodrigues, J., L/Cpl., S.V.C.	
Rozario, L.L.L. de, Cpl., S.V.C.	
Salleh bin H. Asghar, L/Cpl., S.V.C.	
Silva, E.F. de, Private, S.V.C.	
Souza, C.A. de, Private, S.V.C.	
Stewart, E.C., Sergt., S.V.C.	Medal & Clasp
Stewart, S., C.S.M., S.V.C.	Medal & Clasp
Stuart, E., Cpl., S.V.C.	Medal & Clasp
Syed Mohd. bin A. Kadir, L/Cpl., S.V.C.	
Swithinbank, W., L/Sergt., S.V.C.	
Soakara Shunmugam, Sergt., P. & P.W.V.C.	
Stewart, F.W., Sergt., P. & P.W.V.C.	
Stevenson, A.D., C/Sergt., M.V.C.	
Santa Maria, W., Private, M.V.C.	
Tamby bin Kassim, Cpl., S.V.C.	Medal & Clasp
Tamby b. Mohamed Salleh, Sergt., S.V.C.	
Tan Beng Chin, Aux., S.V.C.	
Tan Mong Heng, Second-Lieut., S.V.C.	
Tan Ah Ling, Cpl., S.V.C.	
Tham, J.P., Sergt., S.V.C.	
Tuxford, I.R.B., L/Cpl., S.V.C.	
Theseira, C.E., C.S.M., P. & P.W.V.C.	
Tan Cheng Chye, Lieut., A/Captain, M.V.C.	

IV (b)   APPENDICES   179

EFFICIENCY MEDALS (1930–1937)—*continued.*

    Ung Guan Hoe, Sergt., P. & P.W.V.C.
    Vincent, S.J., Sergt., S.V.C. .. .. .. Medal & Clasp
    Watt, G.A., Lieut., S.V.C.
    Whitham, E., Private, S.V.C. .. .. .. Medal & Clasp
    Williams, E.S., Spr., S.V.C.
    Wilson, D., B.S.M., S.V.C.
    Wyllie, H.M., Private, S.V.C.
    Wembeck, J.G., C.Q.M.S., P. & P.W.V.C.
    Watts, H.R., Sergt., P. & P.W.V.C.

MEDALS COMMEMORATING THE SILVER JUBILEE
of
THEIR MAJESTIES KING GEORGE V & QUEEN MARY
1935

    Major E.J. Nettlefold, S.O.L.F., Malaya.
    Comdr. L.A.E. Johnson, M.V.O., R.N., S.S.R.N.V.R. (Retired).
    Acting Sub-Lieut. O.H. Eustace, S.S.R.N.V.R.
    Acting Leading Signalman Ahmat bin Bujang, S.S.R.N.V.R.
    Lt.-Col. R.H.L. Fink, O.B.E., M.C., Commandant, S.S.V.F.

    Lt.-Col. G.A. Potts, M.C., S.V.C.
    Lt.-Col. L.H. Chidson, M.B.E., S.V.C.
    Major A. Chamier, O.B.E., S.V.C.
    Major B.E. Ablitt, M.C., S.V.C.
    Major F.H. Robinson, S.V.C.
    Major C.C.B. Gilmour, S.V.C.
    Major J. Lee, S.V.C.
    Major Wong Siew Yuen, S.V.C.
    Captain A.P. Goldman, S.V.C.
    Captain R. MacDonald, M.C., S.V.C.
    Captain W. Rose, S.V.C.
    Captain W.A. Aeria, S.V.C.
    Lieut. and Quartermaster J.G.H. Grey, S.V.C.
    R.Q.M.S. E.W. Slight, S.V.C.
    Captain C.E. Collinge, S.V.C.
    Captain H.A.J. Woodfall, S.V.C.
    Lieut. (A/Captain) R.H. Pennefather, S.V.C.
    Lieut. R.C. Stewart, S.V.C.

Lieut. S.F. Ho, S.V.C.
Lieut. Rahmat bin Abass, S.V.C.
C.S.M. C. Constable, S.V.C.
B.Q.M.S. J.P. Learney, S.V.C.
C.S.M. E.H.R. Bowermen, S.V.C.
C.S.M. Cheng Kang Nghee, S.V.C.
C.S.M. G.S. Miller, S.V.C.
C.S.M. S. Stewart, S.V.C.
C.Q.M.S. Mohd. bin Tahir, S.V.C.
C.S.M. R.F.W. Leonard, S.V.C.

Lt.-Col. G.D.A. Fletcher, M.C., P. & P.W.V.C.
Major H.W. Esson, M.C., P. & P.W.V.C.
Major E.A. de Buriatte, P. & P.W.V.C.
Captain P.T. Hutchings, P. & P.W.V.C.
Captain A.C. Trotter, P. & P.W.V.C.
Lieut. (A/Captain) G.W. Somerville, P. & P.W.V.C.
Lieut. (A/Captain) S. Mortimer, P. & P.W.V.C.
Lieut. (A/Captain) Mohamed Noor, P. & P.W.V.C.
Lieut. (A/Captain) A.T. Dougal, P. & P.W.V.C.
Lieut. S. Toolseram, P. & P.W.V.C.
C.S.M. Abu Baker, P. P.W.V.C.
Sergeant Ooi Chook Teik, P. & P.W.V.C.
Lieut. E.A. Fisher, P. P.W.V.C.

Lt.-Col. A.A. Lermit, O.B.E., V.D., M.V.C.
Major G.R. Percy, M.C., M.V.C.
Captain Tan Seng Tee, M.V.C.
Captain W.J. Curran-Sharp, M.V.C.
Captain A.M. Drysdale, M.V.C.
Lieut. (A/Captain) E.V. Rodrigues, M.V.C.
R.S.M. T.G. Peddie, M.V.C.
Sergeant A.D. Stevenson, M.V.C.
Sergeant Leman bin Mamat, M.V.C.

Medals Commemorating the Coronation
of
Their Majesties King George VI & Queen Elizabeth
1937

Major J.D. Wyatt, M.C., S.O.L.F., Malaya.

Comdr. L.A.W. Johnson, M.V.O., S.S.R.N.V.R.
Lieut. W.I.L. Legg, S.S.R.N.V.R.
Lieut. G.C. Ashworth, S.S.R.N.V.R.
Master-at-Arms Adnan bin Raji, S.S.R.N.V.R.
Petty Officer Mohamed bin Haji Yunos, S.S.R.N.V.R.

Lieut.-Col. V.G. Stokes, M.C., S.S.V.F.
Lieut.-Col. L.H. Chidson, M.B.E., S.S.V.F.

Major R.B. Henly, S.V.C.
Lieut. H.J. Rae, S.V.C.
Battery-Sergeant-Major D. Wilson, S.V.C.
Sergeant R. Crawford, S.V.C.
Major C.G. Burt, O.B.E., S.V.C.
Captain R. Caunce, S.V.C.
Sergeant J.B. Best, S.V.C.
A/Major F. Bedford, S.V.C.
Captain R.E. Earle, S.V.C.
Sergeant Beppo Wahid, S.V.C.
Lieut.-Col. A. Chamier, O.B.E., S.V.C.
Major W. Rose, S.V.C.
Major A.P. Goldman, S.V.C.
Captain J.F.A. Swallow, S.V.C.
Captain A.F. Cornelius, S.V.C.
Lieutenant L.V. Taylor, S.V.C.
R.Q.M.S. J. Broadbent, S.V.C.
C.Q.M.S. J. Nairn, S.V.C.
Lieut.-Col. D.G. MacLeod, O.B.E., S.V.C.
Major W. Penrice, S.V.C.
Captain N.E.B. Graburn, S.V.C.
Captain Wee Kah Kiat, S.V.C.
A/R.S.M. Cheng Kang Nghee, S.V.C.
C.S.M. C. Pennefather, S.V.C.
C.S.M. Hamid bin Omar, S.V.C.
Captain A.L.B. Swaine, S.V.C.
Captain C.E. Collinge, S.V.C.
Lance-Sergeant E.H. Hanson, S.V.C.
Captain E.G. Holiday, S.V.C.
Major W.E. Hutchison, S.V.C.
C.S.M. Lye Nam Hong, S.V.C.
Captain J.E.A. Clark, P. & P.W.V.C.

Captain J.A. McEvoy, P. & P.W.V.C.
Captain S. Toolseram, P. & P.W.V.C.
Lieutenant (A/Captain) Leong Sin Kwee, P. & P.W.V.C.
Lieutenant Mohamed Noor bin Mohamed, P. & P.W.V.C.
C.S.M. S.M. Hussain, P. & P.W.V.C.
C.S.M. Lim Teik Hock, P. & P.W.V.C.
C.Q.M.S. A.M. Oliveiro, P. & P.W.V.C.
Sergeant A. Shipwright, P. & P.W.V.C.
Sergeant Jamaludin bin M. Hassan, P. & P.W.V.C.
Sergeant S. Shunmugam, P. & P.W.V.C.
Major W.J. Curran-Sharp, M.V.C.
A/Major A.M. Drysdale, M.V.C.
Captain Mohamed Ali bin Maidin, M.B.E., M.V.C.
Captain R. Watson-Hyatt, M.V.C.
Captain E.V. Rodrigues, M.V.C.
A/Captain Tan Cheng Chye, M.V.C.
Lieutenant A.W. Frisby, M.V.C.
A/Captain Abbas bin Mohamed Saaid, M.V.C.
Second-Lieutenant C.E.R. Darby, M.V.C.
Squadron-Leader D.S.E. Vines, S.S.V.A.F.

Mentions in Despatches
for
Valuable Service in Malaya during the War

The following names were brought to the notice of the Secretary of State for War and the Army Council for valuable services rendered in connection with the war (*Straits Settlements Government Gazette* Notification No. 907, July 26th, 1918):—

x. Adams, Lieut.-Colonel A.R., K.B.E., V.D., Commandant, P.V.C.
Blair, Captain F.Y., S.V.A.
Brown, Captain E.A., Chinese Coy., S.V.I.
Campbell, Captain J.G., S.V.A.
Darbishire, Major C.W., S.V.R. (attached from 1/6 R.W.F.).
x. Derrick, Lieut.-Colonel G.A., C.B.E., V.D., Commandant, S.V.C.
Dilley, Lieutenant F.E., S.V.A.
Elliot, Major F.M., O.B.E., Reserve of Officers, S.V.C.
Ellis, Major Sir E.C., Kt., Retired List, S.V.C.
Glennie, Major J.A.R., Second-in-Command, S.V.C.
Hay, Captain T.C., Malay Coy., S.V.I.
Le Masurier, Captain J., S.R.E. (V).
x. Lewis, Major D.T., S.V.A.
Middleton, Major W.R.C., S.F.A., Coy.
x. Smith, Captain S., Adjutant, M.S.V.R.

Temperley, Lieutenant, F.H., S.V.A.
x. Thompson, Major A.M., S.R.E. (V).
x. Tyte, Lieut.-Colonel J.H., Assistant Commandant, M.S.V.R.
Webb, Captain G.R.H., S.R.E. (V).
David, Private P.A.F., Veterans' Coy., S.V.C.
Hutchison, Private G., Veterans' Coy., S.V.C.
Pierrepont, Sapper J.D., S.R.E. (V).

In addition to those marked with an x. above, whose names were again brought to notice for further valuable services rendered in the Local Forces during the war, the following names were also mentioned:—

SINGAPORE VOLUNTEER CORPS.

Adams, Lieutenant J.W., S.F.A. Coy.
Addie, Lieutenant R.J., Veterans' Coy., S.V.C.
Bartley, Captain W., Malay Coy., S.V.I.
Black, Major N., M.C., S.F.A. Coy..
Clarke, Lieutenant F.S., Eurasian Coy., S.V.C.
Elder, Captain E.A., S.F.A. Coy.
Everitt, Captain C., Veterans' Coy., S.V.C.
Hashim, Captain N.M., Malay Coy., S.V.I.
Hunter, Captain P.S., S.F.A. Coy.
Mayson, Lieutenant W.J., Veterans' Coy., S.V.C.
Murdoch, Lieutenant W., S.V.A.
Song Ong Siang, Captain, Chinese Coy., S.V.I.
Tan Soo Bin, Lieutenant, Chinese Coy., S.V.I.
Tongue, Captain H., Maxim Coy., S.V.C.
Wace, Captain G.G., 1/4th K.S.L.I., Adjutant, S.V.C.
Abubakar bin Hadji Airshad, Serjt., Malay Coy., S.V.I.
Barrett, Sergeant-Major J.G., S.V.C.
Branson, C.Q.M.S., G.W., S.F.A. Coy.
Chater, C.S.M., R.W., S.R.E. (V).
Finlay, Gunner J., S.V.A.
Lewis, Corporal P.R., Motor-cyclist Scouts Section, S.V.R.
Lim Liang Quee, C.S.M., Chinese Coy., S.V.I.
Lobb, C.S.M., H.R.W., Maxim Coy., S..VC.
McDougall, 2nd Corporal A.G., S.R.E. (V).
McMillan, Sergeant K., S.V.A.
Noon, C.S.M., H.W., Veterans' Coy., S.V.C.
Orchard, Sergeant H.A., Veterans' Coy., S.V.C.
Peh Wah Kok, Chief Clerk, S.V.C. Headquarters.
Stuart, Sergeant E., Signalling Section, S.V.R.
Todd, C.S.M., A.H., S.V.R.
Wodehouse, Private R.L.D., S.V.R.

PENANG VOLUNTEERS.

Brown, Captain D.A.M., "D" Coy.
Cheeseman, Lieutenant H.A.R., "D" Coy.

Goatly, Captain C.R.A., "A" Coy.
Hamilton, Captain W., late Adjutant.
Hogan, Captain C.D.D., "A" Coy.
Muir, Lieutenant H., Quartermaster.
Rose, Captain J.S., late Adjutant.
Sellar, Major J., Second-in-Command.
Thorne, Lieutenant W.H., Maxim Coy.
Alsagoff, Pte. Syed Salleh, "C" Coy.
Evens, Sergeant L.S., Maxim Coy.
Fitzgerald, Coy.-Sergt.-Major C.B., "A" Coy.
Lim Ah Lin, Private, "D" Coy.
Murray, Bn.Q.M.S., A.E.T.
Syer, Sergeant F.N., Maxim Coy.
Ward, Sergeant W.A., "B" Coy.
Webb, Reg. Sergeant-Major.
Williams, Sergeant T.J., "B" Coy.
Yap Swee Lin, C.S.M., "D" Coy.

MALACCA VOLUNTEER RIFLES.

Campbell, Captain J.W., Chinese Coy.
Courtney, Second-Lieutenant J., Malay Coy.
Graham, Captain E.N., Field Ambulance Coy.
Rippon, Second-Lieut. F.W., European Coy.
Sime, Major W.M., Commanding Officer.
Sinclair, Second-Lieut. J., European Coy.
Tan Soo Hock, Second-Lieut., Chinese Coy.
Butler, Sergeant E.D., European Coy.
Cunningham, Private C.E., European Coy.
Ee Toon Lim, C.S.M., Chinese Coy.
Mohammed Noor bin Bachi, C.S.M., Malay Coy.
Nunn, Private B., European Coy.
Sharp, Corporal F.H., Ambulance Coy.
Sharp, Sergeant J.M.C., European Coy.
Tan Seng Tee, Sergeant, Ambulance Coy.

PROVINCE WELLESLEY VOLUNTEER RIFLES.

Duncan, Captain W., Commanding Officer.
Richards, Lieutenant R.M., Adjutant.
Mallett, C.S.M., N.W.
McLeod, Sergeant K.M., Platoon 1.
Rickeard, Sergeant H.W., Platoon 3.

MALAY STATES VOLUNTEER RIFLES.

Armstrong, Second-Lieutenant H.W., "A" Coy.
Evans, Second-Lieutenant F.D., "A" Coy.
Fisher, Lieutenant N., "B" Coy.
Fox, Lieut.-Colonel A.J., Commandant.
Harris, Lieutenant H.G., "D" Coy.
Kindersley, Captain R.C.M., "A" Coy.

Mathews, Lieutenant J.C.M., "A" Coy.
Reeve-Tucker, Captain W.S., "B" Coy.
Robbins, Second-Lieutenant H., attached "C" Coy.
Shelley, Captain M.B., "C" Coy.
Swettenham, Major J.P., "E" Coy.
Thomson, Second-Lieutenant R., "B" Coy.
Tobutt, Lieutenant H.K.C., "C" Coy.
Topham, Lieutenant D.F., "A" Coy.
Atkinson, Sergeant C.B., "B" Coy.
Barnard, Private B.F.H., "D" Coy.
Bell, Private Carlyle, "B" Coy.
Bidnell, C.Q.M.S., A.F., "D" Coy.
Braddon, Private A., "E" Coy.
Braddon, Lance-Corporal W.L., "E" Coy.
Chapman, C.S.M., C.L., "B" Coy.
Clodd, Private H.P., "A" Coy.
Coales, C.S.M., F.G., "D" Coy.
Duff, C.Q.M.S., R.M., "C" Coy.
Gilman, Corporal A.P., "B" Coy.
Graham, Private H.C., "C" Coy.
Green, Private C., "A" Coy.
Holloway, Private J.M., "B" Coy.
Hose, Lance-Corporal E.S., "C" Coy.
Kenneison, Sergeant-Drummer E.J., "A" Coy.
Lathan, C.S.M., T., "A" Coy.
Latter, R.S.M., H.
Le Sueur, C.Q.M.S., "B" Coy.
Martin, Private T.A., "A" Coy.
Millner, Corporal W.A., "A" Coy.
Mustard, Sergeant A.C., "B" Coy.
Peake, Sergeant A.G., "D" Coy.
Powell, Corporal C.U.T., "D" Coy.
Quarterley, Private H.R., "B" Coy.
Talbot, Private F., "A" Coy.

MALAY STATES VOLUNTEER INFANTRY.

(a) PERAK.
His Highness the Sultan of Perak.
Chapman, Lieutenant W.T., Commanding Officer.
Worley, Second-Lieutenant N.A., Chinese Platoon.
Ng Kim Kooi, Q.M.S., Chinese Platoon.

(b) SELANGOR.
Eaton, Captain B.J., Commanding Officer.
Palmer, Lieutenant A., Tamil Platoon.
Perkins, Second-Lieutenant C.J., Malay Platoon.
Tungku Makhota, Second-Lieutenant, Malay Platoon (Bandar).
Abdul Rahman bin Abdullah, Corporal, Malay Platoon.

Barre, Sergeant A.L., Mixed Platoon.
Che' Ariff, Sergeant-Instructor, Malay Platoon (Bandar).
Lim Hock Hye, Sergeant, Chinese Platoon.
Raja Haroun bin Yahya, Sergeant (since deceased), Malay Platoon.
Rozario, Private C.W., Mixed Platoon.
Thambiah, Sergeant V., Tamil Platoon.
Thambipillay, Q.M.S., Tamil Platoon.
Teh Chock Soon, Corporal, Chinese Platoon.
Towle, Sergeant-Major Instructor W.
Tribe, Sergeant L.F., M.S.V.R., attached Malay Platoon (Bandar).

(c) PAHANG.
Jones, Second-Lieutenant H.W., late O.C., Kuantan Platoon.
Laidlaw, Second-Lieutenant G.M. (since deceased), Pekan Platoon.
Parr, Captain C.W.C., Commanding Officer.
Bakar, Corporal, Kuantan Platoon.
Che' Ungku Mohammed, C.S.M., Pekan Platoon.
Dollah, Sergeant, Pekan Platoon.
Hashim, Lance-Sergeant, Pekan Platoon.
Hashim, Lance-Sergeant Drummer, Pekan Platoon.
Mahat, Corporal, Pekan Platoon.

(d) NEGRI SEMBILAN.
Abdul Rahman, Lieutenant Tungku, Commanding Officer.
Grist, Second-Lieutenant D.H., Kuala Pilah Platoon.
Hanson, Second-Lieutenant W.H., Seremban Platoon.
Bux, Corporal S.J., Seremban Platoon.
Hussain, Corporal, Seremban Platoon.
Mahmood, Corporal, Seremban Platoon.
Syed Junid, Lance-Corporal, Seremban Platoon.

JOHORE VOLUNTEER RIFLES.
Griffiths, Captain J., Commanding Officer.
Pretty, Second-Lieutenant E.E.F.
Bodger, Sergeant W.
Bush, Sergeant-Major T.D.
Buyers, Q.M.S. A.L.

KELANTAN VOLUNTEER RIFLES.
Anderson, Captain H.A., Commanding Officer.
Graeme-Anderson, Lieutenant W., Adjutant.
Ham, Private G.L.
Johnston, Sergeant W.B.
Pepys, Sergeant W.E.

APPENDIX V

COPY OF LETTERS FROM THE GOVERNOR, STRAITS SETTLEMENTS,
SIR C. CLEMENTI SMITH,

TO LT. W.G. ST. CLAIR, S.V.A. AT RAUB VIA KLANG.

GOVERNMENT HOUSE,
SINGAPORE, 28th *June*, 1892.

Dear Mr. St. Clair,

I have just got your telegram, for which please accept my thanks.

I am very greatly obliged to you for the assistance which you are evidently giving to Colonel Walker, of whose departure for Lipis I was not aware when I telegraphed to him.

Yours most truly,

CECIL C. SMITH.

The S.V.A. is always ready at the call of duty as you have again exemplified in your own person.

C.C.S.

GOVERNMENT HOUSE,
SINGAPORE, 26th *July*, 1892.

Dear Mr. St. Clair,

I have telegraphed today to Colonel Walker—a message which you will doubtless see en route,—that I approve of your being put in charge of the Forces in the Raub District.

I have, as this will show, every confidence in you, and I know that no keener man could be found anywhere.

I thought it right to ask Mr. Shelford if there was any objection on the part of the Proprietors of the Free Press, and he replies, after referring to Mr. Freeman, that there is no objection to your giving us the benefit of your services.

The letters which I and the Sultan of Johore have received have satisfied us that the Sultan of Pahang really does intend to move down to Pekan.

I expect that he will get there about the 10th prox. The rebels will then have lost the support which they have hitherto relied upon.

Yours most truly,

CECIL C. SMITH.

APPENDIX VI

Royal Warrant – 1923
to
The Singapore Royal Artillery (Volunteer)
and
The Singapore Royal Engineers (Volunteer)

(S.S. Government Gazette No. 9 of the 9th February, 1923)

"It is hereby notified that His Majesty the King has been pleased to approve of the grant to the re-organised Artillery and Engineers units of the Straits Settlements Volunteer Force of the privilege of using the title "Royal". The titles of these units will accordingly be:—

    Singapore Royal Artillery (Volunteer).
    Singapore Royal Engineers (Volunteer).

Note.—The Engineers of the S.V.C. received their first Warrant entitling them to the use of the title "Royal" on the 29th May, 1902, but after re-organisation of the Corps as part of the S.S.V.F. it was necessary to confirm that the re-organised and reformed unit was allowed the same privilege as the old one and this was done as shown above, in the same Warrant that conferred a similar privilege on the Volunteer Artillery.

APPENDIX VII (a)

Singapore Mutiny February, 1915

Summary of Casualties

	Killed			Wounded
	Officers	Other Ranks	Total	Total
Regular Military Forces 5th L.I.	2	..		..
R.G.A.	3	2		3
A.S.C.	..	1		..
			8	3
Regular Naval Forces H.M.S. "Cadmus"	..	1		
			1	
Volunteer Forces S.V.A.	..	1		..
S.R.E. (V)	..	1		1
S.V.R.	1	6		3
S.V.M.C.	1	..		..
M.S.V.R.	1	1		1
			12	5
Johore Military Forces European	1	..		
Malay	1	2		
			4	
European Civilians	..	..	13	1
Russian Sailors	..	..	..	2
Chinese Civilians	..	..	3	..
Malay "	..	..	2	..
Total Killed	..	..	43	..
Total Wounded	..	..	..	11

A List of Casualties in the Singapore Mutiny
February, 1915

Captain P. Boyce	5th Light Infantry	Killed
Lieutenant H.S. Elliott	do.	do.
Major R.H. Galwey	Royal Garrison Artillery	do.
Captain F.V. Izard	do.	do.
Captain M.F.A. Maclean	do.	do.
Corporal J.R.V. Beagley	do.	do.
Gunner J. Barry	do.	do.
Sergeant G. Keeble	do.	Wounded
Gunner A. Hind	do.	do.
Gunner F.W. Saby	do.	do.
Sergeant E.H. Sexton	Army Service Corps	Killed
Stoker C.F. Anscombe	H.M.S. *"Cadmus"*	do.
Gunner P. Walton	Singapore Volunteer Artillery	do.
Sergeant G. Wald	Singapore Royal Engineers (V)	do.
Sapper W. Flint	do.	Wounded
Second-Lieut. J. Love Montgomerie	Singapore Volunteer Rifles	Killed
Corporal D. Mac Gilvray	do.	do.
Private F. Drysdale	do.	do.
Private J. Harper	do.	do.
Private A.J.G. Holt	do.	do.
Private G.O. Lawson	do.	do.
Private B.C. Cameron	do.	do.
Private A. Gardener	do.	Wounded
Private R.L.V. Wodehouse	do.	do.
Private J. Robertson	do.	do.
Lieut. A.F. Legge	Singapore Volunteer Medical Co.	Killed
Captain P.M. Gerrard	Malay States Volunteer Rifles	do.
Private W.H. Leigh	do.	do.
Private E.E.F. Letts	do.	Wounded
Captain H. Cullimore	Johore Military Forces	Killed
Captain Jabar	do.	do.
Corporal Salleh	do.	do.
Private Yakub bin Fali	do.	do.
Dr. E.D. Whittle	Govt. Service S.S.	do.
Mr. C.V. Dyson	do.	do.
Warder J. Clarke	do.	do.
Mr. G.B. Woollacombe	Eastern Extension Telegraph Coy.	do.
Mrs. G.B. Woollacombe		do.
Mr. L.P. Smith	do.	do.
1st Officer T.A. Flett	E.E.T. Co., Cableship "Recorder"	Wounded
Mr. J.B. Dunn	Messrs. Guthrie & Co.	Killed
Mr. E.O. Butterworth	do.	do.

VII (a) APPENDICES

Mr. D. J. Marshall	China Mutual Insurance Co.	Killed
Mr. A.R. Evans	The Borneo Company	do.
Mr. H. U'S Collins	Straits Bulletin	do.
Mr. M.F. Edwards	Messrs. Paterson, Simons & Co.	do.
Mr. F. Geddes	Messrs. Topham, Jones & Railton	do.
Two Russian Sailors	Names not known	Wounded
Hassan Kechil bin Hassan	The Straits Motor Garage	Killed
Omar bin Ahmat Kaptin	Pulo Brani	do.
Three Chinese Civilians	Names not known	do.

APPENDIX VII (b)

MUTINY OF THE 5TH LIGHT INFANTRY IN SINGAPORE
15TH FEBRUARY, 1915

Summary of Surrenders, Captures and Sentences

Date	Reported or Captured	Killed or Drowned	Still at Large	SENTENCED						
				Executed	TRANSPORTED					Prison
					Life	20Y	15Y	10Y	7Y	
			L.I. MSG							
22nd February	T 614	T 52	..	..	..	..	..	..	..	..
23rd "	..	..	..	2	..	..	..	..	..	..
27th "	+ 9	..	125	..	..	..	..	..	..	..
1st March	..	..	113	..	..	..	..	..	..	..
2nd "	..	T 56	62 +3	..	..	..	..	..	..	..
4th "	..	..	49 +2	..	..	..	..	..	..	..
8th "	+ 1	..	..	3	..	..	1	..	..	1-1Y
10th "	+16	..	28	..	..	..	..	..	..	..
11th "	+ 4	..	..	..	..	..	..	..	..	..
12/15th March	+ 7	+ 3	..	..	..	..	..	..	..	..
25th "	..	..	..	22	8	7	..	7	1	..
1st April	..	..	..	6	9	..	4	1	..	1-5Y 1-2Y 1-1Y
26th "	..	..	..	1	10	..	4	2	1	3-1M 1-3Y
17th May	..	..	..	3	14	1	7	..	..	3-2Y 1-1Y
	651	59	..	37	41	8	16	10	2	12

T = Total accounted for up to the date shown.   Total Sentenced .. 126.

Note:—The total strength of the 5th Light Infantry was 818. The figures above include many Malay States Guides under headings "Reported" and Still at Large". The figures published, however, were obviously not complete hence the discrepancy.

APPENDIX VIII

SINGAPORE FORTS

The following notes have been collected in order to give Volunteers some idea of the positions of the old, and now obsolete, Forts and Barracks of Singapore, many of which have been mentioned in this history.

Fort Canning, Singapore.—Is the hill overlooking the Cathedral and Padang, was originally (before Raffles' time) the burial place of Malay Rajahs and called Bukit Larangan (The Forbidden Hill) being supposed to be haunted by the ghosts and spirits of long forgotten Malay Sultans. It became a fort early in 1819 when Raffles built a commodious block-house there capable of mounting 8 or 10 pounders, and it is recorded that Raffles appointed Lieut. Ralfe of the Bengal Artillery as his Assistant Engineer in charge of works for this purpose. In 1822 Raffles built a small bungalow for himself on Bukit Larangan, which afterwards became the first Government House and was added to by Crawfurd. The hill was known as Government Hill until Government House was removed in 1859. After this and due to the fort extensions or "field redoubts" built by Col. Collyer (Madras Engineers) the hill was named Fort Canning after Lord Canning, Governor-General and first Viceroy of India, 1857 to 1862. In 1861 the European Artillery moved there from Pearl's Hill.

In 1867 there were nineteen guns at Fort Canning, seven 68-pounders, eight 8 inch, two 13 inch Mortars and "a few" 14-pounder carronades. The distance of these guns from the beach put them at a great disadvantage against an enemy's ships at sea and fire from this fort and Fort Fullerton would have drawn fire right upon the centre of the town, while the two small works at Mount Palmer and Mount Faber were really of very little use.

Fort Fullerton, Singapore.—Named after Mr. Robert Fullerton who arrived in Singapore in 1826 as first Governor of the incorporated Settlements of Prince of Wales Island (Penang) Singapore and Malacca. The Fort was established in 1830 "at the point of the Singapore River" but more or less on the beach level and not the present day point as much land has since been reclaimed all round it. It was then the barracks for native artillery. In 1859 it was enlarged at a cost of about $840,000 to nearly three times its original size and armed with 56 and 68-pounders and the road leading to it was called the Battery Road.

In 1867 it contained ten guns, nine 68-pounders and one 13-inch Mortar though it began to be dismantled in 1865 as it was admitted that it would draw fire on the most richly stored warehouses of the place. In 1874 the old Post Office was built on the site of Fort Fullerton as the previous one on the other side of the river was found to be too far away from the commercial part of the town which was then only served by Cavanagh Bridge. In 1890 when the Singapore Volunteer Artillery was firmly established, Major McCallum built the Drill Hall on the eastern end of the site of the then obsolete Fort Fullerton. For the benefit of the S.V.A. an emplacement was also built for a 7-inch M.L. Gun. The building of Anderson Bridge in 1910 finally wiped away the last of Fort Fullerton though many traces were found while excavating for the foundation of Fullerton Building, which, housing the present General Post Office more than covers the whole site of the old Fort.

Fort Faber, Singapore.—An earthwork situated half way up Mount Faber, overlooking Keppel Harbour, and named after Captain Faber of the Madras Engineers who arrived in Singapore in 1844. The road to this fort is a steep and narrow one leading off Kampong Bahru Road. It was never a really good fort. There were two gun emplacements half way up the hill to which the S.V.A. Mountain guns were hauled by ponies for firing practices in later years. There are also two granite emplacements at the top of the hill laid down for Mortars. The emplacements, of a very rough type, can still just be seen.

In 1867 the fort contained two 56-pounder guns and, on top of the hill, two 13-inch Mortars (which now stand in front of the Victoria Memorial Hall).

Fort Palmer, Singapore.—On a hill known as Mount Palmer situated near Teluk Ayer overlooking the Eastern Entrance to Keppel Harbour. It was named after Mr. John Palmer "The Father of the Indian Mercantile Community" who died in Calcutta in 1836 and whose mercantile connection with Singapore dated from before 1820.

In 1867 Fort Palmer had five 56-pounder guns and in the Eighteen nineties this fort possessed a, for that decade, formidable defence with four 10-inch breech loaders, one of which now lies on the ground near the remainder of the hill which was used for the second Teluk Ayer Reclamation when Fort Palmer was finally dismantled. "One Hundred Years of Singapore" tells us that an Indian contractor bought one of these 10-inch guns for $40, one of the conditions being that he had to take it away under penalty of $200. He presumably paid the fine because the gun is still there.

Fort Pasir Panjang, Singapore.—Situated on the ridge running from Labrador Villa to the point above "Lot's Wife", called Belayer Point, which is the nearest to Blakan Mati at the Western narrow entrance to the Port. Fort Pasir Panjang was built in 1892 and had six gun emplacements, two for 7-inch muzzle loaders which can be seen dismounted behind the emplacements and two for 9.2-inch R.B.L. guns, which latter can also be seen dismounted in front of the two old emplacements nearest Labrador, while the two centre emplacements contained two 6-inch R.B.L.

This fort is charmingly situated and although in the days of its first existence it was not easily accessible except by sea to the ammunition pier opposite Siloso, it can now be gained by following the continuation of the road past Labrador bungalow. It is equipped with a portcullis at the Belayer Point entrance, and an ammunition passage runs from the sea level, where the old Harbour Obelisk (Lot's Wife) used to be, up to where the Signal Station now stands.

Fort Tanjong Katong, Singapore.—Was situated at the sea end of Fort Road, Katong.

Tradition has it that its origin lay in the fears of the merchants of Singapore, who asked "What is to prevent a man-of-war coming in from the East and shelling the town?" On which the military authorities, with great guile, murmured, "We never thought of that", and built Tanjong Katong Fort on the sea-shore—most substantially—with the Colony's money. Two 8-inch Armstrong guns, come by through the accident of their passing through Singapore at the time of the Franco-Chinese war (two others were landed at Fort Serapong), were placed in position at Katong Fort as "they were no earthly use elsewhere" and orders were given that on the outbreak of war the fort was to be abandoned.

The guns being on the sea level, a high tower was erected for range finding instruments, but being built on sand it shook so that the delicate operation of determining the range was impossible; in addition the range of the guns was useless, and there was no adequate supply of ammunition for these guns which were of a calibre outside the British Artillery scheme. A landing party could have taken the fort without much effort and without serious losses. When, therefore, during practice the R.G.A. blew the chase off one of the guns, declared (and denied through the tampion was never found) to be due to failure to remove the muzzle tampion, the fort became, as it had always been called by old Singapore residents, "The Wash-out Fort". The last traces of it disappeared when the Municipality made a People's Park on the site.

BARRACKS

1. 1824. Cantonments near Stamford Road on the north bank of the river under Government Hill (Fort Canning) were removed, as the land was required for other purposes to,
2. ROCHORE but the ground here was found to be too low. Up to and during this time there was an Arsenal on PEARL'S HILL.
3. The Infantry Cantonments were then moved to SEPOY LINES (near the present General Hospital) where they continued until European regiments took the place of native troops.
4. 1858. European Artillery which arrived in Singapore this year were quartered in the old Tan Tock Seng Hospital on PEARL'S HILL.
5. 1861. The Barracks on FORT CANNING were completed and the European Artillerymen were removed there from PEARL'S HILL.
6. 1868. TANGLIN BARRACKS having been completed, were first occupied by European troops. Prior to the building of barracks, this was the site of Mr. William Willan's nutmeg plantation of 1,600 acres and included Mount Harriet which is the site of the present Officers' Mess.
7. 1886. Blakan Mati Artillery Barracks.

APPENDIX IX

COLOURS

The use of some symbol as a rallying point and an indication of position dates back to the early days of history. Originally the symbols used were primitive poles, with some distinguishing figure which could be held aloft to be plainly visible over the heads of the combatants.

In Roman times, the "standard" was a metal eagle, and the part played in battle by the standard bearers is familiar to all students of history, for, carried in the forefront, the "Standards" served as a great incentive to the "legions".

In feudal times the "lords" raised companies from their domains to fight in specific battles, and each company usually carried as its "colour" the personal emblem of its "lord". When such companies were retained in readiness for battle, and combined into regiments, the number of the colours carried was reduced to three per regiment, and later to two.

About 1751, the Union Jack became the first or King's Colour, and a flag with the regimental badge became the second or Regimental Colour. There has been little change since that date.

The Colours were carried by Regiments whenever they went into battle and many are the chronicles of heroic deeds performed in advancing the Colours and safe-guarding them. Captures or losses are special events, glorious or the reverse, written into the history of every regiment.

In the Zulu War of 1879, where battles were being fought on an extended front, it was found that without the necessary protection afforded by concentration, casualties in Colour Parties made great inroads into the strength of the Regiment. This was therefore the last war in which Regiments of the British Army carried their Colours into battle.

The "COLOURS" however have the same significance, symbolic of the corporate life and unity of a Regiment, and they are to-day given the same reverence and respect as in the days when the prowess of a Regiment centered round them more actively.

The evolution of the present day Sovereign's and Regimental Colours dates from about 1743, when the first General Order was issued on the subject. The Journal of the Society for Army Historical Research[1] gave a very comprehensive note covering the changes from 1743 to 1931, from which the following main points of interest have been extracted:—

> *Warrant, 14th September, 1743.*—Two Colours only approved for the future (Some regiments had had three or more); the first to be the Great Union, the second Colour to be the Colour of the facing of the regimnet, with the Union in the upper canton. Royal regiments and a few others had special regulations as to their Colours. The cords and tassels to be of crimson and gold mixed.

---

[1] Vol. XVI No. 53 p. 48.

Warrant, 1st July, 1751.—Size of Colours to be six feet six inches flying and six feet two inches on the pike. The pike spear and ferrule included, nine feet ten inches in length. The official name for the first Colour to be the "Sovereign's" or "King's Colour".

Warrant, 17th December, 1768.—Gives the size as six feet six inches flying and six feet deep on the pike.

Horse Guards Circular, 5th December, 1800.—The Great Union Flag to have the St. Patrick's Cross on it by 1st January, 1801, also the shamrock in the wreath.

Horse Guards Letter, 2nd June, 1806.—The Inspector of Regimental Colours (at Heralds College) first appointed.

War Office Letter, 27th July, 1813.—Ordering appointment of one Sergeant in each company of infantry as Colour-Sergeant. Such Sergeant to wear an "honourable badge" and "to attend the Colours in the field".

1815.—Painted Colours as opposed to embroidered ones were rarely "given out" to regiments after Waterloo 1815.

King's Regulations, 1st June, 1837.—States "No regiment is henceforth to display a Third Stand of Colours. No alteration permitted without the King's approval".

Queen's Regulations, 1st July, 1844.—Introduces the Imperial Crown on both Colours and directs that the 1st, Queen's or Sovereign's Colour is only to bear in the centre the Imperial Crown with the number of the regiment underneath in gold roman characters.

Horse Guards Order, 6th November, 1855.—Reduced the size to six feet flying and five feet six inches on the pike, the larger size being "cumbrous and difficult of carriage".

Horse Guard's Letter, 11th May, 1858.—Again reduced the size to four feet by three feet six inches with the Crest of England (the Lion and Crown) on the pike in place of the spear-head.

Queen's Regulations, 1st December, 1859.—Gives the size as above, "Exclusive of the fringe (2 inches)".

Queen's Regulations 1st January, 1868.—Reduces the size to that of the present day "three feet nine inches flying and three feet deep on the pike, exclusive of the fringe which is about two inches in depth, the length of the pike, including the Royal Crest, to be nine feet ten inches.

Queen's Regulations, 31st December, 1873.—Finally settled the length of the pike by reducing it to eight feet seven and a half inches including Royal Crest and ferrule.

H.Q., W.O. Confidential Letter, 17th January, 1882.—Stated that in future Colours were not, necessarily, to be taken on Active Service, owing to "the altered formation of attack, and extended range of firing". G.O.C.'s to decide in special cases.

Clothing Regulations, 1898.—Lays down that Colours when replaced become "the property of the State and should be deposited in some Church or other public building". "No one is entitled to sell old Colours or deal with them in any way". This was enlarged upon in Clothing Regulations 1909, which stated that "in no circumstances may Colours be allow to pass into the possession of any individual".

Clothing Regulations, 1926, App. XI, paras. 8-11.—Details the *King's Colour* and states that it is to bear in the centre the territorial designation on a crimson circle with the Royal or other title within, the whole surmounted by an Imperial Crown. The ten selected Battle Honours for the Great War to be emblazoned on the Colour.

The *Regimental Colour* to be the facing of the regiment with territorial designation displayed as on the King's Colour on a crimson circle within the Union. A wreath of roses, thistles and shamrocks, the whole Ensigned with the Imperial Crown. This Colour to bear the ancient badges, devices, distinctions and mottoes as given in the Army List which have been conferred by Royal Authority, except the ten Great War Battle Honours. If the number of other Battle Honours exceeds nine, laurel branches to be introduced and the scrolls bearing the names of the actions entwined thereon.

Army Order 170, September, 1930.—Gives the King's approval for a badge to be selected by each regiment, not already entitled to bear one; such badge to be carried in the centre of the Regimental Colour, instead of the battalion number which is to be placed in the dexter canton.

APPENDIX X

S.V.A. CAMP SONGS

1894 CAMP SONG FORECASTING 1915

Oh! When the row shall start in Singapore,
You will wish you was a member of the Corps
And you could have your fun,
Round a comfortable gun,
Instead of marching 'till your feet get sore.
Rahand the Town,
Up and down,
Keeping civil order for the Crown.
While those they don't require
Can come and 'jadi Tukang Ayer'
And bring us 'ayer batu'
From the Town.

TELOK AYER BAY
by James Graham 1895

Beyond the new Fish Market, underneath Fort Palmer's frown,
    Lies a piece of reclamation which is slowly settling down;
Where the stones are sharp as bayonets and the smells
    As sweet as hay
And no one ever goes there but the gallant S.V.A.
    Down in Telok Ayer Bay
    Where they drills the S.V.A.
Can't you hear the bullets pinging as the Maxims blaze away?
    Down in Telok Ayer Bay
    Where the smell is sweet as hay
And the Sergeants swear most 'orrid on the firing practice day.

CIVILYUN AN' SOJER TOO
(With Apologies to Rudyard Kipling)

As I was a-strollin' roun' Collyer Key—by the orfices mercantile,
    I seed a man in a karki soot of a semi-Regular style,
'E 'eld 'imself up like a sojer-man, an' I sez to 'im—"Oo are you?"
    Sez 'e, "I'm a gunner, a Volunteer gunner—Civilyun an' Sojer too."
'Is own work starts at nine or ten, an' 'e works the 'ole day through,
    An' afore an' after an' in between 'e learns wot a Tommy should do,
'E's a kind of a giddy amphidextrum—Civilyun an' Sojer too.

An' after I met 'im at Katong Camp—adoin' all kinds of work,
    Like draggin' about a Maxim Gun—w'ich is wot most men would shirk,
'E'll sleep in a tent w'en 'e can't get a 'ouse, and to give the feller 'is doo,
    'E drills like a jolly 'Er Majesty's Tommy, though 'e's a Civilyun too.
There ain't a thing on a Maxim gun the feller don't know an' do,
    'E can draw a bead on a bald mans pate an' riddle it through an' through,
'E's a regular juggling prestigidatrix—Civilyun an' Sojer too.

We've slanged 'em in papers, we've grinned as they pass, but we're fond of 'em all the same,
Though they call us the shirkers, dandified shirkers, an' we answers some other name,
But w'en we are made to do "Speshul" work with a 'owlin' coolie crew,
    We'll wish we wos Gunners, Volunteer Gunners, Civilyuns an' Sojers too.
They'll think for 'emselves an' because we can't, they'll be tellin' us wot's to do.
    An' some of the shirkers will find that this is a bally tough bullet to chew.
Ho! They'll each be a bloomin' Nepolyumpart—these Civilyuns an' Sojers too.

You may say you are fond of your old long chair, an' ong familee cup of tea,
    But there ain't no doubt you're a lazy lout (w'ich ain't wot I want to be.)
It'll make you feel fitter for troubles to come, an' the work you may 'ave to do,
    To know you're a gunner, a Volunteer gunner—Civilyun an' Sojer too,
Oh yus! by Jove, we'll wish we wos that, w'en the first war bugles blow,
    So 'ere's my advice, if you take it you 're wise—Jes go an' be one of their crew,
An' you'll thank your stars, w'en it comes to spars—You're a bit of a Sojer too.

THE SERGEANT-MAJOR
(after Gilbert & Sullivan)

1. When our energetic Major's not a-drilling, not a-drilling,
   When our Adjutant's not doing the attack, the attack
   Our zealous Sergt.-Major's always willing, always willing
   To do his best to stop us getting slack, getting slack
   Every Monday now, our wit we try to smother, yes to smother
   Till lecturing our Sergt.-Major's done, yes done,
   So taking one consideration with another, with another
   His life is just a very active one-oh!

   CHORUS—
   Yes, when regimental duty's to be done, to be done,
   A Sergt.-Major's life is not an idle one, idle one.

2. When that Gun Drill is over in the morning, in the morning
   And a very drowsy day we have made, we have made
   We hear that beastly bugle sound the warning, sound the warning
   To dress ourselves for five o'clock parade
   Our men with new manœuvres then they bother, yes they bother
   For an hour or seventy minutes in the sun, in the sun
   So taking one consideration with another, with another,
   A Sergt.-Major's life's a drilling one-oh!

   CHORUS—
   Yes, when regimental duty's to be done, to be done,
   A Sergt.-Major's life is not an idle one, idle one.

3. Twice a week the N.C.O.'s with his assistance, his assistance
   Of Preliminary Practice learn the art, learn the art
   Both at aiming drill and also judging distance
   That amusement dear to every soldier's heart, soldier's heart
   We stand about and try our yawns to smother, yes to smother,
   For Preliminary Practice takes the bun, takes the bun
   So taking this consideration with that other, with that other
   A Sergt.-Major's life is not a fattening one-oh!

   CHORUS—
   Yes, when regimental duty's to be done, to be done,
   A Sergt.-Major's life is not an idle one, idle one.

A SELANGOR CRICKETER'S ODE TO THE S.V.A.

At a Smoking Concert in the Drill Hall, Singapore shortly after Major McCallum arrived in Lagos

There is one of your great institutions
   Which must not be left out in the cold,
It increases and flourishes daily
   And is now up to strength I am told,
The scene of their works, Tanjong Katong,
   At the 8-inch they labour all day,
They leave Johnsons Pier in the morning
   And at Maxims you'll find them au fait.
Their Commandant's flitted away,
   He's a Governor now, so they say,
He's left them folorn and to Lagos he's gone,
   He'll be missed by the S.V.A.
      Hurrah for the S.V.A.
      Hurrah for the S.V.A.
Merewether and Dunman will still find some fun man,
      Hurrah for the S.V.A.

INDEX

A

Adams, A.R. 40, 151, 173, 174.
Advisory Committees. 94.
Alexandra Barracks. 62.
Allowances. (See "Finance").
Ambulance—Bearer Section S.V.A. 44, 45, 58; Medical Coy. S.V.C., 45, 59; Volunteer Field Ambulance, 45, 86, 106, 116, 119.
American Volunteers. 76.
Anti-Aircraft. 113, 114, 116, 119.
Armament:—
    Artillery. 11, 23, 39, 50, 53, 58, 75, 90, 94, 114.
    Light Machine Guns (Lewis). 89, 99, 103.
    Machine Guns. 26, 28, 29, 30/1, 50, 89, 97.
    Rifles. 7, 12, 14, 35, 74, 89.
Armoured Car Section. 98, 102, 107, 114, 117.
Artillery:—
    F.M.S. Volunteer. 104.
    Hong Kong Volunteer. 10, 29.
    Rangoon Volunteer. 15, 24, 35, 49, 74.
    Regular. 8, 14, 29, 33.
    Singapore Volunteer. 11, 21/41, et seqq., 86, 92, et seqq.
Auxiliary Service Volunteers. 84, 94/5, 96.

B

Badges and Buttons. 7, 30, 55, 100/102, 103, 104.
Badges of Rank (Officers). 15.
Band. 12, 76, 124.
Bearer Section S.V.A. (See "Ambulance").
Bisley, Rifle team sent to. 57.
Buckley, C.B. 5, 13, 14, 20, 129, 147.
Burma Auxiliary Force. (See "Rangoon Volunteers" and "Artillery Rangoon").
Butterworth, Colonel W.J. 3, 5; Mrs. Butterworth 5.
Buttons. (See Badges and Buttons).

C

Cadets. 14, 49, 72, 75.
Camps. 24, 28, 30, 33, 94/5, 96, 98, 105, 106, 108, 111, 112, 116, 119, 120, 124.
Cavenagh, Colonel Orfeur. 8, 9, 11.
Ceylon Light Infantry. 43.
Chaplain. 29.
Cheang Hong Lim. 27.
Chidwheel, the. 114.
Chinese Volunteers Club. 54, 96.
Chinese Volunteers. 43, 44, 49, 54, 55, 61, 74, 86, 118.
Civil Disturbances, Quelling of. 90.
Clementi Smith, Sir Cecil. 21, 38.
Coast Defence Volunteers—Singapore and Penang. 78/9.
Colours. 5, 17, 112, 115, (also Appendix IX).
Command, time limit of. 109; Eurasian and Chinese Coys. 118.
Competitions. 55, 89, 92, 96, 97, 98, 109, 111, 113, 117, 120.
Composite Company—87, 89.
Concessions. 93.
Constitution. 4, 5, 44, 51, 58, 86/7, 89, 92, 93/4, 102, 117, 119.
Contemporaries. (See under names of various Corps).
Cornwall, visit of the Duke and Duchess. 45.
Coronation:—
    King Edward VII. 45.
    King George V. 58.
    King George VI. 123.
    Medals. (See "Decorations").
Courses of Instruction. 83, 99, 103, 105, 114, 116, 119.
Cyclist Section. 39, 59.

D

Decorations and Medals. 53, 78, 121, 124, (also Appendix IV (a)).
Defence Electric Light. (See under "Engineers").
Defence Forces Volunteer—Change of Title to. 79.
Derrick, G.A. 21, 55, 62, 147, 157, 160, 161, 163, 164, 173, 174, 182.
Dress and Equipment. 10, 13, 16, 17, 23, 30, 39, 40, 52, 55, 56, 58, 89, 90, 92, 95, 97, 98, 103, 118, 122.
Drill Hall. 22, 29, 54, 110, 111, 119.
Drills and Training. 23, 52, 55, 58, 61, 75, 86, 88, 96, 105.

E

Edinburgh, visit of Duke of. 12.
Efficiency. 100.
Electric Light Section S.R.E.(v). 83, 97.
"Emden", activities of. 59.
Engine Room Section S.R.E.(v). (See "Engineers").
Engineers Volunteer. 44, 49, 61, 83, 92, 108.
Ensign (rank of). 11.
Equipment. (See "Dress").
Establishment. (See "Constitution").
Eurasian Volunteers Club. 96, 97, 99.
Eurasian Volunteers. 19, 28, 44, 49, 50, 55, 56, 82, 86, 99, 118.

F

Federated Malay States Volunteer:—
  Force. 110.
  Infantry. 74.
  Rifles. 49, 62, 83.
  Regiment. 110.
Field Ambulance, Malacca. 106.
Field Company S.R.E.(v). 108.
Finance. 27, 45, 52, 53, 54, 109, 111, 119.
Foreign Volunteers. 97.
Fort Blakan Mati and Pulo Brani. 24, 33.
Fort Canning. 5, 10, 29, 75, 90, 193.
Fort Faber. 11, 194.
Fort Fullerton. 11, 26, 193.
Fort Palmer. 11, 23, 194.
Fort Pasir Panjang. 28, 32, 194.
Fort Siloso. 23.
Fort Tanjong Katong. 23, 30, 194.
Fortress Company S.R.E.(v). 83, 106, 107.
Forts—Notes on Singapore Forts and Barracks. 193.
Frankel, Mr. Julian. 124.

G

Games. 34, 40, 115, 119.
Gloucester, visit of the Duke of. 105.
Guards of Honour. 12, 45, 98, 105, 106, 110, 111.

H

Hashim, N.M. 57.
Headdress. (See "Dress").
Headquarters—Volunteer. 13, 98, 99, 110, 111.
Historical Committee, S.V.C. 125.
Hong Kong Volunteers. 10, 29, 80, (See also "Artillery—Hong Kong").
Honorary Members. 53.

I

Inspections. 8, 26, 28, 32, 93, 98, 109, 112, 117, 124.
Intelligence Sections. 97, 116.

J

Johore, H.H. Sultan Abubakar of. 27.
Johore Volunteer Engineers. 104.
Johore Volunteer Rifles. 61, 83, 86, 104.
Jubilee—King George V. 121.
Jubilee—Queen Victoria's Diamond. 40.

K

Kedah Volunteers. 60.
Kedah Volunteer Force. 114.
Kelantan Expedition. 72.
Kelantan Volunteer Rifles. 60, 72; Force 121.

L

Labuan Defence Corps. 74, 86, 94, 96, 99, 103.
Lavender Street—"Battle" of. 90.
Lermit, A.A. 152, 161, 166, 173, 174.
Lewis, D.T. 55, 88, 161/162, 166/167.

M

Machine Gun Company. 50, 76, 119.
Macpherson, Capt. R. 4, 147.
Magazines, Gazettes and Publications, Volunteer. 39, 47, 99, 115, 119.
Makepeace, W. 149, 158, 161, 163, 164, 173.
Malacca Company S.V.C. 49.
Malacca Volunteer Corps. 83, 94.
Malay Volunteers Club. 96.
Malacca Volunteer Rifles. 72, 73, 76, 86.
Malay Volunteers. 56, 57, 61, 72, 86, 112, 120.
Manuals. 23, 75.
Maxim Guns. (See "Armament—Machine Guns").
Mayhew, T.O. 45, 88/9, 161/162, 164/170, 173, 175.
McCallum, H.E. 15, 21, 22, et seqq., 35, 39.
Medals and Decorations. (See "Decorations").
Medical Company S.V.C. (See "Ambulance").
Meetings. 17, 53.
Mess Dress. (See "Dress").

INDEX

Membership. 23, 53, 130.
Militia Bill. 13.
Mobilization. 59.
Motor Cyclist Section. 97.
Motto. 6, 8, 9, 21.
Mutiny—The Mutiny of the 5th Light Infantry in Singapore. 61, et seqq.

O

Ordinances, Volunteer. 1, 6, 12, 15, 26, 59, 60, 71, 73, 75, 76, 77, 79/82, 83, 93/4, 115.

P

Pageant 1926. 97.
Pahang Rebellion. 35.
Pantomime S.V.C. 115, 119.
Paymasters Honorary. 28.
Penang Volunteer Rifle Corps. 9.
Penang Volunteers. 40, 66.
Penang and Province Wellesley Volunteer Corps. 83, 85, 86, 94.
Piracy. 105.
Prince of Wales, visit 1922. 88.
Promotion. 23, 52, 106, 107, 110, 114, 119, 130.
Province Wellesley Volunteer Rifles. 73, 76.
Provost Section. 106.

R

Ranges, Artillery. 14, 40.
Ranges, Rifle. 13, 14, 45, 83, 92, 95, 97, 98, 103, 113.
Rangoon Volunteers. 14, 15, 16, 49, 61, 74, 80.
Read, W.H. 3, 4, 5, 11, 12, 13, 147, 154, 155, 156.
Recruiting. 93, 95, 105.
Regulations. 7, 51, et seqq., 58, 130.
Re-organisation. 21, 42, 44, 83, 86, 102.
Reserve of Officers. 45, 94.
Reserve Service Volunteers. 84.
Rifle Association (S.R.A.). 14, 39, 58.
Rifles—Volunteer. Chap. I, 44, 50, 60.
Riots and Gang Robbers. 2, 5, 13, 90, 91, 98.
Royal Singapore Flying Club. 110.

S

Scottish Company S.V.C. 87, 88, 95, 119, 122.
Scottish Platoon P. & P.W.V.C. 106.
Second Captain. 4.
Shanghai Volunteer Corps. 2.
Siam, visit of the King and Queen of. 105.

Signal Sections. 97.
Singapore Royal Artillery (Volunteer). (See under "Artillery—Singapore Volunteer").
Singapore Royal Engineers (Volunteer). (See under "Engineers").
Singapore Volunteer Field Ambulance. (See under "Ambulance").
Singapore Volunteer Rifle Corps Disbandment. 19.
Song Ong Siang. 44, 46, 54, 74, 77, 174.
Spencer, Lt.-Col. F.E. 85, 90, 147.
St. Clair, W.G. 15, 17, 21, 22, et seqq., 35, 36, 40, 41, et seqq., 149 187.
Staff, H.Q. 54, 97, 105, 106, 107, 108, 111, 113, 115, 127.
Straits Settlements:—
    Volunteer Air Force. 121.
    Volunteer Force. 83.
    Volunteer Royal Naval Reserve. 115.
Strength. 11, 19, 21, 51, 57, 60, 71, 73, 112, 119.
Sub-Lieutenants. 11.
Sub-Officers. 5.
Surgeons Honorary. 5, 28, 44, 154, 155.

T

Tan Soo Bin. 44, 118, 175.
Tanglin Barracks. 62, 195.
Traffic Control Section. 106.
Training. (See "Drills").

U

Uniform. (See "Dress").

V

Verse. 32, 34, 46, 48, 49, 199/202.
Veterans Company S.V.C. 75.

W

Wars:—
    Crimea. 3.
    Indian Mutiny. 1.
    South African. 40, 42, 50, 51.
    1914–1918. 59 to 84.

Z

Zehnder, H.R.S. 82, 99, 118, 173.

www.ingramcontent.com/pod-product-compliance
Lightning Source LLC
Chambersburg PA
CBHW060339010526
44117CB00017B/2882